# Auction This!

## Your Complete Guide to the World of Online Auctions

Dennis L. Prince

A DIVISION OF PRIMA PUBLISHING

A Division of Prima Publishing

Prima Publishing and colophon are registered trademarks of Prima Communications, Inc., Rocklin, California 95765.

Microsoft, Windows, and Internet Explorer are trademarks or registered trademarks of Microsoft Corporation. Netscape, Netscape Navigator, and Netscape Communicator are trademarks or registered trademarks of Netscape Communications Corporation.

*Important.* Prima Publishing cannot provide software support. Please contact the appropriate software manufacturer's technical support line or Web site for assistance.

Prima Publishing and the author have attempted throughout this book to distinguish proprietary trademarks from descriptive terms by following the capitalization style used by the manufacturer.

ISBN: 0-7615-2316-2

Library of Congress Catalog Card Number: 99-64752

Printed in the United States of America

99 00 01 02 03 BB 10 9 8 7 6 5 4 3 2 1

**Publisher**
Stacy L. Hiquet

**Associate Publisher**
Nancy Stevenson

**Marketing Manager**
Judi Taylor

**Managing Editor**
Sandy Doell

**Senior Acquisitions Editor**
Deborah F. Abshier

**Senior Editor**
Kim V. Benbow

**Assistant Project Editor**
Estelle Manticas

**Technical Reviewer**
Chris Aloia

**Copy Editor**
Hilary Powers

**Interior Design and Layout**
Scribe Tribe

**Illustrator**
Christine Shields

**Cover Design**
Prima Design Team

**Indexer**
Sherry Massey

# Contents

Introduction                                        xi

**PART 1   Understanding the Internet Impact       1**

**Chapter 1   When Bids Meet Bytes       3**
The Auction, Briefly Stated ................................................. 3
The Internet in a Nutshell ................................................... 6
When Worlds Combine ....................................................... 10
The Good, the Bad, and the Bizarre ................................. 13
Time to Go Shopping! ........................................................ 15

**Chapter 2   How and Why Do Auctions Work?       17**
The Role of Auctions in the Economy ............................... 17
Who's Auctioning? ............................................................. 18
It's Better to Barter ........................................................... 20
Bidders Can Be Choosers .................................................. 21
Sellers Find Their Market .................................................. 23
Leveling the Playing Field .................................................. 25
More Whys and What-Fors ................................................ 27

**Chapter 3   Safety, Security, and Privacy Online       29**
What, Me Worry? ............................................................... 30
You Have Nothing To Fear Except . . . ............................. 31
Who's Out There? .............................................................. 32
Who's In There? ................................................................. 34
Spam Doesn't Just Come in a Can Anymore .................... 37
A Virus Is Nothing to Sneeze At ....................................... 38
A Quick Lesson in Netiquette ........................................... 39

What About Fraud? .................................................... 41

A Few More Thoughts to Ease Your Mind ......................... 43

**Chapter 4    Another Trend or a New Tradition?    45**

Why Will This Work? ................................................. 46

The Amazing Colossal Market ...................................... 49

Oh, What a Profitable Web We Weave ............................. 50

Does the Little Guy Really Matter? ................................ 51

Are You Ready to Play? .............................................. 52

 **Seeing the Sites    53**

**Chapter 5    The Online Auction Landscape    55**

Sifting Through the Sites ............................................ 55

Assess the Sites ...................................................... 57

What Kind of Shopper Will You Be? ............................... 59

Do You Have the Time? ............................................. 62

Common Auction Formats .......................................... 63

Understanding Auction Culture .................................... 65

Setting Your Expectations .......................................... 67

Stay in Control ....................................................... 68

Register to Win ...................................................... 69

Start Your Engines (and Other Supercharged Searches) ......... 71

A Preface to What's Coming ........................................ 73

**Chapter 6    The Merchant Sites    75**

What's the Story? ................................................... 75

Onsale.com ...................................................... 78

uBid.com ......................................................... 88

Bid.com ................................................................. 96

FirstAuction.com ................................................. 103

Some Final Thoughts ................................................. 109

**Chapter 7   The Person-to-Person Experience          111**

What's the Story? ..................................................... 112

The Power to Sell ..................................................... 113

Who's Hangin' Around These Auction Sites? ................. 114

I Don't Want Any Trouble, OK? ............................... 115

Oh, The Places You'll See ......................................... 116

eBay.com ............................................................ 116

Yahoo! Auctions ................................................... 132

Amazon.com Auctions ........................................... 142

Hey! Is That All? ..................................................... 152

Voices and Choices ................................................. 152

**Chapter 8   The Elite Few          155**

Traditional Sights ..................................................... 156

Untraditional Sites ................................................... 157

The Price of Participation ....................................... 158

Sotheby's ............................................................ 158

Christie's ............................................................ 164

Butterfield & Butterfield ....................................... 168

Biddington's ....................................................... 172

The Final Hammer ................................................... 176

**Chapter 9   Charity Auctions          177**

What's It All About? ................................................. 177

Who Gets the Money? ............................................. 179

How Can I Help? ..................................................... 180

WebCharity.com ................................................. 180

Universal Studios Charity Auctions ....................................... 182

TheBroadcaster.com Hollywood Auction ........................... 183

Charity Auctions at Other Sites ....................................... 184

## Chapter 10   Specialty Auctions                    187

What's the Story? ............................................................ 187

Is Smaller Better? .......................................................... 188

Does a Smaller Site Equal Smaller Profit? ......................... 189

Do You Deserve Special Treatment? ................................. 190

AuctionGuy's Top Ten Specialty Auctions ......................... 190

Collecting Nation ......................................................... 191

Beanie Nation ............................................................. 192

Just Glass ................................................................... 193

WineBid ..................................................................... 193

Collectors Universe ....................................................... 195

StampAuctions .............................................................. 197

Tickets.com ................................................................. 197

Magic Auction .............................................................. 198

Pottery Auction ............................................................ 200

Gibson Global Auction ................................................... 201

Bonus Site!—URLMerchant ........................................... 201

Hey AuctionGuy! There's Still So Many More! .................. 202

## PART III   After the Gavel                          203

## Chapter 11   When the Auction Ends                 205

Keeping Track of Your Auctions ..................................... 205

Buyers ....................................................................... 206

Sellers ...................................................................... 208

Basic End-of-Auction Rules & Etiquette .......................... 210

Notification ................................................................... 212

Your Key to Successful Communication ......................... 214

Post-Auction Prep Work ................................................ 215

**Chapter 12  Money, Merchandise, and the Mail Carrier    221**

Which Comes First? ....................................................... 221

How Would You Like to Pay Today? .............................. 223

Protecting Your Payment ............................................... 225

    Cash ............................................................................ 225

    Personal Checks ......................................................... 226

    Money Orders and Cashier's Checks .......................... 226

    Credit Card Payment ................................................. 227

    Escrow Services ......................................................... 228

    Does Anyone Still Use COD? .................................... 230

Speaking of Payment . . . ............................................... 230

Ship Shape .................................................................... 232

    Assessing the Item ...................................................... 232

    Getting Supplies ......................................................... 233

    You-PS (Your Parcel Service) ..................................... 235

    Determining the Cost ................................................. 236

    Do You Charge for Anything Else? ............................ 237

The Waiting Game ........................................................ 238

**Chapter 13  Reaching Out and Speaking Up    241**

First Impressions and Last Rites .................................... 241

I'll Show You My Feedback If You'll Show Me Yours .......... 242

    Feedback in a Nutshell ............................................... 242

    How to Post Feedback ................................................ 243

    But What If It Was a Bad Deal? ................................. 245

    Should I Read Between the Lines? .............................. 248

    Can Feedback Be Faked? ........................................... 248

So Does It Really Work? ................................................................ 249

Building a Better World Online ..................................................... 249

## Chapter 14  Auction Scams, Shams, and Other Flim-Flams    251

What Makes Them Think They Can Get Away With It? ...................... 252

Who's At Risk? ............................................................................ 252

The Seven Deadly Scams ............................................................. 252

Is There Anything Else I Should Know? ......................................... 259

## PART IV  Tips, Tricks, and Traps    261

## Chapter 15  Pastime or Full-Time Job?    263

Preserving the Magic .................................................................... 264

If You Love It, Can You Bear to Part with It? ............................... 266

How's Your Inventory Look? ........................................................ 266

If You've Got the Time, We've Got the Place ............................... 267

Who's Driving This Ship? ............................................................ 268

Economy ................................................................................... 269

Who Invited Murphy? ................................................................ 269

Enjoy the Ride and the Thrill of the Chase .................................. 270

## Chapter 16  Put Your Money Where Your Mouse Is    273

What Were You Really Looking For? .............................................. 273

Work Within Your Means .............................................................. 274

Know When to Quit ................................................................... 274

Keep Realistic Expectations ........................................................ 275

Don't Give the Proxy All the Power ............................................. 276

Short- and Long-Term Gains ...................................................... 276

When Bids Go Bad ....................................................................... 277

Something Suddenly Came Up .................................................... 277

What If I've Changed My Mind? ............................................. 278
Are There Valid Reasons for Pulling Out of an Auction? .................. 279
Your Solid Gold Guarantee ................................................ 279

## Chapter 17   Bidding and Selling Strategies                          281

Bidding Tips and Tactics ................................................. 281
  Spread the Wealth ..................................................... 281
  Use Selective Searches ................................................ 282
  Going, Going, Grab It! ................................................ 282
  When to Bid First .................................................... 283
  Outbid the Outbidder ................................................. 283
  Win It with a Penny .................................................. 284
  Bid Big .............................................................. 284
  Explore the Joys of Sniping .......................................... 284
  Mix It Up ............................................................ 286
  Pay Quickly .......................................................... 286
  Post Feedback ........................................................ 287
Selling Strategies ....................................................... 287
  Know Your Stuff ...................................................... 287
  Do Your Market Research .............................................. 288
  Craft Tempting Titles ................................................ 288
  Give Detailed Descriptions ........................................... 289
  Post Pictures ........................................................ 290
  Price For Persuasion ................................................. 291
  Answer All Questions ................................................. 292
  Announce Your Guarantee Policy ....................................... 292
  Post Feedback ........................................................ 293

## Chapter 18   Do You Think I Have a Problem?                          295

What Is Internet Addiction? .............................................. 296
What Makes the Internet So Addictive? .................................... 297

Can Online Auctions Be Hazardous to Your Health? ........................... 298

What Are the Warning Signs? ............................................. 300

Is There Hope? ...................................................... 303

Learning More about Online Addictions................................ 305

**Chapter 19  Honorable Mentions: More Online Auction Sites      307**

More Merchant Auctions ................................................. 307

Person-to-Person Auctions .............................................. 309

More Art and Antique Auctions ......................................... 311

More Specialty Auctions and Other Venues ............................. 312

**Appendix A  Additional Sources of Information      313**

Auctions in General ..................................................... 314

Books................................................................ 314

Web Sites ........................................................... 315

Online Auction Search Sites ........................................ 315

Learn More about PCs, Web Browsers, and the Internet .................... 316

Books................................................................ 317

Web Sites ........................................................... 318

Internet Safety and Good Practices ...................................... 318

Books................................................................ 318

Web Sites ........................................................... 319

Price Guides and Useful Publications .................................... 319

**Appendix B  Seldom Asked Questions      321**

Index      329

# Acknowledgments

This book has been a pleasure to prepare. I've had the good fortune to work with a team of folks with whom I've worked on previous projects. Their commitment and support have been invaluable to me and for which I simply can't express enough thanks (but I'll try).

For starters, there are my publishers, Stacy Hiquet and Nancy Stevenson. Thanks for your endorsement of this new title. Then, thanks to my acquisition editor, Debbie Abshier. Thanks for your belief in this book and all your efforts to help bring it to fruition.

Big thanks to my technical editor, Chris Aloia, who has done a fine job to double-check my facts and bring to light further information to help this book achieve its goals. Next is the remarkable Hilary Powers, copyeditor extraordinaire. You are pure gold in my book, and I would be lost without your input and insight.

My sincere gratitude to Prima Tech's marketing whiz, Judi Taylor. Thanks for everything you've done to help get this new book into the hands of readers everywhere.

And, with this book, I'd like to thank illustrator Christine Shields. Thanks for capturing the spirit of AuctionGuy—I hope the readers will enjoy him as much as I do.

Also, a well-deserved round of applause for the rest of the team. To Dan Foster, Scribe Tribe, and Sherry Massey— it's always a privilege to have you doing your magic behind the scenes on one of my books.

A special *thank you* to Kim Benbow, my project editor at Prima. It's unfortunate that most readers never get to see what it is you do. You have been the "glue" of this project, and I know I never could have done as well without your guiding hand. Thanks for everything you do.

Last, but certainly not least, I must acknowledge the online auction sites and their communities. After all, you're the reason I decided to write this book in the first place. Keep up the good work, team!

# Dedication

# About the Author

**Dennis L. Prince** has been an active member of the eBay community since 1996. He has participated in hundreds of auctions as both buyer and seller. He has literally exchanged thousands of dollars in transactions and has achieved a very respectable eBay community rating. As a seasoned hobbyist and collector, he has worked with long-distance business transactions (businesses and person-to-person) for over 20 years.

# Introduction

Hey! Looking for a great deal on the latest electronic gadgets? Want to be reunited with your long-lost G.I. Joe with kung fu grip? Have you ever dreamed of owning the original Batmobile? Or how 'bout an antique Apple? (the computer, not the fruit.)

Bargain hunters, treasure finders and savvy sellers have been mighty busy lately, seeking out, sifting through, and offering up just about anything imaginable. Always looking for a better deal, an impossible find, or a more promising market, buyers and sellers have gleefully turned to the Internet where they've found the most exciting and innovative approach to trading goods—online auctions.

The hottest form of electronic commerce (*e-commerce*) today, online auctions have captivated the attention of millions of merchants and consumers worldwide. Though less than half the U.S. population has yet to explore the Internet, online auctions have become the compelling draw for many to get off the sidelines and join in the auction action. The promise of finding goods, selling goods, or just having a great time in the booming auction marketplace has mobilized millions and caused an unheralded swell in the online trading business.

Steals, deals, and home-shopping appeal—online auctions seem to promise it all. But with their tremendous popularity, unrivaled growth, and hosting to literally millions of buyers, sellers, and assorted goods, it's become a daunting task for newcomers to determine where (or how) to hop on this train. Beginning a new journey into the realm of online auctions, now with more than 300 active auction sites to choose from, can make an auction amateur (and some of the more seasoned goers) feel lost in the landscape.

Further, there are questions of online security, auction communities, auction lingo, rules, strategies, and all the other nuances that either make the auction experience a joy or a nightmare. It's enough to cause some second thoughts.

But it doesn't have to be this difficult. What if I told you I could spare you the headaches, save you from confusion, and show you a good time? Sure, you can figure it all out on your own—over time—or you can peer over my shoulder to see what I've learned during the past four years of avid auction-going. Interested?

# What's the Big Deal?

Well, that's the question: why are so many people yapping about online auctions? Are they a fad, a fluke, or some other short-lived frenzy? Nope. If you've picked up this book, then I assume someone or something piqued your curiosity enough to learn more about online auctions. Whether you read about them in the news, followed their growth on the stock market, or just heard about them at the office, online auctions have become a way of life for millions of merchants and consumers.

Did you hear about the great computer deals at Onsale? Did your friend find a rare baseball card at eBay? And who was that who just exclaimed, "Wuhoo!" after winning big at Yahoo!? It's auction fever, and it seems everyone's caught it.

Online auctions have become a multi-billion dollar industry. Net surfers flock by the millions to buy and sell both treasures and trash, and the auction sites are making money in the process. Working from the commission-based system, auction sites are earning staggering profits from both professional businesspeople and regular Joes and Janes, providing a dynamic new approach to the ancient art of haggling.

# Why Is This Book for Me?

If you've seen the sea of online auctions, you know there are a host of auction sites to choose from. If you haven't seen them yet, rest assured you will. But if you don't know where to start your auction journey or in which direction to navigate, then this book was written especially for you.

So many people eager to join in the auction action or expand their current online activities are asking all sorts of questions:

- Which auction sites offer the things I'm looking for?

- Which auction sites are safest?

- How long have these auction sites been around?

- Who am I dealing with at the different online auctions?

- Can I sell some of my own stuff at an online auction?

- How do I play?

- How do I pay?

- Can someone please tell me which are the *best* auction sites?

These are real questions from real people, and they're asked of me time and again. If you've asked these questions yourself, or just the mere mention of them makes you want to know the answers, then this book is for you.

Whether you're new to online auctions, new to the Internet, or new to buying and selling over long distances, this book will be your guide. Even if you've already trudged through cyberspace to join in the action, this book offers some deeper insight and a bag full of tips and tricks culled from years of my real-life experiences (online and off).

## What's This Book All About?

This book will work for you and with you to help clear up any confusion, ease any apprehension, and provide a better understanding of what online auctions are about. I've been working the online auctions since 1995 and, coupled with over twenty years experience with long-distance business transactions (person-to-person and business-to-person), I can provide you with the facts, figures, and fallacies of online auction involvement. It's been years of fun and excitement for me, and I'm pleased to share what I've learned with anyone who wants to participate. To help present the extensive amount of information here, I've arranged this book in five different sections.

## Part I: Understanding the Internet Impact

In this first section, you'll read about auctions and the Internet and how these two have joined forces to rival other dynamic duos like Batman and Robin, Lucas and Spielberg, and peanut butter and jelly. Yes, it's the sort of background study that will give you a clearer view of the realm you're venturing into and what it all means. I'll start by introducing you to the ways of auctions—historical and present day. Then I'll quickly review the Internet and how it became the cultural icon that has changed the way we think and live.

You'll see how online auctions came about and how they are drawing billions of visitors every minute of every day. And, just when you're about to ask, "*Why auctions?*" I'll tell you why. You'll learn how auctions serve your needs and desires and why an auction might just be the trading vehicle you'll want to climb into time and time again. Of course, safety is always of high importance, and I probably don't have to tell you how large and sometimes unwieldy the World Wide Web has become. To help you build a sense of security, I will offer some good tactics and sound advice to help you plan a safe and successful journey through cyberspace. When you're done with this section, you'll understand the online jargon, excitedly anticipate the auction experience, and see why online auctions are definitely here to stay.

## Part II: Seeing the Sites

As you enter this section of the book, you'll begin exploring what kind of stuff is out in the auction landscape. You'll learn just how many auction sites there are and how to sift through them all to find the ones most likely to have the goods you seek. I'll take you on a tour of what I consider to be the best auctions online today. Whether you're looking for whiz-bang computer hardware, rare art pieces, elusive spotted Furbies, or antique toothpicks, I'll show you around the better sites to help you shorten your search and bring home the goods you want. Here, you'll learn about the different kinds of auction sites: some where you'll be dealing with reputable and well-established online corporations, some where you'll be dealing with regular people who can be just as reputable, some where you'll be in the company of the auction world's most renowned auctioneers and astute bidders, some where your purchases go to the benefit of worthy charities, and some where you can find specialty items that will feed you with those specific things you crave most. I'll show you each of the chosen sites, give you a rundown on its features, qualities, and potential *gotchas*; and when it's all over, I'll give you my personal rating of what I liked and didn't like during the visit. It's the kind of information that will save you time, money, and headaches—and I've got the empty aspirin bottles to prove it.

## Part III: After the Gavel

Clearly, this is the part of online auctions that most people have questions about. *"What do I do when the auction's over?"* Up to this point, it's just been a lot of online searching, reviewing, bidding, and selling. It's all been electronic, fueled by clacking keyboards and clicking mice. When the gavel bangs, then what? If this particular area troubles you, fear not. This section shows you exactly what to expect and how to bring the auction down from cyberspace into the physical world where someone gets the money and someone gets the goods. Sometimes, it's an effortless exchange. Other times, there might be a little more work involved. But there's always a path that leads to mutual satisfaction if you know how to read the signposts along the way. I'll guide you through this terrain and show you how the experts do it.

## Part IV: Tips, Tricks, and Traps

In this section, I'll talk at length about the potential good and bad of your auction activity. Do you want to work the auctions as a full-time endeavor? Are you looking for useful tips and strategies that will stretch your bidding dollar or increase your profits? Will you be able to focus on your auction goals without getting blinded by the excitement? Here I'll touch on the potential dark side of online auctions—obsessions that could lead to situations where you could lose more than just money.

# What Do I Need Before I Begin?

With your curiosity piqued, you're probably wondering if there's anything you'll need to know up front before you can join the auction activities. Not to worry. Online auctions are free to all lookers and are pretty user-friendly for any new kids on the Web. You don't have to be a tech-head or computer geek to join up, but you should have a basic understanding of how to use a PC, how to access the Internet, and how to work a Web browser. I won't be able to cover all the hardware and software in this volume, but if you're a little light in this department, I'll serve up some good references for you in Appendix A at the back of the book.

Of course, I'll expect you have a PC (personal computer) of your own or access to one that you can use whenever you please. I suggest, at minimum, a PC powered by a 166mhz CPU, 32mb of RAM, and a 2.6 gigabyte hard drive. But to get the most from this book immediately, you should also feel relatively comfortable surfing the Net. Though I won't intentionally whiz past you with Net jargon, I'll assume you're aware of the Internet, basic navigation of the World Wide Web, and the usual format of Web site addresses. For the discussion and examples you'll find in this book, I'll be using a PC running the Windows 98 operating system, a standard Internet service provider (ISP) connection to the Internet, and the Netscape Navigator (version 4.6) Web browser.

## Hey, Is This Gonna Be Expensive?

It's a fair question, especially given the assumptions I've made in the preceding section. The answer is a definite. . .maybe. Anything you do that involves a PC and the Internet can get expensive. Of course, it all depends on what you want to do and how extravagantly you want to do it. The PC, of course, will probably be your most expensive investment, but you can find many suitable setups that exceed the minimum recommendations I've suggested without exceeding the $1000 price point. Believe me, that's a great bargain when you're talking about computer hardware. But, if it's the Cadillac of PCs you're looking for, well, the sky's the limit. You decide, but try not to get too carried away—you'll want to save some cash for the auctions, right?

Connecting to the Internet has become quite affordable, with an average hookup costing less than $20 a month for unlimited (unmetered) use. If you think you'll only use the Internet or online auctions for a couple of hours a week, think again. You'll be clocking some serious time faster than you can exclaim, "Holy mackerel! I've gotta get some sleep!" Again, if you're looking for better and faster, there are always ISDN and ADSL (digital) connections or cable modems, but they'll raise your connection costs quickly. Whatever pleases you.

Then, if you want to get into the selling game yourself (and I'll show you where and how), you might want some of the nice little accessories like a scanner or digital camera to photograph your goods. Though not exorbitantly priced, these little bonuses do add a few hundred dollars more to the overall cost.

And, not to be forgotten, are the auctions themselves. Here's where your money might be going, often faster than you realize. Don't bother just yet with any commissions that some sites charge. Rather, keep an eye on what you might be bidding on and what it could cost. Believe me, you can get so wrapped up in the bidding frenzy that you could click away a small fortune in a matter of moments. Not to worry. Later in the book I'll sit down for a nice little chat about budgeting and funding your online habits.

## Help Along the Way

AuctionGuy—he's Net-savvy and free speaking—will come along for the ride to provide his biased and unbiased perspective along the way. He likes to interrupt from time to time, but he always seems to have something to say that's worth listening to. If the discussion's going too fast, he'll slow it down; if too much is being assumed, he'll stop and explain. If he's not convinced you're getting the whole story, he'll throw in his two cents to give you a deeper or different perspective. I should warn you: he has a bit of an attitude, and he's not always the most politically correct guy you'll come across. Don't let that distract you, though, because he usually cuts to the bottom line of what you need to know. So, when AuctionGuy has something to share, he'll get your attention throughout the book in a number of ways.

**DID YOU KNOW?** He's a bright guy, and he'll have little facts or tidbits of information to share with you. It's the kind of knowledge to keep in your back pocket or in the back of your mind.

**GET A CLUE** He's got a keen eye and a real vision for tips and tricks that you should stop and think about. Whether well-timed clues for your online success or ways to help you cut corners to save time, money, or effort, these little key points can really come in handy.

**IN MY MIND** Well, he's just gotta show you what's going on inside his head. With experience comes insight and an almost unnatural need to impart it to others. Don't turn up your nose, nod off, or look for the next exit. These are pearls of understanding that have come from talking the talk and walking the walk—and if you pay attention, you might make some observations yourself that could otherwise go unnoticed. Indulge him, as he will indulge you.

**WARNING!** If there's trouble ahead or danger afoot, AuctionGuy will sound the alarm. Keep an eye open for these alerts that will help you identify and head off potential problems before they can get their claws into you.

## Does The Author Really Care?

Nope. Not at all. Whether you spend minutes, hours, or days online at the auctions, I don't care. If you should be working rather than bidding, I won't tell. If you're late for the holiday dinner because you have to see how the auction ends, that's OK. I'm not here to judge how or when you spend your time online, which auction sites you decide to haunt or even what sorts of things you intend to buy or sell. I don't care.

But, I *do* care that you're having fun out there. I *do* care that you're feeling confident online. I *do* care that you're finding success at the online auctions. I want to know that you're enjoying the auctions and that you're finding the great things you've always wanted, never knew you wanted, or never even knew existed. I believe that online auctions are fun and that they should remain that way. For this, I do care. My goal is to introduce you to a great time if you've hesitated to participate or to propel you to even greater enjoyment than you've previously experienced at the auctions.

The Web is constantly changing, and it's hard to keep up with. If, while reading or after reading this book, you find you still have more questions to ask, comments to share, observations to point out, or you're just having a good ol' time and want to tell someone about it, then I invite you to drop me a line. You can reach me at **dlprince@bigfoot.com.**

# Part I

## Understanding the Internet Impact

# When Bids Meet Bytes

Can you teach old dogs new tricks? Can you force a square peg in a round hole? Do vinegar and oil really mix? Well, I'm not too sure about those, but I do know that auctions and the Internet are two elements that definitely mix well together.

Start with the base ingredients of haggling, bartering, and the well-practiced poker face often used when negotiating deals and season with a vast forum of free expression, instant communication, and entrepreneurial spirit, and you'll cook up the largest virtual marketplace for buyers and sellers the world has ever known. This is not a forced mixture of any sort. Auctions and the Internet have combined to form a tantalizing recipe that will tempt your inquisitive taste, then satisfy your hunger for excitement, and immediately compel you to come back for another helping (and another, and another . . . ).

So, before venturing deep into the cybernetic landscape of online auctions, first take a look at the elements that make up this virtual feast. It's fun to know what's in the batter: bids and bytes, plus a pinch and dash of exciting new flavors that really spice up the meal.

## The Auction, Briefly Stated

First, how about a little auction history? There's a lot to be learned from what has gone before, and I'd be lax not to provide a look back at the cultural institution known as *the auction*. It's the foundation of this online buzz. So let me take you back to the beginning of auctions and show you where and how this whole thing began.

If I were to step into my Way-Back Machine intent on finding the earliest recorded auctions, I'd need to set the dial as far back as 500 B.C. with the destination of ancient Babylon. By my best navigation, that would be the point at which auctioning is generally known to have begun. Naturally, you'd be curious to know *what* was being auctioned back then. Well, those ancient Babylonians weren't auctioning dusty sandals or even copper ingots—they were auctioning women! Back then, gender equality and political correctness simply didn't exist; the hot "commodities" of these early auctions were eligible women. The bidders were, of course, eligible men who were literally shopping for wives. OK, probably not the best start for what would become today's online auction phenomenon, but it was a start all the same.

From that less-than-impressive beginning, let me take you ahead a few hundred years to ancient Rome, where auctions were held in the *atrium auctionarium*. Rome, being the great assemblage of peoples, classes, and toga-clad businessmen, really had its auctions tuned for efficiency. A wide variety of items were auctioned, most of which were actually acquired as the result of bloody battles with the spoils—anything that could be claimed—going to the victors. And it didn't even need to be portable; the most prized commodity in Roman auctions was real estate. Roman auctions took to the road, where a victorious general thrust a spear into a blood-soaked battleground and announced the land officially up for bid. Of particular interest is the fact that many such battles were attended by Roman businessmen who were there solely to negotiate the anticipated exchange of land immediately after the previous emperor's head had been severed and a new "emperor elect" had delivered a winning bid. Pretty much the same way some bloodthirsty businessmen operate today, toga not included.

 DID YOU KNOW? At one time, the entire Roman Empire was put up for auction. In the year 193 A.D., the empire was taken from Emperor Pertinax and thrown on the auction block for new leadership. The highest bidder, Didius Julianus, became the new emperor. How's that for the "sale of the century"?

Perhaps the most poignant piece of Roman auction history is attributed to emperor-philosopher Marcus Aurelius. During his reign from 161 A.D. to 180 A.D., he was truly a *people's emperor*. Committed to his Stoic beliefs, he ruled with good conscience and good will. When he needed to fund his wars in Eastern Europe, he didn't raise taxes—he held a public auction at which he offered his own gold tableware and his wife's exquisite silk and gold-embroidered dresses. Though not exactly a *charity auction*, it was still an auction with a cause for greater good.

Leaving those dusty and bloody beginnings of auctioning, quickly skip over many more centuries to Great Britain, and you'll find what has made the auction into the selling forum that it is today. The earliest British auctions are said to have occurred in the late 1500s, but most information about the actual goings-on can only be traced back to the late 1600s. By that time, auctions had been established in public forums such as local taverns and coffeehouses. There, the common commodity was fine art. In fact, it has been recorded that the works of Rembrandt were offered at auction in 1657. It seems the legendary artist had a debt problem and desperately needed to raise funds in a hurry.

It was in 1744, though, that auctions found their defining moment when the now world-renowned auction firm of Sotheby's came into being. The initial commodity was written works—books, manuscripts, and other printed materials were offered for bid in the salesroom, and auctions were the best way to establish fair market prices. With the laws of supply and demand making their presence felt, the salesroom witnessed the ebb and flow of material availability and desire of ownership, the final value being set by the highest bidder. It sealed a tradition that would define the role of the auction for generations to come.

A little later, in 1766, another high-profile auction house, Christie's, began operation, catering to the desires of collectors seeking paintings and other fine decorative arts. In fact, the goods being auctioned at Christie's were of such high style that it became the preferred auction house of England's most influential families. With Sotheby's continued focus on printed works and Christie's attraction to the finer things in life, the stage was set for a bit of civilized competition. As C. Hugh Hildesley recounts, "Sotheby's was a group of dealers pretending to be gentlemen, and Christie's was a group of gentlemen pretending to be dealers."

Regardless how these two great auction houses were labeled, whether in true competition or just satisfying different interests of the bidding population, Sotheby's and Christie's had evolved into the heart of the professional auction and the home of the astute auction goer. From the ornate wooded interior of the auction parlor to the all-too-familiar sound of the striking gavel, the British auction experience has shaped the bulk of what many people conjure up in their minds when they think of auctions.

But don't think that auctions are only for buying and selling fine art and antique curiosities. On the contrary, auctions have evolved into a major method of commerce that occurs around the world on a daily basis. You've probably heard of police auctions, where confiscated goods are offered to a warehouse full of deal seekers. You've possibly been to a *farmer's auction* where fatted calves, plump chickens, and any other sort of barnyard fare are auctioned to a crowd that has gathered on the hay-strewn floor of a stable. Maybe you've been to an estate sale where interested shoppers come to bid on the personal belongings of others.

Auctions are actively used to distribute just about anything from fish to flowers, from construction contracts to book contracts, from local plots of land to the national debt. Auctions are the chosen method of setting values and making sales on a regular basis. They've become the utility vehicles for dispersing goods, gains, or anything that can be sold to a demanding, dynamic market.

## The Internet in a Nutshell

No doubt you are familiar with phrases like "logging on," "surfing the Net," and "cruising the Web." This is the basic language of cyberspace, where you and I find and develop our virtual habits and online identities. The Internet is the place to be if you're looking for information, looking for people, or looking for neat stuff on which to spend your hard-earned cash.

But if you haven't already heard the story, you might be curious to know how the Internet came into being and how it has grown into a mainstay of our current culture. In 1969, while much of America was captivated by the technology that put a man on the moon, the Department of Defense (DOD) was funding a modest little project called ARPANET (Advanced Research Project Agency Network), a project that established the first navigation points that would lead to the far-reaching expanse of the Internet. The DOD was faced with the dilemma of how to conduct its ongoing research efficiently and effectively while many of the investigative teams were scattered around the country. The idea was that, out of necessity, a central computer network might be established that could work as a hub for the different research groups, providing a core point for sharing data, statistics, and theories. However, because of the nature of the DOD's research, it was also of highest importance that this new network be impervious to outside infiltration or attack. In the event of a natural or manmade disaster, vital communications *had* to be maintained. Therefore, the network was designed to avoid vulnerable "hard-wiring" of communication points, instead using satellite networks, ground based radio networks, and other dynamic communication flows that used the best path available to transmit messages from point to point anywhere in the network.

I'll spare you all the gory technical details, lest your eyes glaze over and your eyelids begin to droop. Suffice it to say, it was that early military project that spawned the first network for sharing information, and it quickly became the envy of other government agencies and of universities who'd caught wind of the breakthrough accomplishment. The idea of connecting individuals and information from across the nation was too good of a thing to be hoarded by a single project research team. When the U.S. government opened the door to these other agencies and universities, the Internet was well on its way to technical stardom.

By 1973, the general design of the Internet was completed, emerging as a basic "network of networks." The linkup to different computers and computer networks was pretty much in the bag, consisting of lots of hardware, cables, and funny little wires. The problem was the lack of a consistent way to send and retrieve the information stored in these electronic vaults. So, Network Control Protocol (NCP) was developed, but could only address the next network server in the network, wherever that might be. Message addressing *and* forwarding was needed, leading to the development of *Internet Protocol* (IP) in 1982. IP worked as a standardized translator, providing a reliable way to communicate across the network. The design involved the creation of *packets* of information that could be shared across the Internet, routing and forwarding these packets from computer to computer until the eventual destination was reached. It's much like addressing an envelope and sending it off in the mail—it goes through a series of sorters and forwarding offices that direct the envelope to the intended addressee. On the Internet, the sorting and forwarding of information packets usually takes place within seconds.

With the Internet protocol well defined, another problem emerged: how can the information in these networks be easily accessed in a simple, user-friendly way? Enter the World Wide Web. Typically referred to as *WWW,* it was developed by Tim Berners-Lee, a graduate of Oxford University, England. His vision was to develop a sort of front-end tool that could help Internet users get around the various network stopping points, allowing folks to send and retrieve information without needing to know very much about computer hardware, network connections, and communication protocol. In 1989, Berners-Lee proposed his point-and-click solution for simplified global information sharing under the project name of *World Wide Web.* The basic concept, as presented, was to enable people to work in a connected, interactive computing environment that would be presented as a *web* of hypertext documents.

GET A CLUE

*Hypertext documents* are simple files containing embedded *hyperlinks* that allow the reader to immediately jump to different areas within a single document or even to entirely different documents that have been made available on the World Wide Web within the space of the Internet.

Certain text within hypertext documents could act as *hot buttons* that would be linked to different locations on Web, those locations usually existing on different computers linked within the Internet. Access to information anywhere on the Internet (literally anywhere in the global connection of networks) could be just a mouse click away.

All that was needed now was an easy way to interact with the World Wide Web, and that need gave birth to the *Web browser*. Browsers, such as Netscape Navigator or Internet Explorer, are those fun little applications that let you point-and-click your way across the Web. The browser was another contribution by Berners-Lee. You have him to thank (or blame?) for your current rapid-mouse-fire abilities and seemingly endless online explorations.

OK. That gives you a quick and dirty background into the development of the Internet. It wasn't until the mid-1990s that Internet use truly exploded and the *Net* and *Web* became household words. To wrap up this little history of the Net, here are a few statistics for you to chew on:

- Between 1994 and 1998 Internet use has grown from roughly 3 million users to over 102 million worldwide.

- In January 1999, revised estimates reported the Internet is shared among 151 million users.

- By 2001, it is projected that the number of online users will reach 700 million and progress to over 1 billion shortly thereafter.

It's these numbers that make the Internet such a big deal. From its humble beginnings at the DOD through the intense research and development in decades that followed, the Internet has grown in a way its originators could hardly have anticipated. Now entering its fourth decade, the Internet has become a part of our culture—a way of life for each of us as we enjoy the opportunity to access more information and services from the comfort and convenience of our own homes.

The Internet is now a driving force in daily life. It directs how information will be shared, who will be sharing it, and what they'll be able to do with it. Although the potential impact of the Internet is seemingly limitless, its eventual outcome is cause for speculation. Will it develop into a utopian existence of knowledge, understanding, and sharing through the Net, or will it fuel an Orwellian world in which people are robbed of their human identities and reduced to nothing more than machine parts? Is this the promise of a shining world of new enlightenment or of a virtual mental dungeon that will shape and control all that we think, do, and believe?

Too heavy, huh? OK. I'll table that discussion for now. In the meantime, how 'bout catching a cyber-wave and getting back to the auction aspect?

# When Worlds Combine

Picture this: you have a garage, an attic, or a storage shed (maybe all three) packed to the rafters with stuff. You claim it's treasure; your spouse claims it's junk. Debate ensues, and the result is that you have to get rid of the stuff. A few solutions spring to mind:

- Take out a classified ad in a local newspaper

- Hold a garage sale on your driveway

- Donate the stuff to a charity (hoping they'll take it all)

- Move to another home and leave the stuff behind

The last option is enticing but probably isn't feasible. The third option is nice, and you can probably write off a portion of the items' value in next year's income tax return. But it's the first two options that hold the promise of profits to be gained. You might be sitting on a veritable treasure trove of rare, unusual, and enticing goods. Your goal in this situation: maximize your profits, cut your losses, and show your spouse how great that "junk" really is. OK, maybe you don't want to get into a petty exchange of *I-told-you-so*; instead, focus on how to pull in the best wad of cash for your no doubt highly desirable cast-offs.

Start with the first option listed above. Many people take out classified ads and get a relatively good response for their efforts. But fielding phone inquiries about your items can be a bit labor intensive and logistically challenging. As some folks keep different waking hours, you might find yourself sleepily grasping for the perfect sales pitch that will clinch a 2 A.M. deal for your estranged Exer-Cycle. In addition, you'll need to arrange for interested lookers to visit your home and inspect your treasure. You can only hope that they'll keep their appointment and that they will actually buy the loot they come to see. But the greatest challenge to selling via newspaper classifieds is this: can you reach enough people to find the *right* buyer, the one who will buy your compelling items quickly and eagerly? Just how far does your local paper reach out into the vast buying public?

Maybe you'll decide to try the more direct method of liquidating your stuff: a garage sale. It sounds pretty easy. All you have to do is lug it out on your lawn or driveway, post a few garish signs around the neighborhood, and the shoppers will come. But hold on a minute: if it's a *garage* sale, why drag the stuff out of the garage? Well, from firsthand experience, I can promise that you'll have looky-loos poking all around your garage if you don't redirect them to your intended sales floor. I once had to escort a woman out of my backyard—she saw the kids' play structure and demanded, "How much?" In garage sale language, "how much" equates not to how much you're asking, but how much you'll settle on to let the buyer steal it away from you. At a garage sale, everyone's a champion haggler and you'll be offered mere coins for what you believe is worth a fistful of bills. Then there's the sticky fingers. Oh yes, the person who just bought the box of books from you for two dollars has secretly grabbed a few extra dishes and an antique iron, stuffing them inside the box before making a hasty getaway. The point is that at a garage sale, you're *truly* liquidating your stuff, getting only pennies on the dollar, and you might find you have less control over your sale as bargain hunters besiege your cozy hamlet turned haggle-ground. And, again, the reach of your homemade advertising is extremely limited. There has to be a better way to reach the right buyers and get the prices you deserve while maintaining control of the situation.

Enter the Internet. Remember those statistics I gave you earlier? Imagine if you could reach those millions of online surfers when hocking your wares. Imagine reaching a variety of social classes, pockets of wealth, bargain hunters, and treasure seekers. Imagine making the perfect sale: getting your price for an item that will be valued and loved by its buyer. Stop imagining. It's real.

Maybe your visions of the Internet are of privacy invasion and pornography peddling. Yes, there is some creepy stuff going on out there. But you'll also find on the Internet magnanimous forums of buyers, sellers, and traders, and a level of courtesy that almost defies comprehension. Your online experience could start with a chat group discussing computer hardware. Eventually, one of the participants will mention, "Hey, I have an extra 17-inch PC monitor just sitting here. Anyone interested in it?" The seed is planted. "Yeah. How much do you want for it?" The seed is watered. "I was thinking $100." It sprouts. "Cool. I'll take it." Leaves appear on the stem. "Wait!" a third person interjects. "My monitor is about to die on me. I'll give you $125 for yours." A spurt of growth. "Hold on. I'll make it $150." In no time at all, a sweet-smelling rose has appeared. And it started so easily, didn't it?

My early experiences with buying, selling, and trading online began in the *newsgroups* (also known as the *Usenet*). You know, that's where you can join in conversations on everything from collecting trinkets to politics to major medical advances to ridding the airwaves of a certain hyper-affectionate purple dinosaur. I'm a collector of various memorabilia and other promotional knickknacks, and I spent much time online haunting the **rec.collecting** newsgroup (see Figure 1-1). There, I could trade stories and information with other collectors while finding listings of various items for sale in the

Figure 1-1

This is where my online bartering began. The rec.collecting newsgroup had more items than I could click a mouse at.

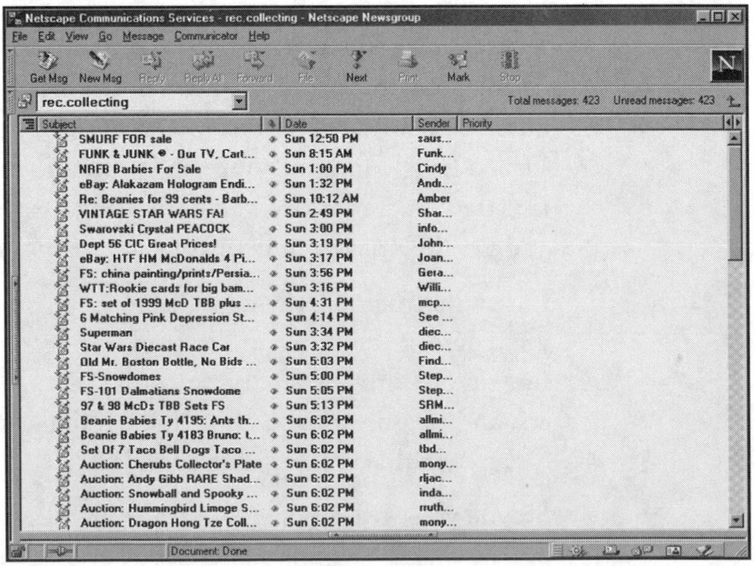

wide-reaching electronic classifieds column. What a great idea! Soon, I began posting some of my own items for sale—and selling them, too. It didn't matter where anyone was geographically; in the newsgroups, participants may as well all be sitting in a circle.

And then it happened. An item was posted for sale, and the seller received a flood of offers. His dilemma: Who would get the goodies? Rather than make the decision himself, he offered the item to whoever made the best offer. With that, the newborn online auction received its inaugural slap on the butt. The cry was heard across the Net.

As you'll soon learn, the Internet has become the platform for a new marketplace, a place where millions of Web surfers can find one another with ease. Merely mention "for sale," and you capture the immediate attention of online shoppers from around the world. Online auctions established a huge virtual auction parlor where more sellers find more buyers, and more items become more available than ever before. So look again at your pile of stuff. Do you want to settle for just selling it to the people down the street or the people across town, or do you want to offer it up to a multitude across the globe? That's a rhetorical question. The answer is obvious: *There's gold in that thar Net.*

## The Good, the Bad, and the Bizarre

Before I go much further, consider again your key goal in reading this book: how to make sense of all the auctions available to you on the Internet and how to make the best use of your time online. Just as you get junk mail in your neighborhood mailbox as well as in your e-mail inbox, you can find a bunch of time-wasters (and worse) on the sometimes "Weird World Web."

While the Internet can be a huge virtual playground, it can also be a huge sinkhole of wasted time and missed opportunities. With so much to see online, it's clear that you won't be able to see it all (nor would you want to). But the lure of the Web can easily ensnare you, and you can find yourself a slave to its offerings. Although I'll go deeper into the traps and trials of the Internet in Chapter 18, for now let me give you some quick advice before you embark on your online journeys.

Having dragged myself into work after many a night of unbridled link-hopping, I've learned to exercise some discipline. If I have a true purpose for going online (research, shopping, bidding, or selling at auctions), I try to limit my destinations to just the appropriate sites. I can't tell you how many times I've dithered about, surfing randomly, only to find that I had less than three hours to sleep before I had to get ready to go to work. I've also had many experiences where my intended online goals were derailed at the sight of interesting links, leading me astray and dashing the possibility of achieving what I had originally set off to do.

If you have time for casual surfing, go for it, but try to set yourself a time limit. Navigating the Web can chew up more time than you realize, and you might never get to the task you originally wanted to achieve. Your butt tends to flatten after a while, too.

The Web offers up a smorgasbord of things to do, places to see, and people to meet. Your goal should be to get the most out of the Internet without it getting the most out of you.

First, the good: the Internet offers more information at your fingertips than any public library or reference center that I know of. If you need to find out, seek out, or look out, start with the Internet. I have yet to enter an online search that didn't return at least some information that I needed. Often, my quests for knowledge have been enhanced as I encountered supporting information or related links to similar subject matter. Whether you're looking for medical advice, legal information, consumer assistance, product data, public opinion, or just fun and games, the Internet is the best place to find it. Try it if you haven't already, and I think you'll agree.

Now, the bad: there are some potentially dangerous places out on the Web. Unfortunately, we share this world with some less-than-honorable and even downright nefarious people. You've no doubt heard that you can learn about making bombs online; it's true. Some hackers are obsessed with breaking into private computer systems to steal confidential information, illegally alter data, or just make their nasty little presence known. I've already mentioned the pornographic element out there; you don't have to try too hard to find it, nor is it hard to accidentally stumble across.

**WARNING!** Watch it folks! Your innocent Internet searches can often turn up some nasty stuff. Some unscrupulous characters will put just about anything in their wicked Web site's *meta data* (that's the information used to match Web searches) to get more people to find their site. It was found that a simple search for the "White House" turned up not only 1600 Pennsylvania Avenue but also a pornographic peep show that you might not normally expect to tour.

**IN MY MIND** Now, before you label me some sort of Web censor, I must assert that I am a proponent of freedom of expression, and I applaud the open forum that the Internet provides. By the same token, I'm also a member of a community. Everything on the Internet serves a purpose, but it should have its proper place, time, and audience. Duping innocent Web surfers into stumbling across potentially offensive or illegal content isn't fair and it isn't nice. My motto: Keep the Internet open and free, but clearly mark each avenue to avoid a wrong turn.

And then there's the bizarre: strange things abound in cyberspace—not all of them bad or dangerous, but definitely peculiar. There are all manner of online freak shows, personal *webcams* (PC cameras that transmit what someone or something is doing), and goings-on beyond anything you can imagine. Remember, the Internet is huge, and there are millions of people using it. If you can think it, you can probably find it on the Net. Don't say I didn't warn you.

## Time to Go Shopping!

OK, I think you've got the idea of what the Internet is all about. Now, before I leave this chapter, let me make one confession: I am an avid online shopper. There, I've said it. E-commerce, for me, has become the greatest convenience to show up in a long time, and I shop online practically every day. Gone are the days where I have to drive the streets and scour the city to find the stuff I want. The Internet has conveniently brought the goods to me.

Online commerce has become a breakthrough development for retailers. Never before have businesses been able to reach so many customers with so little effort. Marketers are learning how large the market really is, about what people are buying, and about why they're buying it.

Web retailers report that most of their online selling activity occurs after 10 P.M. on any given day. It makes sense: in this fast-paced world, many people don't have time to get out to the local mall to shop for what they need or browse for what they want. As time has become such a precious commodity for everyone, online shopping has emerged as the leisurely way to shop for whatever, whenever—24 hours a day. There's something very enticing about strolling the cyber-aisles in your jammies.

 **DID YOU KNOW?**   In January 1999, online sales figures for the 1998 holiday season tallied to an impressive $8.2 billion.

But what happens when you can't find that special item at the online stores? What if what you're looking for is rare, out of production, out of stock, or generally out of reach? And if you do find what you're looking for at the online mall, do you know that you're getting the best price? Do you know what others are paying for the same item? Have you really sampled the total selection that's out there? Your answers lie in the realm of the online auctions, where you can find the hard-to-find, compare prices and values, find the best deal, and have a great time doing it. I mentioned earlier how the online auctions can benefit those who have something to sell. They can also benefit those who are looking to buy.

Why do the auctions work and who's using them? Well, that will be the next stop. Read on.

# CHAPTER 2

# How and Why Do Auctions Work?

Yeah, what's the big deal about auctions? Are they really the greatest break-through in e-commerce, or are they just the product of a collective lapse of sanity and out-of-control whimsical bidding? Do auctions really serve a use-ful purpose, or are they just a playground for folks with tons of stuff to sell or wads of cash to blow? Do auctions offer any benefits for buyers, or are buyers just lining the pockets of the sellers who pit them against one another as they strive to acquire some desirable item?

These are valid questions. To answer them, take a look at how auctions work and how they can benefit both bidders and sellers alike.

## The Role of Auctions in the Economy

People who scoff at the role of auctions in society probably assume that auc-tions in general don't affect them or their lifestyle. After all, they think, if *I'm* not participating in any auctions anywhere, how could they possibly affect me? In case your friends start criticizing your new hobby, allow me to offer you some counter arguments.

Auctions account for billions of dollars being exchanged on a regular basis. Not just in the sale of art, collectibles, or curiosities, either. As I hinted in the preceding chapter, auctions are used to establish wholesale prices for perish-able goods (fish, flowers, or other such commodities) as well as durable goods (land or equipment). But auctions are also used to exchange economic goods. More specifically, governments use auctions to fund their national debt and keep their economies afloat.

The U.S. Treasury conducts regular auctions in which it offers government securities (treasury bills, notes, and bonds) to qualified dealers in order to fund the country's outstanding debt. The dealers are various institutions or banks that bid on the debt being offered at the time of auction. Simply put, the funds the dealers use to pay for the securities (by way of their high bids) are actually loans to the government to cover the debt. The results of these auctions can drive fluctuations in the rates for the securities being offered and are often an indication of how the bidding institutions view the soundness and stability of current fiscal policy. The ripple effect of these auctions can reach you and me by way of influencing interest rates, mortgage rates, and any other form of monetary policy that affects the common person.

In this respect, you are involved in auctions and their results whether you like it or not. But that's what makes the economic world turn, so not to worry, right?

## Who's Auctioning?

OK, now it's clear that our government is using auctions on a regular basis. You also know that high-end auction houses such as Sotheby's, Christie's, and Butterfield & Butterfield make auctions their way of economic life. And you've discovered that even the local seafarer drops his load of mackerel at the docks and auctions it off to the highest bidder. But who else is auctioning? Seemingly *everybody!*

Perhaps that's too much of a generalization; but just take a look at who else is auctioning goods:

- The U.S. government auctions more than just the debt. It also regularly auctions off government surplus and seized goods. Uncle Sam might cut you a great deal on real estate, cars, trucks, boats, office equipment, and more. Anything from autos to home furnishings to toys to jewelry can be found for auction. The proceeds of sales of goods go into the U.S. Treasury Asset Forfeiture Fund.

- Your local post office holds auctions, too. No, not old postal scales or half-licked stamps. The USPS regularly auctions off damaged or unclaimed items that have been relegated to the "where is it now?" closet of misfit mail.

- Public resources and utilities make use of auctions. A recent example was the auctioning of licensing rights for the Broadband PCS services. An auction was conducted to ensure that the ultimate licensees (the highest bidders) would understand the unique value of the technology and would apply the best ideas and innovations to the emerging PCS services market.

Those are interesting, but a little remote from daily life. How about bringing it a little closer to home? Who's auctioning the stuff you really want? Take a look at what you can readily find at some of the online auction sites:

- Major manufacturers of computer equipment auction off manufacturing overruns or recently outdated hardware and software.

- Manufacturers of electronic equipment stage auctions to clear their warehouses to make room for new inventories.

- Wholesalers auction whatever is making their warehouses bulge, often liquidating new merchandise to reclaim storage capacity or to clean out inventories if the building lease has expired.

- Retailers auction just about anything that doesn't seem to be selling via the normal sales methods and look to the auction to spur sales that otherwise would never materialize.

- Collectors buy and sell just about everything under the sun that holds any sort of nostalgic appeal or potential investment promise.

- And that guy with the garage full of stuff—he's auctioning all sorts of things that might otherwise be hauled off to the dump or stored indefinitely. Anyone looking for a used lawn spreader?

The bottom line is if you've got it, someone probably wants it. If you're looking for it, someone probably has it up for auction. The auction has universal appeal to just about everyone who's looking for great deals, great items, and a refreshing alternative to the regular ways of shopping.

Hey, even kids are getting into the auction game. Although you have to be 18 years or older to participate in online auctions, eight-year-old Eric Prince and his classmates have been known to step into the auction parlor in their third-grade classroom. Teacher Cindy Davis has learned that kids like auctions, too, and they're quite resourceful when it comes to earning bidding power. Mrs. Davis awards her students *auction certificates* for good citizenship in her classroom. The more consistent the citizenship, the more often certificates are awarded. The more certificates the kids have to spend, the more bidding power they can assert. And you ought to see these future CEOs in action. It's some of the fiercest bidding you'll ever see as these youngsters clamor for goodies, gadgets, stickers, and Star Wars stuff. Good thing they have about nine more years before they can get into the online auction arena. From bidding wars to bait-and-switch tactics, these junior-leaguers seem to already have the act down pat. They're one tough crowd.

## It's Better to Barter

It's important to understand why so many people are attracted to auctions. Auctions now challenge the market analysts and focus groups that devote so much attention to determining what makes a shopper tick. The auction, with its sometimes competitive, confrontational, or even scavenging qualities, doesn't fit the statistical picture that resulted in the streamlined neon shopping malls of today. So what gives?

First, remember what an auction is as well as what purpose it serves. By definition, an auction is the public offering of goods or property in which a group of potential buyers bid until the highest purchase price is declared. The high bidder wins the right to purchase the item for the value of the high bid and has set the new market value for the item (in that forum and at that moment, anyway). That's the textbook definition, and it's probably much the way you might express your understanding of an auction.

Next, look at the duty of the auction: it is chiefly a means by which values can be determined for goods or property with no specified, quantifiable, or agreed-upon sales price in a direct-sales market. If you have a unique or desirable item, you might not know its true value until you put it to the auction test. This is especially true of items that have no established, recurring sales history (rare artifacts, perhaps). Their value might only be determined by association with similar items that might have an expressed value. That might sound like a lot of

Greek salad to you, but it essentially means that some items defy valuation until you collect a group of bidders and let them perform the valuation ritual for you.

Your original expectations could be far exceeded if a group of bidders actively drives the price of an item through the roof. On the other hand, you might have a sobering experience, learning that there are few buyers interested in your item and what they are offering is much less than the sacks of money you'd hoped for.

And, therein lies the beauty of the auction: no one commands a price unless the buying public agrees it's fair and reasonable. No one can proclaim what's rare, hard to find, or highly desirable unless the auction marketplace agrees. By your bidding, you have control to pay what you think is a fair price and you have the choice to say "not interested" if you're not convinced the item is the steal of the century. At an auction you truly have purchasing power, and the bidding floor will determine what's hot and what's not. And with so many auctions to be found online, you have the power to choose and compare. You'll know what's hard to find and what's hardly a find. Take your time, kick the tires, and get what you *really* want.

## Bidders Can Be Choosers

So now you're bidding. Do you bid on the first thing you see, everything you see, and anything you see? There's a smooth-talking guy up there wearing sleek polyester and a Cheshire grin. He must be dialed in to know what he's talking about, and he's about to let you in on a great deal. As you move forward to get a closer look at his wares, a barker from across the way rings out that *he's* got the goods you really want. Maybe a third or a fourth chimes in, and soon the hot commodity on this floor is *you*. You've got the wallet and you're willing to spend. Where will you spend, though? These guys are clawing for your time and money while you sit back and let them battle it out. And with an obvious selection to choose from, you don't have to be in a hurry to buy anything until you want so.

That's the power of the online auction market. With hundreds of auction sites and millions of items up for bid, you have time for a leisurely stroll through the listings to see what you like most. Gone are the days when sellers claiming their items are "impossible to find" can easily exploit buyers. Maybe at a local show or convention that seller might be speaking the truth—and in that scenario you might have to pay the asking price. But open up your view to the national and international market, and you'll probably find more of the same thing that first seller was offering. Soon, the impossible to find is readily available. Too bad, Mr. Seller.

And how about Mr. Seller? Do you like him? Do you think he's being fair and honest with you? If not, wave him off and move on to the next online merchant. That's the other benefit of the online auctions: those sellers now have to work harder for your business since it's a highly competitive and crowded marketplace that they'll be working in. Honesty, integrity, and good customer service will dictate which sellers get the sale and which ones should just sail away. The wheat is always separated from the chaff, and if someone rubs you the wrong way, just make a mental note and move along. The interesting thing about online auctions is that the good sellers and the bad sellers become well known very quickly.

If you're a new buyer in the online auction realm, here's a tip for you: you'll need to practice some restraint and patience. Your first experiences will probably be marked by the penchant to jump in and bid immediately on everything you see that interests you. You might be thinking, *"Wow! I better get this now while I can. I might not see another."* Let me help you break those shackles of times past. The auctions are a steady stream of goods that you can tap into whenever you feel like it. Most items will be easy to find, some will be a little harder. But more often than not, if you lose out on an auction the first time around, you'll probably find another of the same item (maybe in better condition or more complete than the first) sometime very soon.

**IN MY MIND**

I see it as a sort of *elliptical stream*. Stuff flows through the online auction offerings and people snatch what they want from the stream. If a buyer tires of an item or wants to upgrade it or whatever, that item usually finds its way back into the stream. Eventually, that little goodie you're looking for will come bob-bob-bobbing along through an auction site near you. In the meantime, just stay the course and enjoy the free-flowing current. Remember that sometimes the journey is as enjoyable as the destination (unless you're on your way to a root canal or something, in which case it's a lot better—but at least for the present you won't find dental surgery on the auction block).

Figure 2-1

My most peculiar purchase this year. The Japan-only "Phantom of the Paradise" action figure. A distant cousin to the Ken doll, and a twisted reminder of the kooky things you can find at an auction.

A final point to be made about the online auctions is that you can find just about anything conceivable out there (see Figure 2-1). If you need some hardware to beef up your home PC, you'll find it. If you're looking for a cool deal on sporting goods, you'll find it. If you've lost some trinket from your past that has left a nostalgic hole in your existence, you'll (usually) find it. And if you're just looking for something odd or entertaining to satisfy your whimsical nature, you'll find *a whole lot* of that.

## Sellers Find Their Market

Now sellers aren't all slime, and they don't have to resort to bootlicking to make the online auctions work for them. In fact, sellers will often find incredible prosperity in the virtual auction parlor simply due to the fact that there are millions of ready-and-willing bidders out there waiting for the next item to hit the block.

For sellers, whether they be wholesalers, retailers, or private individuals, online auctions provide an audience that is captivated by the goods flowing across their PC monitors. Someone with a garage full of treasure has access to a group much larger than the local population of garage-sale mavens and passers-by—a group so large, in fact, that it practically guarantees a seller will find a buyer every time.

Think of an electronics dealer who has a huge overstock of a previous year's Dolby Surround receivers in his storeroom but can't seem to sell them as rapidly as before due to the advent of Dolby Digital and DTS technologies. He has a bunch of capital invested in that outdated equipment, and he's looking for a way to move that inventory out fast. Well, with electronics being one of the hot commodities at online auctions, he can either offer them up for bid at one of the merchant sites (like Onsale.com) or list them himself at one of the person-to-person sites (like Yahoo!Auctions). By going this route, he throws the doors of his overstocked storeroom wide open to the buying eyes of millions of online bidders.

But is this electronics peddler going to have to practically give away his unwanted receivers and have to settle for taking a loss on his inventory? Probably not. The unique by-product of auction sales is that bidders often get so caught up in their back-and-forth bidding volleys that they end up paying retail prices for items. That makes sellers happy, and it's a practice on which bidders will be counseled a bit later in this book. To the seller's benefit, online bidding and buying is conducive to whimsical purchases and impulse buys.

**WARNING!**  All right. It's happened to me. I've been caught up in the bug of bidding at auctions to the point that I've lost oback of how much I was really spending. After a time, you can get really used to having little packages arrive at your doorstep on a regular basis. Once they stop arriving, you get a bit twitchy and despondent that there was no little "present" awaiting you at the end of the day. The cure: Buy more! The result: Pay more! The sellers: They're happy as clams.

And, just to prove the point of how bidding can get spirited and sometimes exceed the expectations of the seller, take a look at Figure 2-2. There, you'll see a whimsical little auction that turned to gold for me.

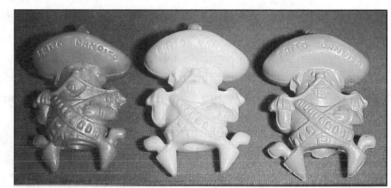

Figure 2-2

From 1969, the easily recognizable Frito Bandito pencil topper. If you were a kid then, you probably had a pencil box full of them. This lot saw some unprecedented bidding on eBay.com and brought a final high bid of $89. Wuhoo!!

## Leveling the Playing Field

In the past, you had to rely on our your knowledge and wits when negotiating purchases. When you stepped into the sales arena—maybe a car dealership or an antique show—it became *us versus them* in a battle of wits, cunning, and cold hard facts. As the offers and counteroffers flow back and forth, someone starts gaining ground while someone starts losing ground. The buyer might be desperate to have the item. The seller might be desperate to make a sale. Weaknesses are exposed and the informational advantage soon takes its toll. The momentum sways to one party or the other, and a deal is signed. Are both parties happy, or is remorse on the way (experienced by either the buyer or the seller)? You know, it doesn't have to be this way.

I already discussed the way the Internet has become a vast pool of information. What do you need to know? Look on the Internet for your answers. What do you want to research? Look on the Internet for the facts. What do other people think? Well, the Internet is overflowing with personal opinion and testimonials. This ties neatly to online auctions in that, if you're considering bidding on something online, you typically have a period of days to comfortably and casually research what it is you want to buy *before* you buy. That way, when you do decide to bid on something, regardless of where it's being auctioned, you can do so with a clear head and a firm understanding of what it is you think is worthy of your well-educated bid.

And remember that the auction sites themselves present invaluable research data. After all, what better way to estimate the value of an item than to review what others have paid in the past or are about to pay in the very near future. At most online auction sites, you can review the outcome of recently completed auctions and determine how many people were bidding and how much they were bidding. You can also find out how many of a particular item have been available in the past, how many are available right now, and how many will probably be available in the coming days or weeks (remember Mr. Impossible-to-find?). And beyond that, if you don't like the prices you're seeing at one auction site, you can often hop the next hyperlink and go to a different auction site to see if the same item is available there.

GET A CLUE

*Big* clue here, folks. Many items you can find at online auctions will be selling for vastly different prices. A bit later on you'll see how you can save some money by visiting the less-traveled sites to place your bids or, if you're selling, which sites will have more people spending more money.

Now, if you're not one to do a lot of heavy research or you can't seem to find what you need to know about what's up for auction, just watch what the other people are doing. Seasoned auction goers are well versed in the value of things online. They're also very vocal about what's fair and what's not, especially within the auction sites they regard as their homes online. Auction communities have the added benefit of "regulars" who spend a lot of time (and money) at these sites. They do so because they're finding the items they want on a regular basis, or they're making profits from their own sales week in and week out. To these community members, it's in their best interest to help keep the neighborhood clean. If anyone's up to any shenanigans, the flares usually go up. Site administrators will be contacted or feedback forums will resonate with reports of wrong-doing in cyburbia. Auction communities even go so far as to converse with one another to warn of potentially bad situations (a dishonest seller or a deadbeat bidder) to the point that it becomes difficult for any slimeball to sneak about in the shadows.

The nice thing you can expect from an auction community is that, if you have a question and want someone's opinion, you'll find the community members are rarely bashful about letting you know how they see it. E-mail addresses of other auction goers are typically available to registered member communities, and most sites encourage interaction among the populace. After all, since auctions are something of a meeting ground, why not strike up some conversation? You'll find a lot of experienced buyers and sellers who can help you when you hit a snag or just want some reassurance.

## More Whys and What-Fors

By now you're getting a feel for why online auctions are a good alternative to "find-and-buy" shopping—online or otherwise. But here are just a few more benefits you'll reap when you choose the online auction venue:

- You've already learned that the impossible-to-find sometimes isn't, and if you're looking for something that is quite elusive, you just might find it at the auctions. On the other hand, if you have something to sell that doesn't seem to turn up very often, you'll stand a chance of making greater profits when you parade it in front of those millions of salivating bidders instead of just listing it in your local fishwrap. It's a good deal either way you look at it.

- Remember, you are no longer confined to geographic boundaries. You now have the whole world at your fingertips. Regional items and imported treasures are just a click away. Besides, money is a universal language.

- Although popular items usually carry a popular price, you can often find some great deals when nobody's looking.

- Get more for your effort by letting the Internet carry word of your merchandise for sale. Remember that those millions of bidders like to keep in close contact with one another. They freely share news of interesting items up for auction by word of, uh. . .mouse.

# Safety, Security, and Privacy Online

You now have a good understanding of what auctions are, where they came from, and why they are sometimes the best way to buy or sell. You've seen how auctions can benefit you, and you've become more aware of how many organizations, businesses, and individuals use them, and how often they do so.

You also have a good understanding of the Internet—what it is, where it came from, and why it came about. It's huge, you know, and the resources it offers are unparalleled. It's the most dynamic tool for research and recreation our generation has yet to see.

Now with the Internet's wide open cyber wilderness comes a warning: take care and be safe in the online jungle. Do you feel comfortable with all the Net has to offer? Do you feel you can safely navigate the Web without taking a wrong turn down a back alley and encountering unsavory characters with wide grins and evil intent? Well, if you're like most Web surfers, these are concerns that you ponder.

It can be a jungle in there, filled with dangerous critters in a perilous landscape. But it can also be a lush paradise filled with sites of wonder and enjoyment. You need a map to avoid the pitfalls and a guide to point out dangers and undesirable elements. This chapter will help ensure that your eventual journeys will be safe and worry-free.

Take a momentary break from the specific auction discussion to be sure you're clued in on the safest way to enjoy the Internet and the online auctions you'll soon be visiting.

## What, Me Worry?

Whenever I talk to anybody about Internet safety, I first try to bring the whole matter into reasonable perspective. Remember, as large as the Net and the Web have become, expect that you are surfing with millions of other Web-riders out there. They're all looking for the perfect cyber-wave, and they're usually too interested in how good they're looking to worry about who you are and how well you're taming your own wave. So in my experienced opinion, you don't need to fear that someone on the Net is out to get you. I can almost guarantee that they don't even *know* you, let alone care. Of course, there are some Web jerks out there who don't have much more to do in their lives than to pick, poke, and peek into the doings of others. You've heard of Net fraud, hacking, stalking, and other unpleasantness. But it's rare that someone will single you out online—you and I are just more peas in the pod. Unless you go about truly making your presence known while you're online (maybe in newsgroup postings or in chat rooms), it's likely that none of these cyber-buggers is ever going to notice you just scooted by on the fiber-optic freeway.

If you're new to the Internet and feeling a bit squeamish about jumping into the mix, just plot a course for yourself, go where you want to go and do what you want to do for as long as you want to do it. While you're out there, mind your own business and take in the sights. Check your paranoia at the entry portal and relax. And don't worry—this is fun place.

**IN MY MIND**   What's that, you say? We're just putting blinders on? Well, you're probably right. I agree that there's more danger out there on the Net than you or I could ever click a mouse at, but isn't that just the way of life in general? You can worry about getting in an auto accident every time you pull the car out of the garage. You can agonize about salmonella every time you crack open an egg. Or you can take reasonable precautions and arm yourself with enough skill and knowledge to make your life a little more light-hearted. Maybe I'm just whistling past the graveyard, but until the dead begin to rise from the Earth, I'm going to take in the beautiful craftsmanship on each of the tombstones I see.

# You Have Nothing To Fear Except . . .

The first thing that probably comes to mind when you think of your Web safety is your identity and the availability of your personal information online. Can others out there *see* you when you're surfing? Can they tell what you're up to, and are they taking notes? Can they learn enough about you to use your personal information in any sort of wicked or unauthorized way? The answer: probably not with wicked intent, but possibly unauthorized. It all depends on how you define *authorized*.

Believe it or not, a lot of information about you is readily available online. It's typically nothing new and usually didn't involve anything devious to put it there. Right now, you can go online and find your name, address, phone number, and even directions to your home. "*Scary*," you say? "*Who cares?*" I respond. Open up a phone book and you'll find most of that information anyway. Drop by your local post office and you'll get even more. Are you and I interesting enough to be sought out and tracked down? I think not.

**GET A CLUE** If you want to try the exercise for yourself, go to **www.infoseek.com**. Once there, choose the selection *White Pages*. You can enter a name or an e-mail address and find some pretty basic information about a person. If it comforts you, just think about Steve Martin in the movie, *The Jerk*. *"The new phone book's here!"* He was pretty excited to see that he was worthy of being listed.

Before you get too alarmed at what you can easily learn about yourself or others online, remember that all of this same information is also available offline as well. Granted, the Internet does make it easier to retrieve this data, but it's been available to the general public for decades all the same. If you haven't been targeted by some Nosy Norman by now, chances are you never will.

But what else about you is out there for others to peruse? Well, how about your shopping habits and your purchasing preferences? That's the kind of information that gets big attention because it tells how you have spent your time or money in the past and how you might be inclined (or encouraged) to spend it in the future. Marketing trends and buyer profiles are big business in the consumer world. For all the products and services that people buy, countless hours have been devoted to making sure that bottles of ketchup fit the hand comfortably and the electronic voices on the phone are pleasant and reminiscent of favorite aunts. If you've ever responded to a telephone survey, you've provided personal information. If you've ever returned business reply mail (maybe a product warranty card), you've provided personal information. If you've ever responded to an e-mail message from an online retailer, you've provided personal information. And if no one's yet blown up your car or harassed your Chihuahua, you'll probably be fine.

The information you provide, though, is all stored in huge databases. That's often how the phone survey people got your number in the first place. The information in these databases is of high value to other marketers and retailers. They're buying your information in hopes that they can make you one of their future customers. It's not dangerous, although I'll admit it can be annoying when the Culligan Man calls just as you're settling into the tub. My advice: get an answering machine and let it screen your calls.

**GET A CLUE**  Here's something you should know: whenever you purchase or inquire about a product online, be sure to carefully review any screen where you will be entering your personal information. You've got to provide your name, address, and so on when making a purchase—the supplier has to get your item to you somehow. But, while you're in that online order form, keep a watchful eye out for innocent little sentences or paragraphs that ask if it's OK to provide your information to other businesses that might offer similar products. Often, these "permission statements" will be preceded by a little check box that is prechecked—*your permission has been assumed*. Turn those little check boxes off if you want to reduce your incoming junk mail.

## Who's Out There?

It all seemed to start with some real brainiacs that designed the Internet, the Web, and the browsers. Then the coders came along. They began developing Web sites, chat rooms, and newsgroups. They brought HTML, Java, and CGI Script. They spoke with one another online in seemingly cryptic languages that only they understood. They were geeks, machine-heads, and code-crunchers—and we owe a lot to them. They made the Internet and World Wide Web what they are today. Sure, they might have seemed peculiar upon first meeting, but they're generally good people and very helpful to newcomers.

Since the early days of the Internet, millions of new people have gotten online and millions more are catching the wave every year. Today you'll find business professionals, artists, celebrities, teachers, students, moms in tennis shoes, and gray-haired grannies in housecoats. It's society, and it's potentially everybody, including you. As a Muppet once sang: *"Who are the people in your neighborhood . . . the people that you meet each day?"*

Now there are a fair share of creeps, crooks, and cruddies online, too. They're looking to stir up some trouble or get some attention. They might be looking to exploit you or rip you off. They're often masters of disguise, too. The Internet is a funny place in that you can assume any identity you want while you're online. It's a faceless interactive meeting ground, and you're never 100 percent certain who you're meeting when you go person-to-person. You don't necessarily want to run scared while you're online, but you do want to develop a certain awareness. Most folks you meet online are the same kinds of nice people you meet at the local grocery store, and most will respect you and your personal privacy. Others, though, have different ideas in mind while trying to act as your best friend.

If you're looking for some ways to determine who you're meeting out there, use this simple checklist to help you decide if you've found a good witch or a bad witch:

- Have I initiated this person-to-person contact or has the other person?

- What does this other person seem to want?

- Has this other person requested personal information from me?

- Does this other person seem to say all the things I want to hear, have all the items that I'm looking to buy, or generally seem to be the exact person I'm trying to track down?

- Does this person seem to know a lot about me already?

- Is this person *too friendly?*

It is a shame that we have to exercise a certain amount of distrust when we meet others, but it's better to be safe than sorry. Usually, in my online meetings, I can tell if another person is genuine—in good part by seeing that person share the same sorts of reservations about me as I have about them. The really wise folks out there know better than to start digging in your personal affairs or information. They know how important it is to be protected online, and they'll often extend that belief in an effort to help you protect yourself. After a few brief interactions, you'll generally have a feeling whether you can trust another person. But never let your guard down completely.

If you do encounter someone who seems questionable, don't overreact and don't panic. That might be playing right into their hands. Simply deny their request for sensitive information or any other inquiry you don't feel comfortable answering. Don't duck and hide; a simple *"No thank you"* or *"Not at this time"* will usually do the trick. Often, a fleece-clad individual who sees you have a certain amount of Net savvy will simply take off and look for someone less informed to dupe. Just by showing you're aware shows you're no pushover.

## Who's In There?

What about when you're not interacting with another person or business? Are you still offering information about yourself while you cruise the wonders of the Web? Actually, yes, you are.

Remember that while you're online—researching, auctioning, shopping, or just playing—you are leaving a trail of electronic bread crumbs behind you. And there are little electronic critters that will follow the bread crumbs right into your PC. They're real quiet, and you might not even notice they've nested in your cozy little hard drive.

When you log on to the Net, you start an electronic conversation with other computers that act as the switching stations for your journey. Your PC regularly exchanges IP addresses with other computers as a result of your navigational requests. By your mouse clicks, you're identifying that you wish to go somewhere online and the different cyber-conductors recognize and route you along your way. The only way they can effectively do that is to identify your PC during the trip.

Now picture what happens when you walk into an electronics store. You're looking for a new high-definition television, and you might ask someone at the counter where those are. That person acknowledges you and points you in the right direction. Soon, an eager clerk scoots across the sales floor and greets you with a big smile, an aura of cheap cologne, and his business card. This is Chuck, and he's going to be your best friend today. You ask about the televisions and Chuck asks about you. You want to know how much the TV costs, and Chuck wants to know if you'd like to finance it. You want to know if delivery is free, and Chuck wants to know where you live. You want to open an in-store line of credit, and Chuck wants to know where you work, what your average income is, and if you can offer up two forms of picture ID. Chuck's not being invasive; he's just doing his job. But now Chuck knows a lot about you. If you're not sure you want to make the purchase, you might leave the store and think about it, away from the overpowering scent of Old Spice. If you return to the store, Chuck might recognize you and might even remember your name. He goes to his little computer-thingy and pulls up the information you gave him last time you visited. If you don't return to the store, Chuck may place a friendly follow-up call to your home to see if he can answer any more of your questions.

Now, this is all very cute but I assure you there is a point to the illustration. When you travel about online, the sites you stop off at are filled with *Virtual Chucks*. As you click through a Web site, the site is taking note of your IP address (your computer offered it as admission on the cyberspace transport), what areas of the Web site you visit, and even how long you hang around browsing. In many sites, especially those where you'll do some shopping, you might be asked to register in the customer database. This is Virtual Chuck. He wants to know more about you and what sorts of things you're looking for so he can be of more assistance to you during this and hopefully future visits. Virtual Chuck is so pleased you've registered that he goes so far as to offer you a cookie. And from here on out, Chuck will recognize you every time you visit the site.

On the Internet, *cookies* are those little electronic treats that are stored on your PC. They are identifying codes that Web sites use to recognize a particular PC when it returns to the site. If you registered at a site, the cookie can find the information you've previously offered up and you will receive a nice warm welcome upon your return:

"Hi Dennis. Welcome back. Here are some new products you might be interested in."

Isn't that special?

GET
A
CLUE
Sometimes, Virtual Chuck will slip a cookie into your back pocket when you browse his showroom. Most often, cookies are dropped onto your hard drive without much fanfare or notification of any sort. If you want to prevent that from happening or at least want to know when the plate of cookies is coming your way, read on.

Cookies are really not too much to concern yourself over, but they do represent your being identified online. Some Web sites will even sell their cookie information to other sites and, before you know it, Virtual Chuck has told all his other sales buddies in the area who you are and what sorts of things you want to buy. Typically, though, cookies are neither destructive nor of much danger to you or your PC. However, if you think you've been taking in too many free cookies, you can put your PC on a diet.

First, you can *just say no* to cookies at the source. Web browsers like Netscape Navigator or Internet Explorer have settings that either warn you of incoming cookies or let you deny the placement of incoming cookies, or both (see Figures 3-1 and 3-2).

The downside to not accepting cookies is that you'll need to reenter your information upon your return to Web sites you frequent. But if you already have cookies on your PC (or maybe you're not sure), just do a file search on your PC's hard drive and look for a file named "cookie.txt." There, you'll find cookies and the URLs of the Web sites that gave them to you. Start up a simple text editor to modify the cookies.txt or cookie.txt files (you might have more than one). Keep only the cookies you want and throw out the rest. It's that simple.

IN
MY
MIND
Sometimes, I *do* like cookies. If I find a Web site that I think I'll be visiting a lot, I'll accept and keep those cookies. Reputable business sites leave cookies that are no trouble to me and speed me along to my intended business while I visit.

Figure 3-1

To manage your cookie acceptance using Netscape Navigator 4.6, you'll find this dialog box when you choose Preferences from the Edit menu. Click on the Advanced category on the left and select your cookie preferences on the right.

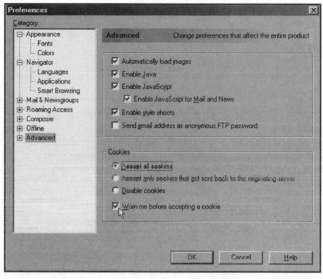

Figure 3-2

In Internet Explorer 4.0, you can manage your cookie settings by choosing Internet Options from the View menu, then clicking on the Advanced tab. Scroll down to the heading labeled Cookies and make whatever changes you like.

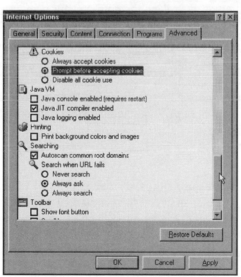

# Spam Doesn't Just Come in a Can Anymore

At one time, Spam simply existed as that heavily marbled meatlike product that sat in the dark recesses of your pantry, only emerging for camping trips or occasional power outages. Its one charm was that you didn't need a can opener to get into it—it came with its own key.

Today, though, spam is the common name of unsolicited e-mail messages that come to you from anyone who's looking for your attention, time, or patronage. Spam is typically not dangerous, although it is annoying. It's usually the result of someone's lifting your e-mail address and using it as a means to interest you in their products or services. As an online auction user, I receive a small but steady stream of spam from start-up auction sites: they're hoping my current auction interest will be incentive enough for me to try their spam-heralded site. To me, that's a sign of desperation and a general turnoff. I'll just delete the spammy message.

**WARNING!**   Look out! Some spam can be dangerous. Beware of unrecognizable messages whose subjects urge you to *"Read this message"* or *"Open this right away."* Naturally, any message that contains any sort of file attachment should be an immediate cause for suspicion. There are some no-goodniks out there who revel in corrupting or destroying the data on your computer. They can easily disrupt your computing life by inserting little e-bombs inside seemingly innocuous file attachments.

It's the attachments that pose the threat. At least as of this writing, the text of the message itself is perfectly safe, except for the threat to your peace of mind—there's no way that simply reading an e-mail message can damage your computer—and warnings to the contrary are generally hoaxes. When a friend forwards a panicky message to you, check it out at **http://kumite.com/myths/** or one of the other virus-hoax sites before you worry about it.

**DID YOU KNOW?**   In some states, distributing spam is illegal. If that's the case where you live, you can forward the unwanted messages to the appropriate law enforcement agencies where they'll go to work to "calibrate" the offender's activities.

And most ISPs try to keep spam out of their servers. If you get a message you don't want, you can often help cause trouble for the spammer by forwarding the message to abuse@[yourispname] and abuse@[spamispname].

## A Virus Is Nothing to Sneeze At

Look out, because sometimes it's an all-out germ war going on in cyberspace. You've probably heard about *viruses*—those destructive little scraps of code that can wreak havoc on your PC's files before you realize it. Viruses are dangerous and can literally wipe out the information you store on your PC. They usually live inside executable application files (those with the .*exe* extension) or in program macros inside document or spreadsheet files (look for the extensions of .*doc*, .*dot*, and .*xls*). And where do these viruses come from? Well, just about anybody online can have and pass along a virus. It usually starts with someone developing a virus and then tucking it away inside one of the file types I just mentioned. The evil virus inventor sends that nasty little creation off to the Internet by placing it on a Web site, posting it to a newsgroup, or spamming it through e-mail. Once it gets out, its growth rate can be exponential. It proliferates among online users like a disease among people in a crowded building.

How can you protect yourself from viruses? First, *never* open any message attachment from someone you don't know, especially if they've sent you one of the above-mentioned file types. Second, be sure you have a good virus protection program running on your PC (McAfee's VirusScan or Norton's AntiVirus are two of the most widely used; these days, one or the other is often installed on most of the newer PCs when they're sold). The virus protection programs normally run constantly on your PC's desktop and scan for infected files every time you boot up. These utilities also provide updates and information about new viruses that have been discovered as well as the appropriate antidotes that you can download for free. Just visit their Web sites to be sure your PC's anti-viral medicine chest stays stocked up (go to **www.mcafee.com** or **www.symantec.com**).

Finally, if you decide you do want to open a message attachment that has been sent to you or download something from the Web, save it to your hard drive first and then run your virus check. If the file has a recognized virus, the virus utility should catch it. Oh, and always wash your hands when you're through.

## A Quick Lesson in Netiquette

The next thing to think about is you and your behavior. After all, safety and security is really up to each person on the Net. Everyone must take appropriate steps to ensure they take care in what they do online and how they present themselves when in the company of others. And for that, it's appropriate to take a quick course in *netiquette.*

Netiquette, by its name, is the online answer to good manners, appropriate behavior, and mutual respect. To be treated well online, you must treat others in the same way. The general tenet of netiquette is the use of the Golden Rule: "Do unto others as you would have them do unto you." If you think that sounds corny, think again. It's really the only thing that keeps a society civilized. The Internet is a society, and it's a powerful asset to everyone who takes part in it. People who "pee in the pool," so to speak, ruin it not only for other swimmers but for themselves as well. There's a certain amount of self-policing that needs to occur, and it's everything that everybody's parents taught them. Use the Golden Rule generously when you interact with others online, and you'll be pleased at how well others interact with you.

Another thing to keep in mind while online is that others can't see your facial expressions or hear the inflection in your voice. What you mean as funny might come off as rude. What you intend as sincere might be received as sarcastic. How can you help ensure your intentions are properly understood? Simple, use *emoticons.* You know, those little facial representations that better describe your mood as you converse electronically online. Take these, for instance:

:^)   :^}   :^|   :^(   :^D

If you can't immediately figure out the emoticons illustrated, rotate the book clockwise a quarter turn and you'll see five different facial expressions: smiling, embarrassed, indifferent, sad (or disappointed), and laughing out loud.

Along with emoticons, you can also make use of acronyms. Those are alphabetic representations or abbreviations for commonly used phrases. Take a look at these few examples:

- <g> = grin (a sort of online wink of sarcasm)
- LOL = Laughing Out Loud
- IMHO = In My Humble Opinion
- ROTFL = Rolling On the Floor Laughing

Remember, in cyberspace, no one can hear you laugh or see you wink. You might have to let people know your mood to make sure you won't be misunderstood.

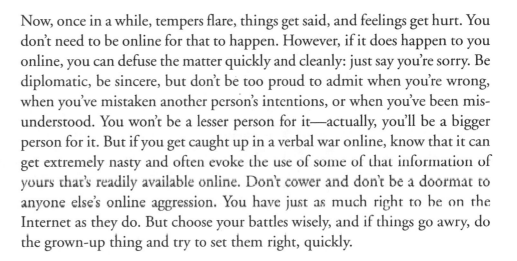

Now, once in a while, tempers flare, things get said, and feelings get hurt. You don't need to be online for that to happen. However, if it does happen to you online, you can defuse the matter quickly and cleanly: just say you're sorry. Be diplomatic, be sincere, but don't be too proud to admit when you're wrong, when you've mistaken another person's intentions, or when you've been misunderstood. You won't be a lesser person for it—actually, you'll be a bigger person for it. But if you get caught up in a verbal war online, know that it can get extremely nasty and often evoke the use of some of that information of yours that's readily available online. Don't cower and don't be a doormat to anyone else's online aggression. You have just as much right to be on the Internet as they do. But choose your battles wisely, and if things go awry, do the grown-up thing and try to set them right, quickly.

**GET A CLUE** Don't forget your most reliable ally if you get into an online feud: your PC's power switch. Just shut down and shut off the whole situation. *If they throw a fit, you should quit.*

Also remember the underlying theme I've been pushing throughout this discussion of online safety: *don't be paranoid!* It's OK to be quietly cautious and it should be expected, but if you're running about online crying "*wolf!*" or screaming "*foul!*" and generally distrust everyone you come in contact with, you may as well hang it up. The Internet has become the phenomenon it is because it involves people. You and I meet, work, and play out there, and at some point you're going to have to exercise a bit of trust, just as I do. Especially when I take you into the realm of online auctions, you're going to have to trust me and the sites that I show you or you'll only succeed in confining and restricting yourself. Be careful, but have some faith.

## What About Fraud?

This is probably one of the biggest sore spots about online commerce, and it usually gets the most press. Internet fraud is, undoubtedly, a real problem. According to the National Consumer's League, this is the list of the top five Internet fraud leaders:

1. Online auctions

2. General merchandise

3. Hardware and software

4. Internet-related services

5. Work-at-home schemes

Well, it's clearly sobering to see my beloved online auctions at the top of the fraud-heap. Should I just stop writing now? Should you just put this book down and go leaf through the Sears catalog instead? Don't be too hasty. There's more to it than meets the eye.

First, there's help. The FBI has just created a new unit, the *Internet Fraud Complaint Center*, which helps the long arm of the law reach into cyberspace itself. This unit will be a bastion of help to online consumers who believe they are being scammed at their stops along the Information Superhighway. Conveniently enough, consumers who need help can file their complaints while already online. The high-priority cases will be forwarded immediately to the FBI for thorough investigation while lower-priority cases will be forwarded to state and local authorities.

Then there's your state attorney general and the U.S. Postmaster General. If you ever send money for something you've bought online (especially at one of the person-to-person auction sites) and then don't receive your goods, well, chum, that's mail fraud and it's a serious crime. You can file claims with either officer just mentioned and set the wheels of justice in motion.

Closer to the action, most online auction houses have now involved themselves in the business of self-policing their sites. That includes monitoring user activity when necessary, monitoring infringing or illegal items that might become available on their sites, reviewing and restricting certain vendors or users from participating at their sites, and actively engaging in resolving user disputes that might arise. That might sound like a tangle of bureaucratic by-laws at first glance, but these sites are prospering because of the patronage of netizens, and it's in the auction sites' best interest to be sure most of those patrons return time and time again. If you want to know more about some of the self-policing policies and programs being used by online auction sites, refer to Appendix A. I think you'll be impressed by what these sites are doing to make your auction experience better and safer.

**GET A CLUE** Be sure to review Chapter 14—it offers an in-depth look at some of the most common auction frauds, how you can recognize them, and what you can do if you wind up on the bad end of a bad deal.

On a final note about fraud, the finger tends to occasionally point back to you and me. Even though there are agencies to investigate shady doings and policies to bolster user confidence at the auction sites, the bottom line is still *buyer beware*. Again, the National Consumer's League chimes in, stating that the single most common underlying reason for online consumers to get scammed is because they often believe everything they're told—no questions asked. Let's face it, if you're being promised a deal that's too good to be true, then it probably isn't true. Hey, *Sea Monkeys* were just tiny shrimp and none of mine were ever seen wearing a crown. X-ray glasses were just cheap and dark and they never helped me see anyone's underwear (probably a good thing, actually). But, all kidding aside, it's really important that you do a bit of thinking and investigating for yourself before you start sending money to complete strangers. Remember, don't be paranoid, but do be careful.

## A Few More Thoughts to Ease Your Mind

To help you get past any online trepidation you might have, here's something that should give you some reassurance: there are many additional sites and organizations that are devoted to ensuring the Internet stays safe. Their goal is to make the Internet pleasant and safe for all of us. They're acting on our behalf and in our best interest.

Also keep in mind that there's a lot of money being made online, and the individuals and corporations making the money want to make sure as many people log on as possible. If people are too scared or too distrustful of the Internet, then they won't log on, they won't spend money, and they won't come back. You're the one with the cash—by expressing your willingness to spend it in a *safe environment,* you're again exerting control over how your online shopping experience will play out.

These days, most commerce sites offer the use of *secure servers:* screen programs and routines that will ensure any information you provide online (your name, address, credit card number) is properly encrypted (scrambled) so any line-tappers can't intercept your information and use it for their own dishonest purposes.

Next, look for references or recommendations from others online regarding certain businesses or even certain individuals you're considering buying from. At the online auctions, you'll usually find feedback forums that let you see how others have characterized their experiences with certain persons or businesses. You're even encouraged to leave feedback of your own that might be of help to others in the auction community. There is a certain power of the people, and you'll see it in action soon.

And, one more time, don't forget to see Appendix A at the back of this book. There you'll find even more help sites and organizations that will give you a greater sense of safety and security, giving you more time to enjoy the fun and excitement of online auctions.

C H A P T E R 4

# Another Trend or a New Tradition?

And now you face the question of whether this whole online auction business is just a fad or a new staple of online existence. The *e-gateway* is a portal into a new way of exchanging goods, services, and money in the worldwide economy. It's easily arguable that online auctions (especially the radically successful eBay) have been the flagships that take the average Joes and Janes out of the physical world and into the virtual world to do their shopping, haggling, and investing. Online auctions are a place to do all three: find that odd little item to satisfy the Christmas wishes of the person who has everything, get into a little back-and-forth bidding or offline bartering to strike a deal that leaves both the buyer and seller feeling like winners, and track down those future hot collectibles that will balloon in value and leave you the enviable owner of the hot-ticket item for which everyone will be clamoring.

There is no doubt in my mind (nor should there be in yours) that, if you get bitten by the online auction bug, you'll be spending a lot of time, effort, and money in the virtual auction parlors. What assurance, then, do you have that whatever you invest of yourself will have the opportunity to blossom and bear the fruit of long-running success? Rest assured.

# Why Will This Work?

First, some facts:

- In the United States alone, 67.5 million PCs regularly access the Internet.

- Across all industries, 37 percent of businesses report they have full-fledged e-commerce operations up and running.

- Among the people who shop online, 24 percent believe their e-purchases are decreasing the time they spend in neighborhood and regional stores. And 23 percent of online shoppers confessed that they are spending more money on Internet shopping than they would have had they been shopping the traditional brick-and-mortar storefronts.

- Online music sales (one of the e-industry's hottest markets) alone accounted for $170 million in Internet sales during 1998. If current predictions pan out, sales figures will reach nearly $4 billion by the year 2004.

- I spent $365—on an impulse buy—shopping online today, just before writing this chapter.

Now, in a general view, consider why e-commerce is so successful. Never before has there been a medium that could reach so many individuals in so many places around the globe 24 hours a day, seven days a week. The product offerings are staggering in number, and the overhead is next to nothing. Think about it: a flashy Web site becomes the virtual storefront, and the tantalizing inventory is essentially an online catalog. The items for sale, though pictured nicely in photo images and adorned with flashy animated text and other *eye candy*, are really just boxed merchandise stored in some dark warehouse. There are no physical counter displays to set up and maintain, there are no smiling salespeople to employ and pay, and there is no customer damage or theft to worry about. For the *e-tailer* (electronic retailer), it's like having a store where everyone can shop, even though nobody has to open a physical door. E-commerce seems to be the greatest new development in buying and selling since the appearance of the first indoor mega-mall, only there are no floors to vacuum and mop and no mall walkers to dodge. For the e-tailer, overhead costs and inventory loss have just been significantly reduced. That helps drive bottom-line profits up.

Now meet Dan, an entrepreneur who's looking to get into the business world. He's just invented *Jumpin' Jobbies,* and he's certain they'll make last year's Furby appear about as exciting as the fur ball your cat just coughed up. But for Jumpin' Jobbies to really take off, they need exposure and promotion. Well, it turns out that clever Dan is also pretty handy with HTML, the simple programming language used to create Web sites. In no time, he's developed a slick Web page that heralds the arrival of his creation and, with a bit of meta data thrown in, his *Jumpin' Jobbies Jamboree* site is popping up on all sorts of Web searches. He then adds an online order form as well as an order tracking and customer support page and, poof, he's just launched a bona fide online business.

**GET A CLUE** What if Dan auctioned a few of his early Jumpin' Jobbies online? Think of the traffic dropping by to see what he's got to sell. Being good with HTML, he makes his auction page a dazzle for the eyes and an enticement to the curious. He includes a link back to the Jumpin' Jobbies Jamboree site, and now he has virtual visitors roaming his online store. How's that for easy advertising?

When it comes to e-tailing, there's another leveling of the playing field that occurs, allowing *Moe's Magnificent Stuff* to go head to head with *FAO Schwarz Online.* To the Web surfer, online stores become part of the huge virtual marketplace and entrepreneurs can thrive in cyberspace whereas they might not be able to start up a brick-and-mortar shop due to high costs of rent, insurance, and other real-world roadblocks. The big businesses know this, and they know the cult following that can propel the little guy's business right through the roof, leaving the staid corporate store eating dust. The competition, then, is fierce, and it's now up to the e-tailers to cater to the wants and needs of online shoppers.

**GET A CLUE** Online shoppers are usually not a very loyal bunch. They'll bounce from site to site as the whim or trend guides them. If you don't agree, watch how quickly you profess your new favorite online store as the one that just announced all of its inventory is for sale at 30 percent off retail prices, every day! If another site announces a 35 percent discount, well, you're off and packing to your *new* favorite Web site. Get the picture?

And then there's you and me—the online shoppers. Online shopping just might have replaced the credit card as the easiest way to shop. Set up your customer account—once—and start clicking your mouse. Since the online shopping experience is a point-and-click, WYSIWYG (what you see is what you get) activity, it's easy to fill those virtual shopping carts and wheel them over to the cyber checkout stand. The online stores, both professional and semiprofessional, know that online shoppers are easy to entice with fancy designs and easy-to-use Web sites. Before you know it, you're caught up in impulse buys and unplanned purchases. To an extent, that's OK. After all, since you're no longer bound by the physical constraints of your particular geographic area, you can find great stuff you wouldn't otherwise have been able to locate, and it will be delivered right to your doorstep. Cool, huh?

Then, think about the status and acceptance you receive in social circles when you proudly state that you are an *e-shopper*. Maybe that sounds silly at first, but since so many people work or play in the nontechnical sector of society, there are many who have yet to buy a book at Amazon.com or rent a DVD from Netflix.com or complete their kids' Christmas shopping at eToys.com. When it comes to online auctions, you're practically nobody if you haven't been to the biggest, eBay.com, or done your comparative homework at uBid.com. Have you bid at Sothebys.com? Oh my, you do have expensive tastes as well as Net savvy. The emerging online society is experiencing a newfound love affair with e-commerce; people get goose bumps whenever they see "www" or hear "dot com," and the e-businesses know this.

And then there's the "dot calm" that comes with dot com. Perhaps the most enticing thing about e-commerce is that it allows buyers to shop from the comfort of their own homes, dressed as they like, keeping the shopping hours that are most convenient. Ask yourself how easy it might (or might not) be to get to the mall after a full day's work. You might not have the time or energy to make the trek, even though there is some shopping you want or need to do. Now consider the convenience of shopping online during a lunch break or late at night after the kids have gone to bed. You place your order and your item lands on your doorstep within three days. That's probably the fastest way to get the goods in your hands—you'd have to wait for the weekend to get to the mall anyway. *That's* convenience, *that's* stress free, and *that* works.

# The Amazing Colossal Market

In 1994, the first online auction made its humble appearance. The brainchild of entrepreneur Razi Mohiuddin, already enjoying the success of his company, Software Partners, Onsale.com was the first online auction place—a calculated experiment designed to tap into the natural competitive spirit of the American people. The experiment was a success. Although traffic to the site was initially low, it received a major surge of click-through activity when Onsale teamed up with the Boston Computer Museum to auction antiquated computer equipment. Publicized as a charity auction (the first of its kind on the Internet), the novelty of the event drew the attention of the world press and put Onsale in the public spotlight. From there, Onsale drew the participation of major manufacturers who put their branded merchandise (computers, electronics, sporting goods) up for auction with ridiculously low starting bids of $2. The bidders came, did their work, and Onsale.com became a pioneer of a new online experience.

When the Internet experienced the wave of acceptance and excitement in 1995, online auctions were one of the hot topics of interest to Web surfers. Later in that same year, the second major pioneering event occurred: Pierre Omidyar launched eBay. Touted as the first person-to-person online auction site, eBay (then known as AuctionWeb) began operations on Labor Day as a place to buy and sell Pez dispensers. eBay had a simple appeal: people could use the site as a virtual classifieds column where they could post their private wares for auction while also chatting with one another to share information and tips about Pez and other collectible curiosities. Soon, eBay/AuctionWeb was being discussed and publicized on many of the collectibles-oriented newsgroups of the Usenet, and new user participation skyrocketed. The rest is *histor-e*. (Don't shoot me; I won't do it again!)

Since those fledgling days of the mid-nineties, the number of online auction sites has grown at an astounding rate. As of this writing, there are more than 400 active auction sites online.

GET A CLUE    Don't let the staggering number of auction sites overwhelm you. This book will boil it down to the best from each of the major categories. But if you have time to hit them all, be my guest.

Auctions aren't just for start-up companies anymore, either. Established and immediately recognizable businesses have also jumped on the auction bandwagon. Universal Studios has a successful online auction site that features real Hollywood memorabilia up for bid. Knowing the appeal of Tinsel Town trinkets, Universal quickly capitalized on its access to star-studded loot. More recently, CompUSA, the brick-and-mortar computer superstore, has launched its online auction site, CompUSAAuctions.com. The site features items that are new, returned, refurbished, closeouts, or discontinued.

On the Internet, existing e-commerce biggies have erected their own virtual auction parlors. Amazon.com introduced online auctions to its supersite in March 1999 and has gotten the attention of the online community as well as the stock market. Yahoo! introduced online auctions in 1998 and has seen an impressive amount of traffic and press.

It seems every month that more auction sites are being launched, some big business and some small, but the fact remains that auctions are a major economic draw and will probably not settle out anytime soon.

**IN MY MIND**  OK, so now it's a copycat universe, huh? Someone hears auctions are hot and now *everybody* has auctions. Giving selection is one thing, but blatant bandwagoning is annoying. What does some corporate fat cat know about what made the early auctions so successful? It's the users, not the ad banners and scrolling marquees that ultimately contribute to the bottom line. When the dust finally settles, you'll see who's still standing and who's sucking dirt.

## Oh, What a Profitable Web We Weave

Online auctions aren't just for junk collectors any more. Previously viewed as an amusing pastime with the perceived economic impact of a yard sale, online auctions have emerged as one of the major contenders in the land of e-commerce. They have become so successful that the mere mention of them often sends ripples through the stock market.

If you don't believe it, here are still more facts:

- The online auction industry garnered an estimated worth of $1.4 billion by the end of 1998.

- By the year 2003, the online auction market is predicted to become a $19 billion industry.

It's those kind of facts that make the stock market and investors worldwide stand up and take notice. It seems that any time a business mentions the word "auction" in the same sentence as "future business vision," its stock price sees a healthy boost. That's what happened to Sharper Image, seller of nifty little gadgets and doodads. On January 11, 1999, Sharper Image's stock saw a jump of 8.25 points when it announced it had plans to add an auction component to its already healthy online business. It was the same story for Sotheby's, which saw its stock values more than double in early 1999 at the mere mention that it was *considering* a long-lasting presence in the online auction strata.

Established auction sites found a flood of interested buy-ins on the stock market floor. The performance of these auction sites attracted and excited investors and drove stock prices straight up. eBay saw an incredible gain of 642 percent in the fourth quarter of 1998, compared to the same quarter of the previous year. eBay beat the Wall Street analysts when its stock showed a 7-cent profit per share at the end of that quarter, beating the predictions of only 4 cents profit per share. By the end of 1998, eBay stock had reached $321 per share, which is astounding when you look at its 52-week low—a mere $25.25. To frost the cake, eBay announced a 3-for-1 stock split that took effect in March 1999.

It was a similar story for uBid, CityAuction, and FirstAuction. Each of these sites saw similar economic gains near the end of 1998 and at the beginning of 1999, when online auctions were practically skyrocketing everywhere to the shareholders' delight. Online auctions seem to be irreversible, irrepressible, and immune to the labels and pigeonholes that others try to fit them into. And in an online world where you and I want better selection, better service, and a better way, this is all good news.

## Does the Little Guy Really Matter?

So, in all that Wall Street flurry and press attention, one wonders if the auction sites have gotten so large that they squash out the importance of the *person on the street*. With so much at stake at these online auction empires, you wonder if the little guy still matters.

You bet he and she matters. Online auctions' successes are based on the mind-share and the money of people like you and me. Without us, there's no *them*. That's not just soap-boxing and it's not a rant—it's a fact. The good auction sites have recognized the importance of the users and have taken steps to share the site ownership with them.

The best auction sites will have places where your voice can be heard. There will be feedback forums, FAQs, and public bulletin boards or chat spaces where you can freely interact with the site operators as well as the other auction goers. This is an important aspect of the auction sites' ongoing success because, without listening to the people, how can anyone ever develop a site that's truly useful? They can't. You've seen the industrial cartoons that depict the two opposing panels: what the manufacturer developed and what the customer really wanted. It's good for a giggle, but it's bad for business when it really happens (and it happens a lot).

When you're investigating the different auction sites, keep a keen eye open for those sites that have grown into virtual communities—electronic towns. Many have and you'll see some of the best later in this book. These sites have already begun to understand this aspect of what makes a successful business and what doesn't—it's your indicator that your voice is being heard. All you need to do is speak up.

## Are You Ready to Play?

OK. Enough. You've got the facts. You've got the figures. Hopefully now you've got the itch to get started.

The whole point of this chapter was to show you how viable online auctions have become and, despite some of the negative press that has circulated at times, how hugely successful online auctions are in the realm of e-commerce. Now it's your turn to experience the ride for yourself. You have the foundation of information under you, so it's time to wax your board and get ready to hit the waves.

# Part II

## Seeing the Sites

# 5

# The Online Auction Landscape

So here you are, at the edge of auction cyburbia. You can almost feel the energy as millions of people are in there bidding, selling, and enjoying the different auction venues. Before you begin scouting the wired roadways, you'll do well to take a look at this auction nation from the 30,000-foot view. It's made up of hundreds of different sites—or *auction cities*, if you will. There are millions of citizens, and they're all busy clicking here and linking there; newcomers often get left in the dust.

So before I begin your tour of the different ports of call, let me first explain a bit about the character and culture of this world. In the process, I'll give you a chance to examine your reasons for joining in, helping you narrow your intent so that you can jump in quickly and effectively, and build a firm foundation of awareness—and anticipation—under your feet from the get-go. Soon enough, you'll be in the action yourself.

## Sifting Through the Sites

Clearly, there's much to see. Perform a search from any major search portal (Yahoo!, Alta Vista, and so on) using the words *online auction*. Caramba! Combing through the results could take days. But are the 400+ sites you'll find really so different from one another? Do they all offer such unique products and services that each deserves your valuable time and attention? No. In fact, many sites are quite similar. If this is true, then why so many sites? Simple—market opportunity.

If you've even casually cocked an ear to the business wire, you've heard about new auction sites popping up practically every week. Perhaps you heard the rumble when Amazon.com decided to branch off from being just an online mega-mall and became a new contender for a piece of the auction pie. Maybe you read about many of the new partnerships and mergers of auction sites, brick-and-mortar auction houses, and associated auction services that have kept analysts and consumers on their toes, wondering what will happen next. Boil it all down, and you'll understand that the online auction industry is quite profitable. There's a beehive of activity that's fueled by one thing: your patronage.

Every site wants to build the better mousetrap and is striving to attract your attention. Eager to grow their communities, online auctions are now in fierce competition for your attention (and your money).

But if you've studied this book's table of contents, you'll know I'm limiting your tour to only a handful of eligible auction sites. What about the other 390-some-odd sites? Well, many of those are good sites, but it's too easy to overload on the sheer volume of choices. Your immediate mission is to dive into the major sites that offer the best selection, best features, and best return for your time and money.

Consider this: if you're hunting for a digital camera, a tennis racket, or a peculiar little Pokémon character, why trudge through hundreds of sites to find what you seek? You don't need to. Unless what you're looking for is truly rare, you'll do just fine at a select few auction sites. Even rare and obscure items show up at the major sites. So save yourself some time, effort, and virtual shoe leather; most of what you'll want is within easy reach.

DID YOU KNOW?    Don't think I'm snubbing the specialty auctions—those that cater to a specific collecting interest. Yes, there are a bunch of them out there, and you'll see a rundown on a few of the more compelling ones in Chapter 10.

## Assess the Sites

Just as you wouldn't shop where the selection is stale and the service is bad, so you shouldn't auction where the air is still and the aisles are empty. No, you want to be where the action is, where sales are high and the selection is superior. You want to plop yourself right in the middle of the mix where you're most likely to find what you need and get what you want.

So when it comes to defining the venue of choice, you'll need to pay attention to these discriminating features:

- **Inventory**. Hey, if you're looking for something, why rattle an empty box, right? There are some great sites out there with enough stuff to choke a dinosaur, but there are still more sites where even the dust bunnies refuse to congregate. No matter how zippy the site looks, no stuff is no good. More stuff means better chances of finding what you want. So a site lists many tantalizing item categories—you still need to take a quick journey deeper into those category titles. All too often, you'll find enticing titles but zero inventory. Next window, please.

- **Clientele**. This is pretty much linked to the inventory issue: find a site that maintains an active buzz of buyers and sellers. The more people you find at a site, the better your chances of finding what you want or selling what you have. But don't overlook the reputation of the folks you'll be rubbing mice with. Be sure the site fosters and draws good, upstanding auction activists. More on this topic under "Community Values."

- **Stability**. One of the biggest challenges to any e-business is their site's uptime. If the site is down, so is its reputation. This is especially true of auction sites, running active auctions against a central server clock that continues to tick regardless of whether auction goers can get in or not. Don't forget site response time, either. If an auction site runs slow, the auction goers will leave—fast. A good auction site will have a suitable infrastructure (hardware, software, support staff) to handle the level of user activity. Sites that expect tremendous numbers of user hits better have some beefy machines that can stand the barrage.

■ **Community Values**. This is the one that ties back to clientele. By this, a good site will have an established philosophy that it stands behind and continually promotes. Far beyond simple rules of the site, community values set forth what is expected of everyone who visits and trades there. No dirty tricks, unfair tactics, rude behavior, or other nonsense. Look for a community that promotes fair trading, open communication, helpful forums, and a good dose of clean humor. In the final analysis, it's usually the community that makes or breaks the site.

■ **Usage Terms.** Does the site charge any annual fees, auction commissions (to sellers *or* buyers), premium service fees, or anything else that could make your site account swell while your bank balance shrinks? Typically, auction fees are to be expected, but keep an eye open for "fluff costs," especially those that you pay for by default whether you use them or not. Each site should have a "Terms of Use" statement (or something similar). If you can't find one or don't understand the one provided, you might want to move on to better hunting grounds.

■ **Site Policies**. Be sure the auction site has a published site policy. Why? The site policy tells how the site will protect your privacy and secure your transactions. Does the site offer data encryption (often through an *SSL*—Secure Sockets Layer) when you enter a credit card number or other sensitive information? Is there a method of protecting your personal information (street address, e-mail address, phone number, and so on)? Are there restrictions on the types of things that can legally or legitimately be put up for auction? Are there programs in force to thwart spammers, jammers, and other hackers? Does the site offer assistance to users who may find themselves in the midst of a prickly situation—or does it just lock the door and flick out the light? Make sure you know what the site expects of you and what you can expect of it.

■ **Useful Services**. On top of the list should be stellar customer response. If you have a question, can you get a timely answer? If you need help, can you get useful guidance? If you've got a gripe, is someone from the site truly willing to listen to your ideas? Customer service is what separates the players in the retail arena. Just about anyone can provide access to goods or services, but only the best make sure you can get what you need quickly, completely, and in a supportive environment. Those sites that seem to be perpetually out to lunch will soon be out of business.

Aside from customer service, also look for signs of *feature bloat*—myriad programs, features, and whizzy things that don't add much to the auction experience but probably contribute heavily to the site overhead. You don't want to be wading through or paying for a bunch of gaudy gobbledygook.

After grading an auction site using the aforementioned criteria, you should be able to determine a worthy one from a wannabe. Read through the hype and the hot links: all auction sites, eager for your business, are going to serve up some nifty goodies. Flashy designs, catchy slogans, and promises of profit are all aimed at reeling you in. Not to imply these are misrepresentations, but some sites just can't deliver what they promise. The bottom line for any auction site is this: how much stuff is being auctioned and how much activity is going on there. If you want to buy, look to the sites with the largest inventories and the most variety. If you're looking to sell, find the sites that seem to have the most bidders and a healthy history of completed auctions.

**GET A CLUE** Hey . . . want to know how to check the overall health of an auction site? Try looking for reports, reviews, and essays about your favorite site at places like **www.auctionwatch.com**, **www.cnet.com**, **www.wired.com**, and even **www.nasdaq.com** (for the true financial diagnosis of those auction high-flyers). Search the editorial sites for auction news; as much attention as online auctions are commanding, I can assure you'll be finding some great insight, commentary, and opinion about the different venues. At NASDAQ's site you'll learn what the financial big boys are saying about who's hot and who's not in the auction arena. These "bulls" and "bears" know how to get the real poop on a site and aren't bashful about spreading it around.

## What Kind of Shopper Will You Be?

After you've evaluated an auction site and determined whether it's worth your effort and allegiance, you'll need to take a long look in the mirror. The next element that determines your auction success rests firmly with *you*—what are you looking to get out of an auction and what are you willing to put in to get it? That assessment starts by determining how you intend to approach an auction.

You see, once you've found a worthy site, your next step to success involves knowing what you want—as well as knowing under what circumstances you'd like to purchase it. Do you seek items you simply must possess, regardless of the cost in time or money? Or do you want to scare up the greatest deals and incredible bargains that assure future resale returns at highest possible profits? Either way, you'll find an auction that suits your goals. Going into the auction, try to determine who you'll be. Consider the following auction-going types:

- **Serious Collectors.** They set their sights on certain items and mentally mark them as their own long before the bidding ends. They thoroughly research the items of their desire, make contact with the current proprietors, devise winning strategies, and feel no hesitation about unlocking their bankroll. They're typically difficult to beat at the auctions—especially if cost is not a factor. They could appear abrupt, ruthless, or unconcerned about others. Usually, they're not bad people, just determined. These folks have typically mastered the true skills of online bidding.

- **Hobbyists.** Resembles the serious collector, without being quite as driven. They often find the auctions interesting, fun, and fruitful. They have specific interests, and zero in on exactly the items they seek. Different from the serious collector, though, the hobbyist doesn't often live by the dogma of *"I must have it!"* Hobbyists often take a practical approach to their acquisitions, ever on the lookout for that certain something, but usually not prone to engage in a fierce tug-of-war. After all, it's just a hobby. The nice thing about hobbyists is that they're often helpful to others—they enjoy sharing information and ideas with those who share their same interests. They're not given to hoarding, hiding, or otherwise hovering over items of their desire, hoping to keep all others away. Hobbyists just want to have fun.

- **Bargain Hunters.** Those who can squeeze a penny so tight it practically screams. Bargain hunters are much like serious collectors in that they share a similar drive to get exactly what they want—but in this case, it's an unbelievable bargain. They're research oriented, skilled in negotiations, and aware of the trading going on around them. This is usually the person who always finds the deal no one else noticed, and forever seems to find money lying on the ground. They have a sixth sense about finding things, perpetually tuned to the next deal that's lurking just around the corner. Bargain hunters, often, are tight-lipped in their ways—sharing their methods and secrets would deny them the great deals they seek. If there's plenty to go around, they usually share the wealth; if the deals are limited, don't expect to get a tip-off from them.

- **9 to 5ers.** You've probably heard that many people have made auctions their business. They've left the brick-and-mortar world and have migrated to the online auction realm to draw their income. These are usually folks who were already in the resale business (antique dealers, wholesalers, and so on) and then found an incredible customer base of millions of auction goers right at their fingertips. With low overhead and previously unheard-of customer access, the auction pro is schooled in the ways of selectively acquiring inventory, establishing a market niche, and turning over a profit. This is an experienced auction user, someone who will usually deal in a professional though sometimes impersonal manner.

- **Casual Drop-Ins.** Then there are some who are not on a mercenary mission to stomp opposing bidders, snatch up impossible bargains, or keep bread on their table. You'll find a large population of auction enthusiasts who, much like hobbyists, are just looking for a pleasant distraction. They're window-shoppers and looky-loos, and they have plenty to see at the auctions. They bring an unburdened disposition, and they just stroll up and down the virtual aisles never knowing what they might find. Some are there to find stuff and others are there just to observe.

Of course, there's a certain amount of crossover among these auction personas. You could find yourself schizophrenically switching personalities depending on what you find and where you find it at the auctions. But to get the most out of the auction experience without losing total control, decide what your auction-going goals will be.

**GET A CLUE** Don't forget to see Chapter 18 for a discussion of auction addictions. Many have gone from mildly curious to maniacally obsessed; financially indifferent to financially distressed. It could happen to you.

## Do You Have the Time?

Just how much time do you have? That's another key factor to consider as you choose your auction preoccupation. How quickly—or desperately—do you need that special something? If your time is limited and you need to find an item quickly, then a good search tool will be your best bet. All sites you'll see are equipped with a variety of search and browse tools. Whether it's high-priced treasures, low-cost diamonds in the rough, or something in between, search tools will help you zero in on precisely what you seek. I've built incredible collections of things I never thought I'd own just by performing regular searches, each time spending no more than a few minutes to determine if what I desire is presently up for auction. If I strike out, persistent and repeated searches day after day, week after week, month after month will usually turn up those elusive items. The collection you see in Figure 5-1—albeit still incomplete—was gained with a combined time investment of roughly a couple of hours (spread out over the course of two years).

*Figure 5-1*

*This vintage collection of Aurora creature kits cost a pretty penny but was amazingly time-thrifty, thanks to time-saving auction search tools.*

But maybe you're not in such a hurry. Maybe you're the type who has time to stroll the aisles in anticipation of whatever might jump out at you (much like the casual drop-in type). There's plenty of opportunity for you; all sites feature different item categories such as jewelry, computer equipment, books and movies, toys and collectibles, and so on. Depending on the site, you might be strolling seemingly endless aisles of auction attractions, finding yourself wonderfully lost in a maze of tantalizing and tempting treasures. Just leave a trail of hyperlinks so you can find your way back out.

GET A CLUE  Hey, be careful with that *strolling*. Depending where you meander, you'll probably find all kinds of stuff you'll convince yourself you can't live without, even though you've lived without it up to this point. Remember that casual strolling often leads to casual bidding and before you know it, you've casually committed a bankroll.

## Common Auction Formats

If it's variety you seek, it's variety you'll find, not only in the different auction sites but in the variety of ways in which you can participate. Since their historic beginnings, auctions have been presented in a number of methods, using a varied range of rules, each serving a specific commodity or audience. So, to further prepare yourself for realizing your auction goals, you'll need to understand the different auction formats you'll encounter online.

- **Straight Auction.** This is the most common type of auction, and it's likely to be the one that best matches your understanding of how an auction works. Simply enough, a single item is put up for auction at an opening (minimum) bid price to a gathering of interested bidders. Successive ascending bids are given, and the value of the item continues to rise until no more bids are placed. By rules of this format, the seller must sell at final high bid amount. Equally, the bidder who cast the high (winning) bid must honor that bid by paying the seller. The opening bid in a straight auction can be any value designated by the seller. Lower opening bids tend to stimulate bidder interest, presenting the potential of acquiring the item at a cost possibly below market value, real or perceived. Straight auctions are also referred to as *ascending price* or *absolute price* auctions.

- **Dutch Auction.** This format is specifically designed for auctions where multiple quantities of an identical item are put up for bid. Many times, sellers will have duplicate items (as in the case of bulk purchases or warehouse closeouts) and wish to sell all—or as many as possible—of the item during the course of a single auction event. For the bidder, Dutch auctions are usually the most perplexing. Bidders can bid for as many as they want of the quantity that is up for bid, entering at least the starting bid amount. When there are more bids than items, the Dutch auction will honor the highest bidders, assigning winner's rights from the highest bidder on down the scale until all of the available quantity has been allocated. In these cases, the lowest bidders are excluded from the distribution. The twist is that *all* bidders only pay the lowest successful bid price (that is, the bid entered by the last assigned winning bidder). Dutch auctions are great for bidders hoping to gather multiple units of identical items and usually result in lower final costs to the buyer simply because more than one of the item is available. Dutch auctions are often confused with *Yankee auctions,* where winning bidders must pay their exact high bid price. Don't pay more than the lowest successful bid when you participate in a Dutch auction.

- **Reserve Price Auctions.** When a seller has an item but isn't sure if the bidding public is likely to clamor for (or ignore) it, that seller might choose to set a reserve price, that is, a minimum price at which the item will be sold. This protects a seller's investment or belief of value in the item. A reserve price auction follows the same ascending bid format as a straight auction and usually starts with an opening bid lower than the assigned reserve value (stimulating those bargain-loving bidders). If the seller's reserve is met (or surpassed) during the course of the auction, both seller and high bidder are obliged to complete the sale. If a reserve price is not met during the course of the auction, neither the seller nor *any* of the bidders are required to complete a sale. Of course, the seller can decide to sell at the highest bid price even if the reserve price wasn't met (known as "knocking down" the price), but the highest bidder isn't required to complete the deal. A knockdown sale is typically completed off-line, away from the auction site and outside its guidelines and protections.

DID YOU KNOW? Ever hear a bomb go off online? Well, that's what happened when auction giant eBay decided to levy a $1 fee for using reserve price auctioning (usually a fee-free option) while also forcing reserve price auctioneers to establish an opening bid amount that would be at least 25 percent of their reserve price. Y'see, by eBay's rules, an auction that isn't successfully completed (such as a reserve auction whose reserve isn't reached) brings no official final sale and garners no final value commission to the site. With a large number of reserve auctions ending "unsuccessfully," eBay decided to impose a non-refundable fee to use the format and force the setting of an opening bid. The auction-going community wasn't amused, and fallout resulted in the form of spirited user retorts, reduced listings of new auctions, and heavy press coverage. Whether eBay expected it or not, the hot potato it tossed at its users quickly got tossed back in its own lap. eBay hastily retracted the change as proposed and opened discussions with the using community to determine what change might be more acceptable. In the end, the reserve price auction at eBay carries a usage fee of 50¢ when the reserve price is less than $25; $1 for reserve prices $25 and up. This fee *is* refundable, provided the reserve price is met during the course of the auction. Don't ever doubt the belief system of the auction community—they're pretty serious about this stuff.

- **Proxy Bidding.** This isn't so much an auction format as it is an online auction bidding mechanism. Many auction sites provide a method to enter a *maximum* bid—the most a bidder would ever be willing to pay for an item—even if such a high bid is not required to achieve high bidder status. However, if more bids are placed on an item, a previous bidder's maximum bid will be used by way of a proxy system, essentially bidding in the bidder's absence to outbid other bidders. The proxy system will retain the previous bidder's high bid status until such time as another bidder enters a maximum bid that outbids the first bidder's maximum. At that time, the new high bidder will have the proxy system work on their behalf should additional bids by other bidders be placed. The proxy system is like having a little bidding pal you've entrusted with your money. Check back once in a while, though. Your little bid buddy might use up your cash and need an additional advance to keep you from being permanently dethroned.

## Understanding Auction Culture

And when in Rome, must you do as the Romans? It's advisable if you want to get along in the community. The same holds true for auction communities, especially at the person-to-person trading sites. Just as I explained in Chapter 3, those principles are doubly important as you venture in and make your presence known in any of the auction communities. Remember that most auction sites have drawn worldwide participation—people from different lands, of different cultures, and with differing personal values. As in a United Nations conference, it's important to establish and abide by a common language or understanding that keeps the interactions successful and without incident. To the best of my knowledge and past experience, it is the language of business that fits this bill.

It starts with that Golden Rule: do unto others as you would have them do unto you. Healthy doses of mutual respect and understanding will keep the auction environments stable and more enjoyable for all. Just as in the physical world, people will make mistakes, speak out of turn, or simply misunderstand the events around them. Take the patient approach, help the other person, and remember that you might be the next one to step out of line.

 **IN MY MIND**  The Golden Rule is especially applicable in the online auction realm simply because the trading of goods is involved. In an auction you're not just spouting opinions or beliefs as in a chat room or other online forum, you're buying or selling real goods with real money. Mess with someone's livelihood and they might mess with you. As long as the trading is fair and forthright, keep your wild notions and inflammatory opinions in check. Yes, it's a land of free speech and open demonstration, but that freedom does have a little price tag attached: it's called civility.

Next is the need for professionalism. Whether you live a free-wheeling, spontaneous lifestyle or you toe the proper corporate behavior line until you're blue in the face, the online auction communities still expect you to act in a well-intentioned and tolerable manner. Along with politeness and courtesy, be responsive to and respectful of the auction place and the people within it. Again, it's tempered behavior that keeps the auctions alive and helps them draw more bidders or sellers with every new day. The clean house you keep will be to your own benefit.

Remember that the members of auction communities are pretty serious about their business, whether they're in it for fun or profit. Community members have invested a great deal in their specific online meeting ground, and they typically don't put up with much nonsense from anyone who thinks it's all just a game or, even worse, a gathering of suckers who can be duped and manipulated by unfair and illegal tactics. The communities are quick to sound off if something is amiss. If an injustice is in the works—be it perpetrated by a user or the site itself—the community will often rally together and expose the situation. Again, it's not because they're a bunch of hotheads or displaced activists; they're people from all over the globe drawn to a common meeting ground where they can have fun and find some prosperity. They don't want their oasis spoiled.

## Setting Your Expectations

By now you're getting a general feel for the auction places, the formats, and the people you'll have a chance to meet. Next on your readiness checklist is the setting of your expectations. There's a lot that goes on at the auctions, and there are some fantastic things that have occurred, but by and large it's an evenly-balanced marketplace.

First, forget everything sensational you've heard about auction sites from the media; they've culled only the juiciest scraps of information and presented them as the prevailing ways of the online auction regions. Yes, auctions are quite the attention-getters these days and rightfully so. However, much of what has been printed is, well, sensational: horrible rip-offs, immediate riches, and sure-fire stock market gains. I don't know how, in the past four years of auction going, I was able to miss out on this excitement. Perhaps it happened while I was sleeping. Sure, there have been some pretty interesting happenings over the years, but they've hardly been daily events as you might be led to believe by the creative spin of journalism. Regardless, take what you've read in the press, online or otherwise, with a grain of salt. The select incidents that have been served up don't begin to represent the overall experience.

So what does that really mean? Will you really get a "steal"? Will you really make a million? Should you start shopping for that beachfront cottage in the Bahamas? Well, maybe, but keep your head for now. There have been some interesting occurrences in the auction world, but do you really believe that these rare pearls can be uncovered and exploited again and again, at will? In my experience, no.

IN MY MIND Hey, if I could repeat killer steals and deals whenever I chose, I'd have my teeth capped and invade the late-night airwaves, selling an inspiring collection of audiotapes that will free you from the oppression of your current toil and guide you to the swifter currents of the self-made millionaire. Nope, I think I'll keep my day job for now.

The safest bet, though you might think it a bit conservative, is to enjoy the auction for what it is: a way to find interesting items in a unique new buying venue. Given enough experience and determination, you could harness the sites to turn some of your dreams into realities, but I advise taking it one step at a time.

## Stay in Control

Now, taking that thread a bit further, you'll need to understand there is a lot of emotion at the auctions. Consider how excited you'll be when you find something you really want, whether it be a rare or routine item, and you decide it should be yours. The find itself is exhilarating and will bring immediate joy. But when someone else bids against you, even outbid you, feelings of territoriality begin to creep in. Hey, that's the name of the game when you share the auction space with millions of others who are looking for the same thrills and deals as you. Be prepared for competition, and try to decide before you ever place a bid how much you're willing to pay for an item. I say this because it's all too easy to get caught up in a bidding war where you feel the affront from competing bidders and the temptation to lash back with emotionally charged counter bids. In your frenzy to win you could end up paying too much for an item, maybe more than you can readily afford. If you don't think it really happens, think again.

On the opposite side of the auction, the seller loves it when bidders fight it out, throwing dollars as opposed to throwing fists. The happy sellers are the ones who see their auctions become the object of a bidding war; they feel a euphoria of their own as they see their coffers filling up. That's fine, but does that mean a seller is safe from losing control at the auctions and not subject to the effects of runaway emotion? Not at all. Remember my earlier point about

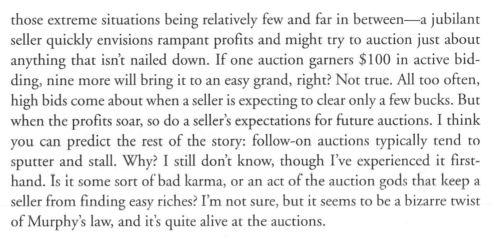

those extreme situations being relatively few and far in between—a jubilant seller quickly envisions rampant profits and might try to auction just about anything that isn't nailed down. If one auction garners $100 in active bidding, nine more will bring it to an easy grand, right? Not true. All too often, high bids come about when a seller is expecting to clear only a few bucks. But when the profits soar, so do a seller's expectations for future auctions. I think you can predict the rest of the story: follow-on auctions typically tend to sputter and stall. Why? I still don't know, though I've experienced it firsthand. Is it some sort of bad karma, or an act of the auction gods that keep a seller from finding easy riches? I'm not sure, but it seems to be a bizarre twist of Murphy's law, and it's quite alive at the auctions.

The bottom line is to maintain reasonable expectations and a decent level of self-control. Otherwise, who knows what you're capable of doing?

## Register to Win

So having said all that, are you ready to jump in? I hope so. Regardless of some of the blemishes I've exposed, online auctions are great fun and a great way to find or sell that special something. But first you have to register.

Practically all auction sites require their users to register before they can join in the bidding or selling. To register, you'll need to provide the site with some vital statistics: your name, physical address, phone number, e-mail address, and sometimes a credit card number. Yeoww! Is that more than you're willing to share? If so, you might resign yourself to just being a looker (which is always free) as opposed to being an active participant.

**GET A CLUE**  It's perfectly OK to lurk at an auction site for a while, watching from the sidelines to see what goes on and how well the site seems to operate. For many people, this is what it takes before they're convinced the site is worthy of receiving the personal information just described.

Why all the vital information? First and foremost, it's for your own protection. Wouldn't you feel better knowing that every auction participant has had to provide the same level of identification? If ever you come into a questionable deal or need a site's assistance in straightening out a troublesome trade, you'll rely on the fact that you can contact the other party by using their personal contact information. If everyone signed up as "Mack," "Bob," or "Jane," it would be pretty tough to settle a difference without much more information to go on.

But before you decide to offer up the personal data, be sure the auction site has a good privacy policy. Recall one of the key factors in determining the worthiness of an online auction site: If you can't find a policy, or you find one that's ambiguous and can't get much clarification from a site's support staff, chances are your information won't be very well secured. In addition, be sure you know what the site will do with that information. Will it offer it to anyone else who asks, or will it give access only to other registered users (if at all)? Will the site be selling your information to direct marketers, partner ventures, or anyone else who wants to know what you do online and how to contact you to tell you of other offers you're sure to be interested in? Hey, some do this, and if it's not the kind of thing you're comfortable with, it's not the auction site for you.

But the sites you'll soon read about in this book all have good privacy policies and make data security a high priority. Therefore, for any site you decide to join while you're reading, you'll typically go through an initial registration process where, once you provide your personal data, you'll designate a user ID and user password (ensuring only *you* can bid or sell with your ID). During the process, you'll be directed to the site's User Policy and Terms of Service. Yes, they're long-winded and full of legalese, but take the time to read them—they tell you exactly what you're responsible for and what the site is responsible for. They should also explain any fees and other commissions you might have to pay for active participation. If you see anything you disagree with, bail out. Most major sites have reasonable terms and policies, so don't get too stressed about it. But read them anyway.

GET A CLUE  Be especially attentive to the site's *dos and don'ts* lists. These are the policies that let you know what sort of behavior is acceptable and what sort will gain you an immediate ticket to the "no longer registered" shuttle. You'll also find out what sorts of things are acceptable and unacceptable to auction (if you'll be selling). Infringing, illegal, and offensively bizarre items are typically not allowed. If you'll be selling, be sure the site allows the sorts of things you want to parade across the auction block.

But assuming that everything looks on the up and up (which it usually will), how soon before you can get into the action? Nicely enough, activation of your registration is virtually instantaneous. Usually, the registration is a multistep process: you submit your information and the site uses the e-mail address you provide to verify that you can be contacted. (It may also dial up your credit card information to verify it.) If you are who you say you are, you'll be provided with a temporary site entry code of some sort. When you receive the temporary code, you go back to the site and complete the registration process. This all happens within a few minutes and before you know it, you're on board.

## Start Your Engines (and Other Supercharged Searches)

And there you are, on the cusp of a veritable gold mine of goodies, gadgets, or unique curiosities. You can *feel* the things you want waiting for you just inside the site's main page, but how do you get to the things you crave? Let the search begin.

As I mentioned before, all good auction sites provide a search tool (or tools) that help you sift through the offerings to help you find just what you want (assuming you're not just there to randomly browse). First, you'll find different *categories* of items, such as computers, music, sporting goods, memorabilia, and so on. Within each category there are usually subcategories that further distill the items within. Use categories and subcategories as your treasure-finding funnel, narrowing the selection and making your hunt quicker and more promising.

To many auction goers, the "thrill of the hunt" is one of the biggest attractions of online auctions. Don't overlook that, or you might miss out on a bit of the inherent excitement.

Besides category listings, you can also use specific search tools that let you locate items based on key words you provide. If you're looking for a special comic book (perhaps *X-Men*, *Spawn*, or *Sad Sack*), you can search for a character name or series title. If there's anything like that up for auction, the search results will show you. Going back to my example in Figure 5-1, I found those kits exactly this way: using key words like "Aurora" along with the particular creepy ghoul I was looking for.

**GET A CLUE** Beware of misspellings: they can prevent you from finding truly elusive treasure. In the person-to-person auctions, it's typically just regular people listing items for bid. If a title is misspelled or otherwise misrepresented, you may miss out on a great item while the seller also misses out on your bids. Buyers, try using spelling variations in your keyword searches; sellers, strive to use correct spelling always!

Take some time to study and understand the different search tools available at a site. Many offer some impressive search routines that help you target and find the exact item you're hunting. In addition, many sites have *search-bots*— special routines that will search the site for you. If your searches are coming up goose eggs, enlist the search-bot (sometimes called *personal shopping agents*) to do the searching for you. If the bot finds a match, you'll get an e-mail alert, typically in plenty of time for you to check it out and bid.

If you're really serious about your treasure hunting, there are also Internet sites that can perform multisite searches per your request. Sites like iTrack (**www.itrack.com**), BidFind (**www.bidfind.com**), and AuctionWatch (**www.auctionwatch.com**) offer auction addicts the ability to enter search-bot criteria and let the bot do the rest of the work. These search sites have Web crawlers that regularly go out to specified auction sites and gather indexes of the items up for bid. If an item you're searching for shows up, you'll get an e-mail note letting you know what the item is and where you should go to stake your claim.

**WARNING!** Be aware that some auction sites are forbidding search sites from accessing the sites' listings. Some auction sites claim search sites' crawlers or indexers are hampering site performance, are inaccurate in reporting results, or are infringing intellectual property rights of the auction site. Whatever the reason, be aware that some of the search sites you use may not include results from *all* online auctions.

And don't forget the Usenet. I've found some great auctions (sites and specific items) by cruising the different newsgroups. If there's a newsgroup that caters to your interest, check it out on a regular basis—many auctioneers use those forums as an additional venue for advertising their goods up for bid.

## A Preface to What's Coming

OK, you have the general sense of what the auction landscape looks like. In the next several chapters, I'll take you on a tour of what I've found to be the best designed, most promising, and most worthwhile sites. Of course, with over 400 sites to choose from, I couldn't possibly cover them all and, if you've seen the sites, you may find that I've skipped over one of your personal favorites. Not to worry. The gist of what you'll see will help you learn the core operating fundamentals of the different types of auction sites. Don't get hung up on the fact that I may have snubbed a site you're particularly fond of. It doesn't mean I think it a waste of time; I just didn't feel it embodied enough of the auction philosophy or features of the sites I will show you.

Remember there's Chapter 19 of this book: a place where I list the honorable mention sites that had good offerings, but got beaten out in the race for page space to provide a detailed review. So with that under your cap, it's time to strike out and see some sites.

C H A P T E R 6

# The Merchant Sites

The first stop on the auction tour will be at the amazing merchant sites. These are the sites you've probably heard something about before—auctions where you can bid on manufacturers' overstock, closeouts, refurbished items, or maybe just last year's inventory.

Whether you're looking for computer equipment (a *very* popular category at these sites), home electronics, sporting goods, travel packages, gadgets, knick-knacks, or other assorted mainstream doodads, the merchant sites are a great place for you to begin your quest.

**DID YOU KNOW?** Here's a poser: What comes first, the Internet or the PC? Most folks would contend the PC since, without it, you can't get to the Internet. However, did you know that some of the best deals on PCs are found on the Internet at online auctions? If you don't yet have a PC, find a friend, relative, or library that has one you can use and do some PC shopping in the virtual auction parlors. You'll be surprised at the incredible offers you'll find.

## What's the Story?

Online auctions have become something of an oasis for merchants, those bona fide businesses who may operate normal retail Internet sites or have a brick-and-mortar presence in your home town. As I briefly explained in Chapter 2, wholesalers and retailers frequently discover they have too much inventory on their hands. Whether they're stuck with a warehouse full of stuff that never sold or they're having to clear out discontinued items in their stores to make room for the new year's models, these merchants often need to dump their goods fast. Sometimes, public liquidation sales, closeout sales, bargain tables, and blue-light specials just can't move the merchandise fast enough. But when merchants venture into the online auction realm, they tap that boundless sea of millions of new shoppers who might be looking for just the sort of thing that needs to go. And, quite often, the bidders can latch on to a steal of a deal.

The merchant auction sites get their inventory through several methods. Most obvious is when the auction host *is* the actual merchant (such as Egghead.com Surplus Auctions). Other times, though, an auction site acts as a hub, hosting product auctions for a variety of manufacturers, wholesalers, and retailers either through direct purchase or consignment of the products (like you'll see at Onsale.com). While at the merchant-operated sites you'll find only those types of items that a merchant usually sells, the multimerchant, megaproduct host sites offer an incredible variety and hefty inventory of different items to bid on.

You can be confident in these auction sites—after all, what you're bidding on is usually some common item that you have seen before or could easily see at a local retail store. Unlike specialty or collector auctions, merchant auctions sell to Joe and Jane consumer, offering goods that you might otherwise buy through conventional retail outlets. The next time you're on the market for a hand-held PC, a new pair of stereo speakers, or a pair of inline skates, check the merchant sites first. You'll probably save time and money for your effort.

Next, homing in on the *premier sites* in the wholesale and retail category, you'll find they're rather straightforward and quite easy to use. In fact, all you need to concern yourself with at these sites is finding stuff and bidding on it. Unlike the person-to-person sites you'll learn about in Chapter 7, merchant sites are really quite simple since all you need to do is register, search, bid, win, and pay. If you think that sounds like a lot to do, it's not, as you'll soon see.

One of the biggest benefits of merchant sites and the reason that I often point first-time auction goers to them is their high level of site safety and security. In Chapter 3 you learned about your personal security as you traverse the open spaces of the World Wide Web. At merchant auction sites, though, you have the added comfort of knowing you're dealing with a solid and reputable business concern. If you head out to *Big Ed's Auction Alley*, you might find yourself venturing out into a site that's run from someone's garage or spare bedroom—and chances are there could be some question to Ed's commitment to your auction security. However, the big merchant sites are fully loaded with secure servers, encryption (data scrambling) routines, and customer support ready to help make your initial auction adventures worry-free.

And what about paying for the things you'll bid on and win? At merchant auctions, you'll typically provide your credit card number when you register (*all* auction sites require you to register before you can bid—looking's always free, though). If you bid and emerge victorious, the moment you exclaim, *"I'm a winner!"* that site has charged your credit card and begun the process of shipping your newly-won treasure. These sites are fast and efficient, striving to complete the transaction without your having to lift a finger. Just lean back in your chair and wait for your package to arrive. What could be simpler?

**WARNING!** Just like any other form of online buying, be careful you don't bid yourself into bankruptcy. Simple clicks of the mouse are easy, and the stuff you'll see at the auctions is super-cool. But be sure you'll still be feeling as giddy when your credit card statement arrives, weighing in at over a pound. If you think you have complete self-control, think even harder—I once thought I had self-control . . . and then the bill arrived. I thought it was a packet of new checks.

Another big bonus feature of merchant auctions is the availability of site and product warranties. That's right, if it's banged up, broken, or not what you expected, these sites will either put you in direct contact with a warranty provider, help you resolve warranty issues, or both. Unlike some of the person-to-person sites where warranties can be as rare as the items you'll bid on, merchant sites operate like full-fledged businesses and take customer satisfaction issues to heart. Of course, exact policies and procedures are going to differ from site to site, and your results may vary. (Don't you just cringe whenever you hear that?) In addition, since many of the items you'll bid on are closeouts or refurbs, they might also come with the dreaded "All sales are final" policy—it's not a bad thing, but you'll have a hard time returning something for the sole reason of just having changed your mind. So to avoid any surprises, be sure you understand each site's policies before you jump in with both mouse buttons blazing.

**GET A CLUE** *"Excuse me, but can't I just go to the store to buy some of the items these sites auction?"* Yes, you can—but many times you'll find better deals online if you don't mind shopping from afar and waiting for your stuff to arrive. But (and this is a big *but*), be careful of the auction allure: many people get caught up in the bidding and winning aspects of auctions. Be sure you haven't set your sights so sharply on winning that you become blind to the fact that you could be spending too much for that object of your desire. If you could've driven a couple of miles and paid less, it's not all that big a victory to win that auction, now is it?

**WARNING!** My sensors indicate suckers are approaching. . . .

Pay little attention to those eye-catching leads such as *"Home Satellite systems starting at $9," "Notebook PCs as low as $1,"* and other such impossible deals. As the adage goes, if it seems too good to be true. . . well, you know the rest. Those are fetching lures, but I've yet to find such a steal. Besides, if I did, do you *really* think I'd tell anyone about it?

So with all that being said, how 'bout if you and I go see what all this auction stuff is about? Bring your credit card . . .

## Onsale.com

The first of the merchant auctions to hit the Web—which you previously learned was also *the first* online auction to ever go live—is also the first stop on this auction tour. Since its initial appearance in 1994, Onsale has grown steadily and has emerged as one of the biggest merchant auctions (especially considering its large offering of closeout and refurbished PC equipment).

**DID YOU KNOW?** Onsale is a publicly offered stock and trades on the NASDAQ board under the symbol *ONSL*.

Onsale is one of the auction hosts, auctioning products purchased or consigned from a variety of established product vendors (manufacturers, wholesalers, or retailers). At Onsale you'll also find items from manufacturers and retailers like Sony, Levi's, Office Depot, Fujitsu, and even Omaha Steaks. Computer biggie Hewlett-Packard, a regular Onsale e-tailer, has recognized Onsale.com as an integral part of HP's own online PC distribution strategy. But this is just a small sampling of the regular Onsale vendors who have turned to Onsale as a viable new distribution channel. And you thought you'd only be bidding on some dusty stuff in an abandoned warehouse.

## Site Presentation

Visit Onsale by entering **www.Onsale.com** in your Web browser's location toolbar. Press Enter on your keyboard, and you're off to the Onsale home page (see Figure 6-1).

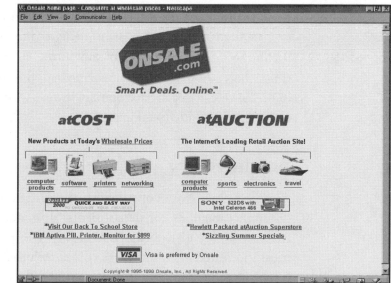

Figure 6-1
The Onsale.com home page offers visitors both an "at Cost" site for flat-price bargains and an "at Auction" site for the thrill of the bid.

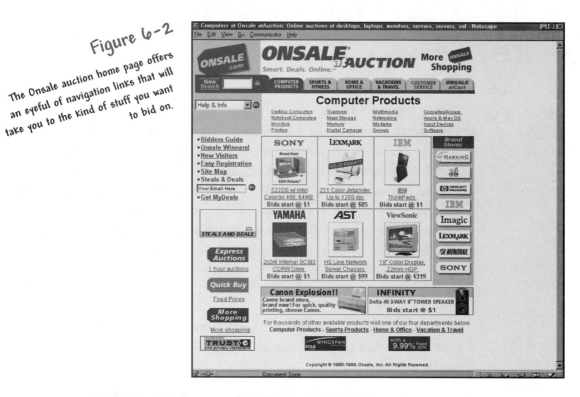

Figure 6-2

The Onsale auction home page offers an eyeful of navigation links that will take you to the kind of stuff you want to bid on.

Well, the first feature of Onsale is to choose your shopping pleasure: go to the *at Cost* site for great items at immediate-purchase wholesale prices, or go to the *at Auction* site to try your luck in the virtual auction parlor. If you have time, check the *at Cost* page, where you'll find mainly computers and related items for sale at decent discounts. However, for now, I'll focus your attention on the auction side (see Figure 6-2).

## Site Inventory

The first thing you notice about the Onsale *at Auction* launch pad is the different categories (or departments) of goods to browse through. The tab strip at the top of the page makes it easy to jump to the department you're most interested in, whether it's computer products, home and office, or customer service. Once in a department, you'll find subcategories (virtual aisles) that you can stroll to find the kind of goods you're after. Don't expect to be gagged by absolutely tons o' stuff—the inventories rotate daily, and what you can't find one day might show up the next. You'll need to pop in from time to time at this site to keep on top of the stream of goods that flows through. Even so, there's plenty to look at, and I'll wager you'll find some little goody you wouldn't mind taking a poke at.

## Registration

So when you think you're ready to start shopping at Onsale, you'll need to register. Just click on the home page link labeled *Easy Registration* that you see in the left-hand column in Figure 6-2. Just enter your name, address, credit card information, and billing address in the online registration form, choose a user ID and password (something cute, clever, or whatever), and click on the *Submit* button. That's it! You'll be assigned your own Onsale account number—use it or your user ID to bid or shop at either of the Onsale sites. So now what? Off to the auctions, what else?

**GET A CLUE** Notice that Onsale will verify your credit card number and especially the billing address. If something doesn't match up, you might be suspected as a potential baddy, and your registration will be rejected. Be honest and be accurate. 'Nuff said.

**WARNING!** Danger Onsale warrior! If you think you're going to take any sort of extended hiatus from Onsale (or *any other* auction site where you register), it's a good idea to close your account. Those folks who are truly savvy about personal data online, especially credit card information, know that it's not a good idea to leave such data idly available where others *could* get to it. If you're not going to be able to watch your auction account for any lengthy period of time (90 days or more), consider closing it out. You can always reinstate it when you return to active bidding.

## Auction Formats

And what kind of auction formats does Onsale offer? Several, including auctions for people who don't like auctions. Here's the kind of formats you'll find at the site:

- **Yankee Auctions.** Though I warned you of this format when you're in the midst of a Dutch auction, Yankee auctions are a viable type of auction and alive and well at Onsale. Since practically all the auctions are for identical units of the same item, bidders win according to Yankee auction rules: each winning bidder pays their exact high (winning) bid value. The strategy is the same as in a Dutch auction: the higher bidders win "rights" to the quantity of units they bid on in a descending fashion until all units have been won. Lower bidders are effectively eliminated from the winner's circle.

- **Express Auctions.** Got some money burning a hole in your pocket? If so, you might enjoy this auction format. Express auctions run for a duration of only one hour and occur many times a day. The selection of items might be less than in the Yankee auctions, but you could find and secure some items really fast—and really cheap. The opening bid is just $1, and who knows—maybe nobody else is watching. . . . The bidding and winning follow the Yankee auction rules.

- **Quick Buys.** Well if you really don't care much for auctions, maybe this is your format (though I'd have to wonder why you're reading this book in the first place). Anyway, Quick Buys are an option if you just want to dart in, find something, and buy it at the designated Quick Buy price. Maybe you're running late on your Christmas shopping, or you just don't feel like participating in the bidding process. That's fine—use Quick Buys to choose from a select inventory of goods that you can buy right on the spot. Quick Buys are in effect until their established closing date or until all available items have been snatched up. Of course, if you're going to go this route, you may as well check into the offerings at Onsale *at Cost,* too.

## Site Navigation, Bidding, and Services

OK, but what about finding the *stuff!?* Sure, Onsale's got lots of it, and it's easy to find. Click on the category that you'd like to browse, then navigate through the subcategories and on to the actual items up for bid. This site has an intuitive layout, and each item listing includes full product details, specifi-cations, sales conditions, warranties, and manufacturer. An even easier method

to get to the stuff you want is to use the site map—you can jump to it right from the home page by using the *Site Map* link in the left-hand column area. The site map displays all item categories and subcategories for your easy use.

**IN MY MIND** As I look at the *Merchandise* links on the Site Map page, I see (and you can, too) that there really aren't a whole bunch of categories to choose from. In fact, though Onsale is one of the major merchant auction sites today, its inventory isn't exactly tremendous. Some folks might contend there are bigger sites to visit, and I'd agree. However, if you're looking for a first auction experience that you can comfortably get your arms around, then Onsale delivers the thrill of bidding without the overload of maneuvering through gobs of stuff.

Besides being able to easily find stuff, you can also find help when you need it. Spend a little more time at the site map, and you'll find topical links that lead you to the information you're looking for: tutorials that help you master the site mechanics, FAQs that give you answers to your questions, and directions for contacting the Onsale staff directly via a toll free phone call if nothing less than human interaction is going to get you on your way. Onsale offices are located in California, and they're currently staffing the phones Monday through Friday from 7 A.M. to 5 P.M. Pacific Time. Go ahead—give 'em a call.

Bidding at Onsale is simple, too. In fact, I've found it to be so easy that I consider Onsale's bidding process one of the best I've ever used. When you drill into one of the item offerings (see Figure 6-3), there's plenty of information readily available to guide you before you bid.

Find an item that appeals to you and click on the item title as you see in Figure 6-3. You'll jump to an item description page that gives all the specifications of the item (often including a picture) and who else has already bid (including their bid amounts and the quantity they've bid for). If you want to bid on the item, just click on the link labeled *Place/Raise Your Bid* on the detail page (see Figure 6-4).

When you bid, you'll enter your user ID or account number, your password, and the price and quantity you wish to bid. Then you'll move on to determining your preferred shipping method in case you win (see Figure 6-5).

Figure 6-3

The Onsale subcategory screen shows the different items currently up for bid, plus easy icons that let you know the type of auction format being used or how long the auction has to go.

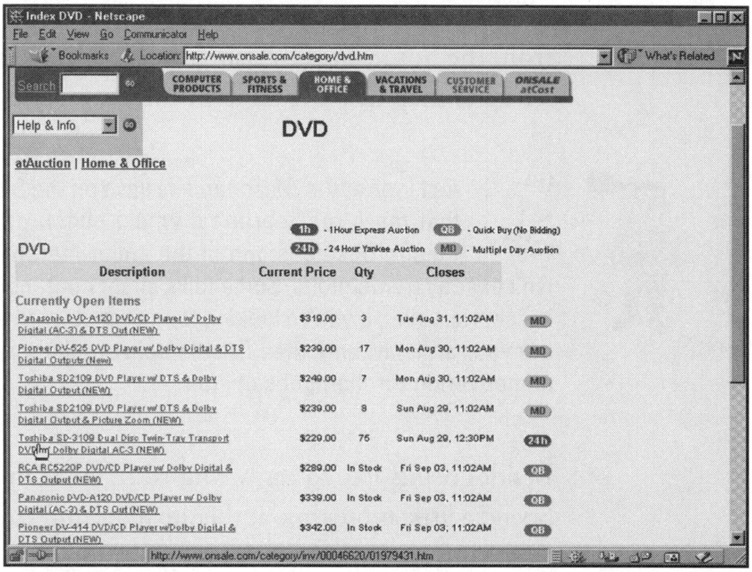

Figure 6-4

You'll find the link to bidding at the bottom of the item status box.

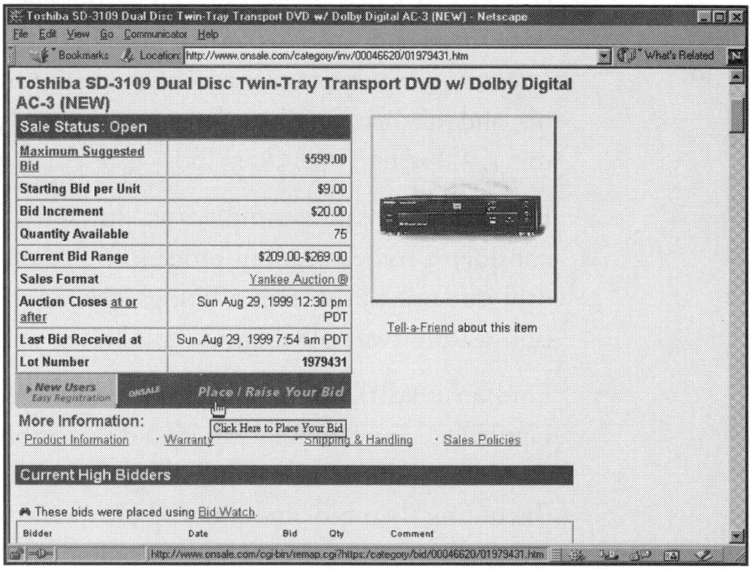

Figure 6-5
The Onsale bidding screen is one of the easiest I've ever used.

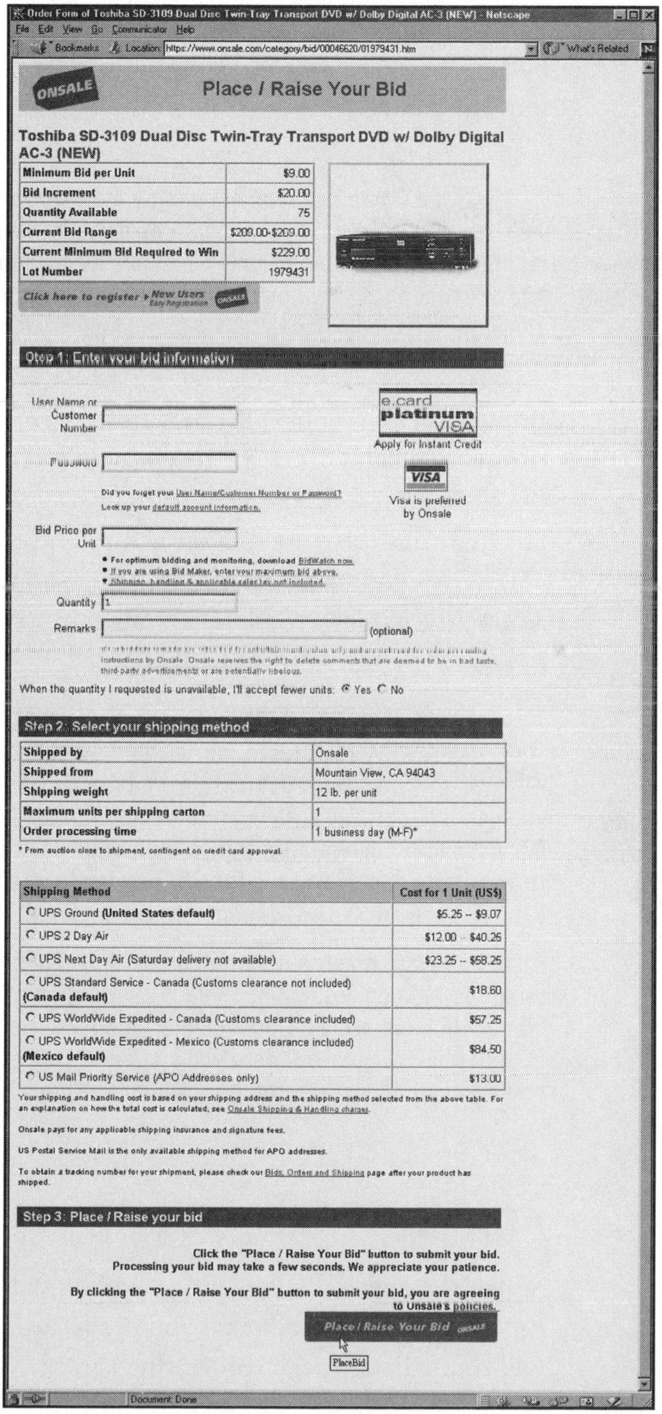

**Order Form of Toshiba SD-3109 Dual Disc Twin-Tray Transport DVD w/ Dolby Digital AC-3 (NEW) - Netscape**

File  Edit  View  Go  Communicator  Help

Bookmarks  Location: https://www.onsale.com/category/bid/00046620/01979431.htm    What's Related

**ONSALE**            Place / Raise Your Bid

**Toshiba SD-3109 Dual Disc Twin-Tray Transport DVD w/ Dolby Digital AC-3 (NEW)**

| Minimum Bid per Unit | $9.00 |
|---|---|
| Bid Increment | $20.00 |
| Quantity Available | 75 |
| Current Bid Range | $209.00-$209.00 |
| Current Minimum Bid Required to Win | $229.00 |
| Lot Number | 1979431 |

Click here to register ▶ New Users *Easy Registration*  **ONSALE**

**Step 1: Enter your bid information**

User Name or Customer Number [              ]

Password [              ]

Did you forget your User Name/Customer Number or Password?
Look up your default account information.

Bid Price per Unit [              ]

- For optimum bidding and monitoring, download BidWatch now.
- If you are using Bid Maker, enter your maximum bid above.
- Shipping, handling & applicable sales tax not included.

Quantity [1]

Remarks [              ] (optional)

Instructions by Onsale. Onsale reserves the right to delete comments that are deemed to be in bad taste, third-party advertisements or are potentially libelous.

When the quantity I requested is unavailable, I'll accept fewer units: ○ Yes ○ No

**e.card platinum VISA**
Apply for Instant Credit

**VISA**
Visa is preferred by Onsale

**Step 2: Select your shipping method**

| Shipped by | Onsale |
|---|---|
| Shipped from | Mountain View, CA 94043 |
| Shipping weight | 12 lb. per unit |
| Maximum units per shipping carton | 1 |
| Order processing time | 1 business day (M-F)* |

* From auction close to shipment, contingent on credit card approval.

| Shipping Method | Cost for 1 Unit (US$) |
|---|---|
| ○ UPS Ground (United States default) | $5.25 -- $9.07 |
| ○ UPS 2 Day Air | $12.00 -- $40.25 |
| ○ UPS Next Day Air (Saturday delivery not available) | $23.25 -- $58.25 |
| ○ UPS Standard Service - Canada (Customs clearance not included) (Canada default) | $18.60 |
| ○ UPS WorldWide Expedited - Canada (Customs clearance included) | $57.25 |
| ○ UPS WorldWide Expedited - Mexico (Customs clearance included) (Mexico default) | $84.50 |
| ○ US Mail Priority Service (APO Addresses only) | $13.00 |

Your shipping and handling cost is based on your shipping address and the shipping method selected from the above table. For an explanation on how the total cost is calculated, see Onsale Shipping & Handling charges.

Onsale pays for any applicable shipping insurance and signature fees.

US Postal Service Mail is the only available shipping method for APO addresses.

To obtain a tracking number for your shipment, please check our Bids, Orders and Shipping page after your product has shipped.

**Step 3: Place / Raise your bid**

Click the "Place / Raise Your Bid" button to submit your bid.
Processing your bid may take a few seconds. We appreciate your patience.

By clicking the "Place / Raise Your Bid" button to submit your bid, you are agreeing to Onsale's policies.

**Place / Raise Your Bid** ONSALE

[ PlaceBid ]

Document: Done

When all information is entered, click on the *Place/Raise Your Bid* box at the bottom of the screen, and your bid will be processed. Yes, it's that easy to get into the game.

**WARNING!**  Your bid does not compute?! If you need to retract a bid (you goofed up or changed your mind), you'll need to do it within 15 minutes of the bid's placement. After that, bids can only be canceled by submitting a cancellation request form and only in cases of bid error (like bidding $1,000 instead of $100). Bid cancellation isn't available for auctions with less than an hour to go or for Quick Buy items.

But what if you're outbid? Can you still get back into the game? Yes, provided the auction hasn't ended and you're prepared to increase your bid amount. Onsale features an *automatic auction extension* feature: bids made within the last five minutes of an auction will extend the auction another five minutes. That gives you plenty of time to place another bid and reclaim your place among the winning bidders. The auction will not end until a full five minutes has elapsed with no additional bids.

**WARNING!**  More bidding alerts! Since you can bid for multiple quantities, you can also instruct Onsale whether you wish to receive lesser quantities should you become partially outbid (another bidder outbids you, but there are still enough items left over that you would get less than your desired quantity). If you decide you want *exactly* the quantity you bid for and nothing less, you can be bumped out of the bidding even if there are still a few items to be claimed.

Also, be aware that the early bid gets the win. A bidder who was previously outbid can raise the bid and outbid you even if their high bid matches your high bid. If that bidder placed their initial bid before you did, when they come back to raise their bid (after being outbid), their original bid date will be considered and the earlier bid will win out over all others, even if the new high bid amount is equal. Get those bids in early!

## After the Auction Ends

When the auction's over, and providing you're one of the winners, you'll receive an e-mail message that you've succeeded in your bidding quest. Onsale will immediately begin processing the payment and shipment of your item.

Remember, they have your credit card information on file, and you specified your desired shipping method when you placed your bid. All you have to do is sit back and wait for the item to arrive (don't forget to clear a place for your new treasure).

## Additional Site Features

Here are a few notable features that you should acquaint yourself with if you intend to become an Onsale regular:

- **Easy Search.** As you can see in several of the figures from this discussion, Onsale provides a product search window near the top of their pages. It's fine for searching for things like "DVD," "MP3," or any other sort of item you're looking for. Click on the *Search* link next to that search window and you'll get to *Easy Search*—it allows you to enter a specific category or manufacturer to search on and also allows you to choose whether your search should be limited to auction item titles or if it should also search in item descriptions. Give it a try.

- **Bid Watch.** This is an actual program that you can download. Bid Watch is a local tool that helps you keep track of your Onsale bidding. It can access the items you've bid on at Onsale, including bid amounts and bid status, and display them all in a single window on your PC. Further, you can use Bid Watch to actually place bids without having to access the Onsale site pages. There's a great tutorial explaining all the details of Bid Watch—just go to the site map and look for a *Bid Watch* link under the heading, *Smart Tools*.

- **Bid Maker.** This is Onsale's proxy bidding system. Use it to place successive bids that will keep you in the winner's circle. Bid Maker will continue to make minimum bids for you until it reaches the maximum bid amount that you have specified. After that, if you're outbid, you'll need to revisit the bidding page and *Raise Your Bid*.

- **E-mail Notification**. Onsale is good about keeping you informed. You'll receive e-mail messages whenever you create or modify your account, place a bid, are outbid, or win an item.

## AuctionGuy Rates This Site . . .

So here's how the rating's going to go: AuctionGuy's pretty particular how and where he spends his money. But when he finds a site he likes, he's ready to throw it down by the fistfuls. Get the idea?

Therefore, on a scale of 1 to 5 (five being best), Onsale earns a 4. The site offers such easy maneuverability, simple presentation of on-screen information, and an overall uncluttered look that it's about as easy to use as it gets. (The only objection: there are a few too many advertiser's banners and ad spots that border on distraction.)

The inventory is good but not boffo. That's OK, though, for new auctiongoers since it keeps from overwhelming them with too much to see. For bargain hunters, the reasonable amount of goods helps them quickly zero in on the best deals. Some of the manufacturer's item details and specifications can get a bit lengthy, though. However, better to have more information than less.

High marks for the site map and the overall helpful nature of Onsale. This can be a real bonus for newbies because they can pretty much master the site and its offerings within a day, giving all future site time to finding and bidding on the things they want.

Finally, the site offers good response, good stability, and terrific security features. It's earned the TRUSTe brand for providing good user privacy policies (see the brand in Figure 6-2). Also, most screens you'll traverse through are secured (notice the little lock or key at the bottom of your Web browser is usually unbroken). This is a safe place to shop and a fun place to bid.

## uBid.com

Another of the top dogs in the merchant auction arena is uBid (**www.ubid.com**). Established in 1997 as a spinoff venture of Creative Computers, Inc. (proprietors of PC-Mall at **www.pcmall.com**), uBid began as another of the sites that offers durable goods (like computers, electronics, and so on) that are manufacturer's overruns, discontinued items, or refurbished units.

**DID YOU KNOW?**    uBid is a publicly offered stock and trades on the NASDAQ board under the symbol *UBID*.

uBid establishes a partnership with manufacturers, purchases merchandise itself, then offers it for sale at the auction site. More recently, though, uBid extended its vendor relationships to include smaller businesses who can apply for vendor status and sell their items directly on the site without first selling to uBid (vendor applicants have to go through a rigorous evaluation first). The inclusion of smaller merchants to the site has increased the inventory and categories of items that bidders can find at the site—an attempt to compete with some of those person-to-person mega-sites.

## Site Presentation

Overall, uBid has a design much like Onsale's: a useful tab strip along with a healthy dose of home page links to take you quickly to specific auction items, other features, and help pages the site offers (see Figure 6-6).

Subsequent category pages provide a similar assortment of quick-jump links and lots of pictures of tantalizing items. It's a busy site to look at, reminiscent of one of those hard-core electronics-lovers' catalogs.

## Site Inventory

uBid has an excellent inventory with plenty of categories boasting plenty of items. In the mainstay offerings (those durable goods) you'll find a big selection; in the newer categories managed by approved small merchants the selection is a bit slimmer. Overall, you'll find plenty of products in each of the categories—not a bunch of alluring category titles with empty shelves inside.

Figure 6-6

The uBid home page is another link-laden launch pad that lets you jump practically anywhere within the site.

DID YOU KNOW? uBid has also established a partnership with S/R Auction, Inc. (Surplus Record Machinery & Equipment Directory) to further promote and propel the S/R auctions. Surplus Record, Inc., was established back in 1924 as the publisher of *The Surplus Record*—a monthly directory of surplus machinery and capital equipment. S/R established a Web presence in 1995 and powered up S/R Auction in 1999. By the recent partnership, S/R Auction is now "powered by uBid" and is the largest auction where business-to-business trading takes place for surplus machinery and other such industrial equipment. Visit **www.srauction.com** if you're interested. Anyone need a fleet of forklifts?

## Registration

Registration at uBid is as easy as 1-2-3, largely because it's a three-step registration form. To begin registering, click on the *Sign Up Here* link you see just below the tab strip in Figure 6-6. In the first part of the registration form, you need to enter some required information such as your name, desired password, billing address, phone number, and e-mail address. The second part of the form is where you enter your credit card information *only if you choose to do so*. This is a real nice security feature: you can provide your credit card information and have it stored with the rest of your account data at the time you register, or you can elect not to store it on uBid's server, entering it only at the time you actually bid on an item. Recalling that warning I issued earlier about leaving an idle account lying about with your credit card data, this option at uBid's site relieves much of that worry if you will be away from the site for extended periods of time. Finally, the third part of the form includes lots of survey-type questions (what kinds of products you like, whether you want to be on a mailing list, and that sort of thing). When you've entered at least the required information, just click on the *Submit Information* button at the bottom of the registration screen. uBid will process your data, then assign you a user ID and account number. Just like that, your account is live.

GET A CLUE There's a great feature for new users at uBid: click on the link labeled *New User? Click Here!*—it will take you to a great *Jump Start Tutorial* page, showing you more tips for using the site.

## Auction Formats

uBid also supports the Yankee auction format. You'll find auctions of identical items up for bid. Bid on the quantity you'd like at the price you think will make you a winner. If you do win, you'll pay your exact winning bid amount, though other winning bidders could pay more or less than you (depending on how high they bid and what quantity of items was available during the auction).

## Site Navigation, Bidding, and Services

On the uBid home page, you're immediately greeted with featured auctions, or you can use the tabs and strike off to find that certain something. There are several other ways to find stuff, too: use the pull-down category browse window you see below the tab strip, click on the *Top 10 Specials* or *Auctions Closing This Hour* links, use the category links in the left-hand column, or use the product search window, also in the left-hand column. And if you're the type who'd like to get more of a bird's-eye view of all the goodies available for bid, click on the *More Categories* tab—it will provide a page full of links to the different categories and subcategories, going so far as to list in parentheses the number of active auctions going on in each of the virtual departments (see Figure 6-7).

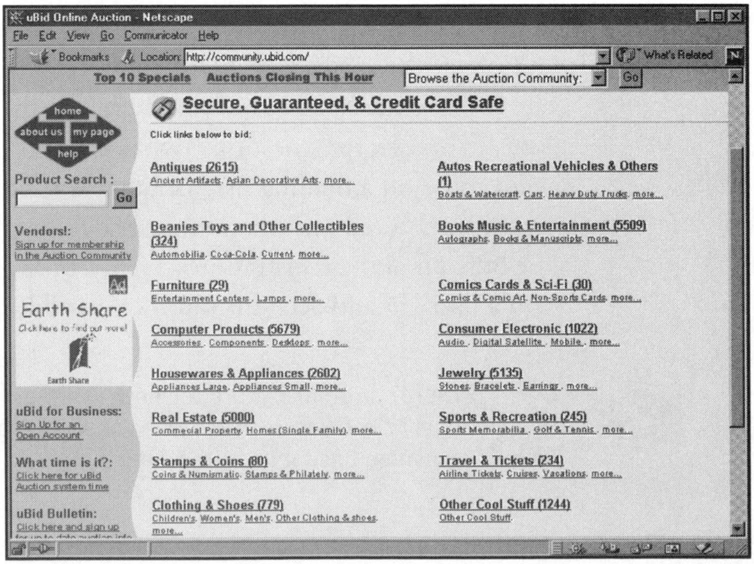

Figure 6-7

Use the More Categories tab to get an overview of all the great stuff you can bid on.

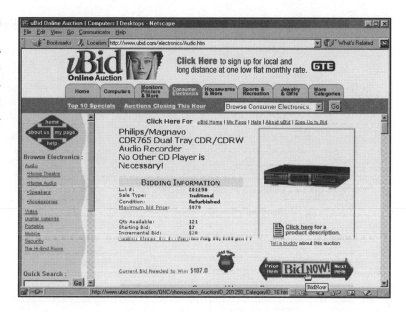

Figure 6-8

Within the top portion of an item detail page, you'll find the major product specifications and current bid status. Use the Bid Now! link if you want to get in on the action.

However you get there, find an item you like and click on its listing title to read more about it. Within the item details, you'll learn the specifications of the product, usually find a picture of it, see who else is bidding, and find out what the current bid range is. If it's something you think you should own and it's still within your definition of a "deal," then place your bid. On every item detail page, you'll find a link labeled *Bid Now!* (see Figure 6-8).

Bidding at uBid is simple (see Figure 6-9). Start by entering your user ID and password. Next, choose your bid amount—uBid uses preset bid increments that you can choose from. Select the quantity you'd like and check (or uncheck) whether you'll accept partial quantities. Select your shipping options and click on the *Place Bid!* button. Congratulations! You're in the running.

**WARNING!**    All bids you make at uBid are non-cancelable. Period. The site managers *strongly* suggest wise bidding.

Just as at Onsale, winning an auction can be determined by how many items you bid on and whether you're willing to accept a partial quantity. Also, uBid follows the "early bid gets the win" rule. It's not always a good idea to wait to place your bid. If you do get outbid, you'll be notified via e-mail, and you

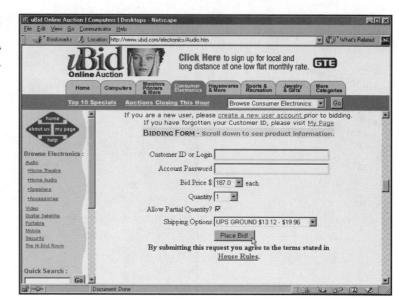

Figure 6-9
Just fill out this simple bid form and stake your claim at uBid.

have a chance to get back into the game. uBid has a similar auction extension feature to the 5-minute wait at Onsale, but uBid requires that 10 minutes pass without any bids being received. If a bid comes in within the 10-minute window, the auction is automatically extended a full 10 minutes more. Yes, these auctions could conceivably go on forever.

## After the Auction Ends

Again, just as at Onsale, you bid using your credit card information. If you win an auction at uBid, the happy little e-elves will charge your card at the value of your winning bid plus the postage per your selection. Your package should be sent out within 48 hours, according to the site's promises.

## Additional Site Features

- **Bid Butler.** This is uBid's proxy bidding service that bids on your behalf. Ol' virtual Jeeves will place minimum required bids to keep you in the winner's circle up to the point that it reaches your designated maximum bid. Not all items on uBid are eligible to use the Bid Butler (guess he needs a day off to press his suit or something).

- **Extended Warranty.** For select items (computer systems, laptop PCs, ink jet printers, laser and dot matrix printers, and monitors) you can purchase an extended warranty at the time you place your bid. It kicks in the moment the manufacturer's standard warranty expires, and it's transferable should you decide to sell or give away the item you win. The cost of the warranty is determined by the final price the item receives when the auction closes.

## AuctionGuy Rates This Site . . .

On the scale of 1 to 5, this site is worth a 3.

Clearly, uBid is one of the retail auction biggies, and it has a good set of product offerings. In fact, I found much more inventory—more things I was interested in bidding on—at uBid than at Onsale. The extra collector-oriented categories were encouraging, though clearly uBid hasn't attracted enough users (buyers or vendors) to really fill the virtual shelves. Maybe that's just a matter of time.

The site wasn't too bad to navigate around, but the lack of a site map was sorely evident. In my mind, site maps are a requirement, especially for some newer users. There's a lot of stuff and a lot of information on this site, but there's no real hub where it can all be easily accessed. The links provided are fine, but they require determined users to click and poke their way along to find just what they need. Also, I didn't like the way the tab strip changed (meaning some tabs disappeared and some new ones appeared) depending on which screen you were in—kind of defeats the purpose of the strip at all.

Bidding at this site is easy, and winning isn't an unreachable feat. High marks for that. The shipping costs, though, are a bit of a problem—they're high. The site could use some more choices in this area.

Site response time is decent though it does suffer from banner blight. Ads and other such animated billboards only make the users wait longer to get to the items they want to bid on. But, overall, the wait wasn't too terrible.

Good ratings for site security (I especially like that credit card option during the registration process). Lots of access to secure servers, which is good. The site has earned the AOL Certified Merchant brand for excellent site security and privacy policies. I feel safe bidding at this site.

All in all, it's another fine site and a good one if you're looking for these types of goods. Financially, it's a solid site and is probably here to stay. As I said before, the increased inventories from the wide variety of manufacturers and merchants works in your favor, helping to hook you up with some neat little something.

## Bid.com

Bid.com is another supersite that offers great stuff that gets bona fide gearheads all in a froth. Lots of PCs, laptops, home electronics, and other goodies that beep, blink, and make beautiful music. In addition, you'll find sporting goods, sports collectibles, and jewelry. The inventory comes from major manufacturers and retailers like Compaq, Panasonic, Technics, and Hamilton Beach (mmmm . . . toaster oven). Not terribly different from the two sites you've just learned about, this site offers some interesting twists from what you've already seen (more on that later).

Bid.com is based in Toronto, Canada (beauty, eh?) and has offices there as well as in Florida. Established in 1995, Bid.com has been another of the successful auction mainstays on the Internet.

 **DID YOU KNOW?** Bid.com is a publicly offered stock and trades on the NASDAQ board and the Toronto Stock Exchange under the symbol *BIDS*.

## Site Presentation

To access Bid.com, use the URL **www.bid.com**. You'll see a screen like the one shown in Figure 6-10. Notice you'll first have to decide if you'll be bidding from the American site or the Canadian site. Make the appropriate selection, and off you go.

Once you actually reach the Bid.com auction launch pad, you'll see it has a really clean design. It's sleek and simple without an excess of eye-garbage cluttering up your PC's desktop (see Figure 6-11).

Figure 6-10

When you first access Bid.com, you'll need to let the site know if you'll be dealing in the American or Canadian flavor.

Across the top, you see the usual tab strip, though this one remains consistent throughout the site. Along the left side, you see the category links that let you jump to the items you want to bid on. In the middle of the page, you'll see the usual pictures of featured auctions. There is some ad-play on this page, but not as much as at some of the other sites.

Figure 6-11

Sleek, simple, and easy to get around—that's what I like in an auction site.

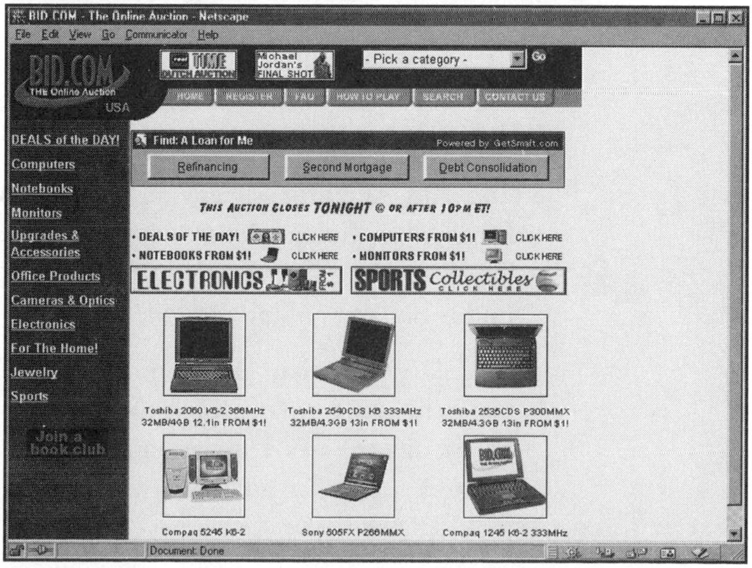

## Site Inventory

Bid.com offers an inventory comparable in size to Onsale. There's enough there that you'll probably find something you like, but not so much that you'll lose two nights' sleep trying to see it all. This is definitely a site to use if you're looking for durable goods and would like to get 'em quick.

## Registration

Registration at Bid.com seems to be the simplest so far. You can register by using the *Register* tab on the tab strip. It takes you to a secure registration form where you'll enter your credit card information (*required* for registration at this site), plus your name, street and e-mail addresses, and phone number.

**WARNING!**  Not sure if this is a true warning, but I'll call in DangerGuy just in case. In a strange move, Bid.com suggests you enter *two* different credit card numbers. The reasoning is that if the primary card hits its credit limit during the billing process, the secondary card can be used to keep from having your great deal denied. Although the data is secure, that was just a bit too much information for this metal-head to provide. The second card information is optional, and DangerGuy opted out.

So, enter the information and click on the *Save* button at the bottom of the page. That be it.

## Auction Formats

- **Top Bid Auctions.** These auctions follow the usual "high bidders win" format, but Bid.com starts its Top Bid auctions daily at 10 P.M. Eastern Time, running them for only 24 hours. Check the site daily to see what's up for bid and ending tonight.

- **Real Dutch Auctions.** Interestingly enough, it took a Canadian site to bring the true form of Dutch auctioning to America. What's that you say— you've already *seen* Dutch auctions? No you haven't—not in their purest form. A real Dutch auction offers an item for bid at a set price, then *lowers* the price by successive decrements every few seconds until all items have been bid on. Yeah, that's pretty different from what you've seen before. The trick of real Dutch auctions is to wait until the lowest price can be achieved before all items in the lot are claimed. As long as items are still available, every bidder can win.

- **Live Dutch Auctions.** Bid.com was the first to offer an honest-to-goodness *live* auction experience to Internet bidders. Using the streaming audio and video technology of *Real* (**www.real.com**), bidders can actually join in a Netcast auction where a real auctioneer will offer goods using the descending-price Dutch auction format.

## Site Navigation, Bidding, and Services

Like the other sites you've seen, Bid.com provides images of featured auction items the moment you land at the home page—but that's just the beginning. Use the category links along the left column (refer to Figure 6-11) to get to the goods that make you most happy. If you're looking for a specific item or brand, use the *Search* tab on the main tab strip (or any page's tab strip—remember, these strips don't change their stripes, er, strips). Bid.com's search engine lets you search by keyword or even by price range (that's a nice feature, especially if you're trying to bid within your means). And if you're just looking for a cross-section of some of the great variety the site offers, click on the *Deals of the Day* link in the left-hand column—you'll find all kinds of randomly selected auctions that will be closing tonight!

I'm sure by now you're getting the hang of finding things at these auction sites (I suspect you've put this book down more than a few times as you've surfed off to find some deals of your own). So, find something you like at Bid.com and click on the item description. As usual, that takes you into the bidding parlor for that item where you can learn more about it and what the bidding status might be.

As you can see from Figure 6-12, Bid.com has added a dash of graphic flair that provides a bit of fun and whimsy. The animated auctioneer calls your

Figure 6-12

An animated auctioneer greets you at Bid.com. I hope AuctionGuy doesn't get any ideas about moonlighting.

attention to an image of the item you're considering bidding on, while to the right of the image you'll see the quantity available in the auction, the *preset* bid increment (yes, Bid.com determines the bid increment for you), and the current minimum bid required to get you in the running. Along the left column of this item screen, you will see the bid history—who's already bid, how many they bid on, and what their high bids are. To learn more about the item, click on its title or the image itself—you'll jump to the product description and specifications page.

The last time I took the family to Disneyland, I wished I had a pair of these handy little radios to keep tabs on the troops (seems everyone else at the park had them, though). So I'll bid. And bidding at Bid.com is just as simple as everything else you've seen so far. Click on the *Bid* button (refer to Figure 6-12) and you'll jump to the bid screen.

As you can see from Figure 6-13, placing a bid only requires you enter your user name, password, bid amount, and bid quantity. The *Comments* are just a little note you can enter that will appear next to your bid. The *Bid Buddy* is Bid.com's proxy bidding system, which I'll explain more in just a bit. Notice also that shipping is precalculated for the item you're bidding on, and Bid.com

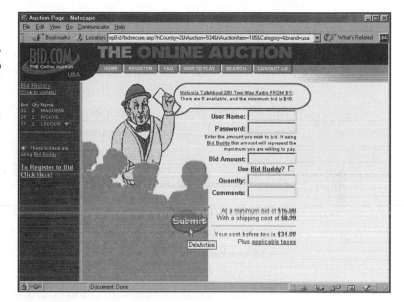

Figure 6-13

More graphics and a simple bid entry screen. The auctioneer is explaining the quantity available and the minimum bid required, so be sure to read what he has to say.

adds that to the current minimum bid so you can immediately see how much this item would cost as you bid (less any applicable sales tax, though tax is only charged—at a rate of 7 percent—*if* you live in Florida). Get your bid information in and click on the *Submit* button.

**WARNING!** DangerGuy's certainly getting some mileage on this one—bids placed at Bid.com *cannot* be canceled. Your bid is considered your irrevocable commitment to follow through with the purchase in the event you win. Be sure about your bids, folks.

Unlike the other sites, Bid.com Top Bid auctions end at 10 P.M. Eastern Time every night without automatic auction extensions. Bid.com's Dutch auctions end at their posted ending time or when all items have been bid on. I tend to like these kinds of auctions better than those that can just go on and on and on.

If you're outbid, you'll get an e-mail notification. However, since the auctions don't have automatic extensions, it's best to stay by your PC to keep up on the bidding if there's an item you simply *must* have.

## After the Auction Ends

When the auction ends and if you're a winner, Bid.com will contact you via e-mail, verify your credit card information, then charge your purchase and begin the shipping process. Expect that your item will ship within a day or two of the auction's close. In this respect, Bid.com (like Onsale and uBid) operates very much like an online retail site.

## Additional Site Features

■ **Bid Buddy.** As I mentioned earlier, this is Bid.com's proxy bidder. You can elect to use it when you're placing your bid. Check the *Use Bid Buddy* option (refer to Figure 6-13) and be sure to enter the maximum amount you want to bid in the *Bid Amount* field. Bid Buddy will only increase your bid enough to meet the minimum bid requirement to keep you in the winner's circle. When your maximum bid is reached, Bid Buddy bows out—you have the option to bid again if you like. Just be sure to check the Bid Buddy option if you'll be entering a maximum bid amount, otherwise that maximum will become your *immediate* bid.

 ## AuctionGuy Rates This Site . . .

On the scale of 1 to 5, Bid.com gets a 4.

I like the very simple design of this site, especially since unnecessary "stuff" makes page loads take longer. Bid.com's slim design helps pages load quickly and makes it easier to focus on what you came to the site for.

Now, in the same breath, I have to admit that the site is devoid of more than just clutter—it's also shy a lot of features that other sites offer. Nowhere is there a site map to give new users an aerial view of the overall landscape. Granted, the site is trim enough that it won't take long to walk it with your mouse, but I'm the kind of user who wants to see the bigger picture, just to make sure I'm not overlooking something. And if you're one of those who likes nifty features with snappy names, you'll be disappointed here (but just wait until you see some of the auction sites in the next chapter). However, some folks believe less is more. I believe that, but you decide for yourself.

Though the inventory isn't as large as you'll see elsewhere, I find a good variety of items that feed the mainstream consumer interest at Bid.com. This site is perfect if you're looking to get in and get out. You can quickly find what you want, find out whether it's available at the present time, and close up the auction within a matter of hours. For people with little time, this site can be ideal.

I like the auction formats Bid.com offers. The true Dutch auctions are fun, and that live Dutch auction is a real hoot—it's the closest thing you can get to being in the auction parlor while still sitting around the house in your jammies.

Not much site help here. The tutorials are skimpy and the FAQ is useful but light (especially for a wide-eyed newcomer who may want a bit more comfort before delving into the bidding). Perhaps this is in response to the site's simplistic design, though I believe more information is usually better.

However, there are enough secure pages to make me feel quite comfortable at this site, and I think Bid.com has done well to present a safe environment—but still, don't leave any stale accounts lying around.

## FirstAuction.com

Now if you're really looking for a mainstream experience, look no further—FirstAuction will be your new hunting ground. It's presented by the Internet Shopping Network, the same folks who bring you the Home Shopping Network, all under the umbrella of USA Networks Interactive (a *mighty big* umbrella, I'd say). If you know anything about the Home Shopping Network and Internet Shopping Network, you'll presume that FirstAuction is going to be big on inventory and big on customer service—and that's a good presumption.

FirstAuction was started in 1997 as a logical extension of the successful Internet Shopping Network. Already drawing large numbers of customers to its television and online retail offerings, the auction venue seemed a natural. When you visit this site, you'll immediately get the feeling this is an auction designed with the average consumer in tennis shoes in mind. So go to **www.firstauction.com** and take a look for yourself.

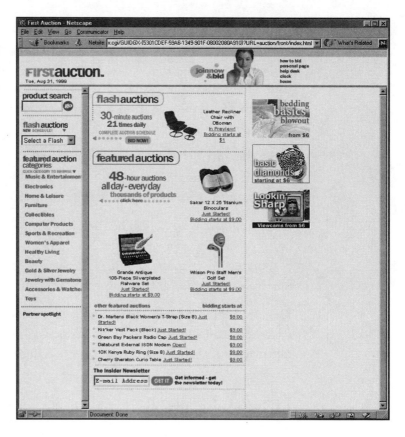

Figure 6-14

FirstAuction.com has a homey feel and boasts some great inventory to browse through.

## Site Presentation

From your first view of the home page, FirstAuction has a look and feel similar to its TV and Internet siblings. But notice that it has a rather diffuse, non-techie look about it (see Figure 6-14).

The site has a "human" feel to it, and its pages resemble last Sunday's newspaper ads. This site has obviously been designed to welcome and comfort those potential bidders who might not be especially Internet savvy or aren't real tech-heads. Of course, that doesn't prevent the gear-mongers from joining in the fun.

## Site Inventory

As you'd expect from the shopping network folks, this site has a bunch of stuff to bid on from a great variety of categories—it's sort of a cross between

CompUSA and Sears. You'll find electronics, entertainment, furniture, bedding, books, videos, computers and accessories, and much more. The varied inventory also adds to the friendliness of this site, helping you find the things you're looking for. FirstAuction leverages from its undeniable presence in the retail market to purchase new, closeout, and some refurbished items to offer to bidders.

## Registration

This site's registration process takes a bit longer than the others I've shown you. If you're ready to become a member, click on the icon labeled *Join now & bid* at the top of the home page (refer to Figure 6-14). When you do, you'll go to the FirstAuction membership form. It asks for the usual stats: your name, address, e-mail address, phone number, and a user ID and password. Enter all that and click on the *Enter* button at the bottom of the page. Next, you'll visit a verification page that lets you review the information you entered. If it all looks good, click on the *OK* button. Now, you're a "member"—but you still haven't registered to bid. Why not? Because you haven't provided your credit card number. As a member, you can fill out an extended membership profile (a survey asking the usual nosy questions) or you're free to link off and start looking the site over. However, since you've come this far, you may as well finish up—click on the *Register to Bid* button. This is when you'll be asked for your credit card information, an alias or nickname to be used when bidding, and whether you'd like to be notified via e-mail when you're outbid. Enter the information and click on the *Enter* button. Again, you'll see a new screen that lets you confirm what you've entered. Click on OK if you got it right the first time. Now, you're in—time to go shopping.

## Auction Formats

FirstAuction offers the typical online rendition of the Yankee auction (multiple units up for bid in an ascending price, quantity, and time-bidding hierarchy; you pay your exact high bid price). Remember, the higher bids win, followed by the highest quantity bid, followed by the earliest time bid. It's like what you saw at uBid.com.

FirstAuction, though, offers some interesting staging variations for their auctions. Consider these:

- **48-Hour Featured Auctions.** Continuously through the day, new auctions start up that run for a 48-hour duration. None of that week-long waiting for an auction to end with these. You can get in, find and bid on what you want, then see how you fare within two days' time.

- **30-Minute Flash Auctions.** If you're really in a hurry, check these out. Twenty-one times a day, Flash Auctions start up and run for a mere 30 minutes. If you miss one, there's another starting right behind it.

## Site Navigation, Bidding, and Services

Just as the site is friendly, it's also pretty easy to get around in. Lots of links to information, and simple links to auction item categories. On every category page, you'll see some nice photos of featured items and the usual text title listings that allow you to link to the stuff up for bid. Don't forget about the search window in the left column of the FirstAuction pages. Enter a keyword and see if there's an auction in your future. When you find what you want, click on it and jump to the details page (see Figure 6-15).

The item page is easy to read and gives me the information I want to see right away—namely, how many of the item are available, what the current bid range is, how many folks have already bid, and when the auction closes. Use the *get more information* link to see a larger image of the item plus the shipping charges that will be tacked on to your (hopefully) winning bid. But my old steak knives are three-time hand-me-downs, and slicing butter's getting to be too much of a task for them; I'm bidding on these.

Click on the *Bid Now* button you see in Figure 6-15. Bidding at FirstAuction is so simple—all you have to do is verify the quantity you're bidding on and select the bid increment (there's a pre-determined list of valid increment values where you see the *Bid Amount* field—just click on the little arrow to see them all). Since the *Comment* field is optional, click on the *Bid Now* button. One more screen after that to verify your bid—click on the *OK* button to place your bid or *Cancel* if you've changed your mind. That's all there is to it.

Figure 6-15

A set of steak knives?? Why not? What—you think I eat like a barbarian or something?

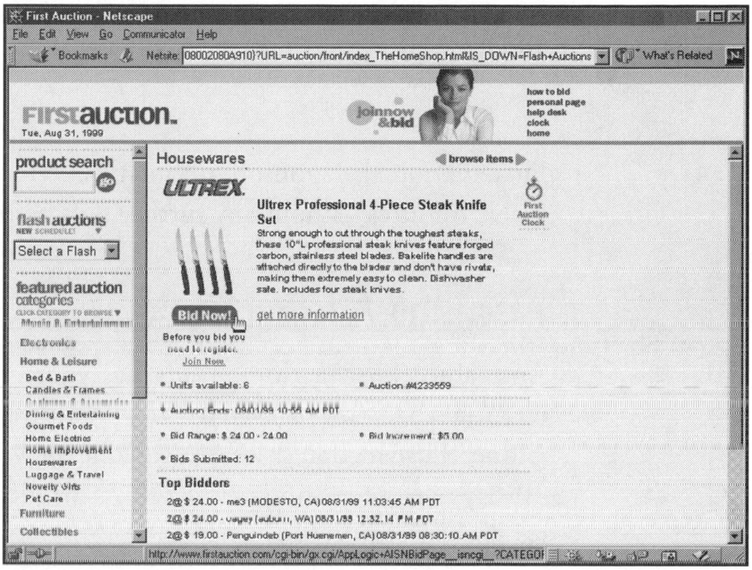

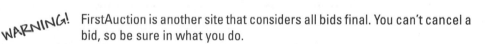

FirstAuction is another site that considers all bids final. You can't cancel a bid, so be sure in what you do.

Here again, if you're outbid, you'll receive an e-mail notice to that effect (provided you elected to receive such messages when you registered). Just head back into that bid page and let those other bidders know you won't be beaten so easily (as for me, I'll be wielding some pointy knives soon). Re-bidding follows the same process as when you placed your first bid. Remember, if you bid early, the time you placed your original bid could help you beat other bidders who bid the same amount as you—the earlier bid time wins out in the case of a bid value tie.

**WARNING!** Note that FirstAuction doesn't provide any sort of bid-bot to perform proxy bidding in your absence. You'll either need to bid high (and pay that high bid price if you win), or keep a close eye on the auction and re-bid right up until the end.

**WARNING!** Hey! Those outbid e-mail messages aren't available for the zippy 30-minute Flash Auctions. Better keep a sharp eye on those to be sure you're a winner.

FirstAuction also sponsors automatic auction extensions: the no-bid window is five minutes without any further bids before the auction closes.

## After the Auction Ends

And, since FirstAuction already has your credit card information (you entered it when you registered), you'll automatically get the charge if you're a winner. FirstAuction strives to acquaint you with your new merchandise within 10 days of the auction's close. Not a whole lot more to say here—just like catalog ordering.

## Additional Site Features

- **Shipping List.** This is a different feature, allowing you to store up to four different shipping addresses to use during your bidding. This is great if you're buying a gift for someone in your house and don't want UPS knocking on the door and handing it to them instead of to you, spoiling the surprise.

- **Personal Pages.** Nope, it's not some lonely hearts club. Personal Pages are a hub of information for your auction comings and goings. They list your active auctions and tip you off when you fall out of the running. In addition, you'll find occasional information here about new auction events that might fit your personal tastes.

- **Bid Summary.** This feature gives you an overview of your FirstAuction bidding activity. You'll see a comprehensive listing of all open auctions you're currently bidding in, all closed auctions you've won in the past, and those other auctions you bid in but lost. Better luck next time on those items—they're mass produced, and will probably be around again.

## AuctionGuy Rates This Site . . .

On the scale of 1 to 5, FirstAuction rakes in a 4.

I like the casual presentation of this site. It has a calm look and soothing approach. For those who were previously only comfortable with mall shopping and catalog ordering, FirstAuction provides a nice segue into the world on online auctions.

There's a great selection of stuff here, and the prices are pretty reasonable. I've yet to get a real steal, but I know I'm getting good merchandise. And the site's customer service is excellent. With all that past experience at the Home Shopping Network and Internet Shopping Network, FirstAuction clearly has customer satisfaction down pat. You'll like that if this is your first auction experience (no pun intended).

The site help was pretty good, but there's no site map that I've ever encountered. However, there are some pretty helpful (though not too detailed) tutorial pages under the *How to bid* link at the top of each page (next to that lady that looks kinda like Susan Dey). A nice plus, though, is a toll-free help desk number (find it under the *Help desk* link at the top of the page) that puts you in touch with a real live person, though only Monday through Friday.

Again, since this is a spinoff of the Internet Shopping Network, you'll know the site security is top-notch. Though I liked the idea of not having to provide my credit card at the time of registration as at uBid, it's not unreasonable to ante up that information, and I saw plenty of secure pages to believe my personal data was safe here.

It's a good site, and it gets a higher mark than a couple of the sites mentioned earlier just because I feel so relaxed after shopping here.

## Some Final Thoughts

OK, so those are my top picks in the merchant auction arena. As you can see, these sites have many common functions and features, though called by different names. But in their similarity, you'll find confidence. The more you become accustomed to how these auction sites work, the easier it will be for you to pop in from site to site as you do your shopping and bidding (and winning).

With so many auction sites, it's useful to find out if they're really so different or if they're often the same animal dressed up in a different fur overcoat. Hopefully, what you've read here boils some of it down for you so you can get off to a good start. Don't hesitate to venture out on your own, though. Much of enjoying online auctioning depends on personal tastes.

A key to being successful at these merchant sites is to do some comparative pricing. One of the sites may be consistently higher on a type of item than competing sites (and vice versa). All sites might be too high on items you can buy cheaper at discount online retail sites (one of my favorites for electronics is **www.800.com**, *hint-hint*). And don't forget the blow-out sale at the store down the street from your home—those are still viable shopping alternatives, even in this time of online everything.

Remember, also, that bidding fever can cause would-be buyers to do crazy things in the name of winning the auction. That often equates to paying too much for an item. Don't get caught up in that yourself. If the auction circuit usually features what you want, wait for the overbid auction to end and watch for the next appearance of that item on the auction block.

Again, because of the nature of these merchant auctions, especially the availability of good customer service and useful warranties, these are good auctions to start at if you're just cutting your auction teeth.

C H A P T E R 7

# The Person-to-Person Experience

But what if you're not looking for a new computer, CD player, or Kitchen Magician for Mom this Christmas? What if you're looking for something really rare, odd, or even outlandish? You could scour the classified ads of your local newspaper, slither about garage sales in your area, or haunt certain newsgroups on the Internet's Usenet, all in the hopes of finding the obscure item for which you yearn. But why mess with all that when there's a better place to hunt right at your fingertips? Now you can wander through the amazing person-to-person auction sites. If you're looking for the unusual, these auction sites are where you'll find it.

Though Onsale.com was the first site to introduce online auctioning to the Net world, person-to-person auctions are what have propelled online bidding and selling to phenomenon status. They're huge, they're exciting, they're a little funky, and they're your place to find some really cool stuff. Better yet, person-to-person auctions are where *you* can sell some cool stuff of your own. From moon rocks to pet rocks, snake lights to strobe lights, Velveteen rabbit to velvet Elvis ("*W'ahl thank yah ver' mushhh*"), you'll find all kinds of wonderful, wild, and weird things at these person-to-person sites. I know you're curious, so take a look at what these sites are all about.

# What's the Story?

Face it: you belong to a society of hunters and gatherers. Everyone seems to be peering at the ground or craning his or her neck to locate some odd little treasure. That stuff your parents and grandparents regularly threw in the old ash can has now become the quest of many collectors. You never know where you'll find that vintage item or rare piece of pop culture. It might be under your nose, across the ocean, or at an online auction.

The merchant auctions are all very nice, but there you're limited to whatever goods the mainstream vendors are offering. But visit any local flea market and you'll find most of the congregating occurs wherever average people are selling their personal junk. Sure, there's a nice selection of new brassware, framed lithographs, and silk plants at the professional vendor booths, but to most market-goers, *that's* the junk. The real goods worth having are in old Sam's dusty box that's been up in his attic for the past 30 years and is now sitting on a patch of pavement waiting to be discovered. Extend this hidden treasure truism to the online world, and you get the person-to-person experience.

I doubt you've avoided hearing about these sites. They're all the rage in the news, in online discussion forums, and in the stock market, to boot. Person-to-person trading has become the latest economic wave, and millions of buyers and sellers have waxed up their cyber-boards to surf the online curl. Who would have thought that sites specializing in helping people sell their junk could result in multibillion-dollar profit statements?

These sites aren't in the business of selling the junk themselves, though. They serve simply as *venues*, virtual hosts to the world's junk dealers (though I should quit calling it junk; there's some great stuff out there). No, these online hosts are there only to offer the Web space for you to buy or sell stuff. They don't get involved in your final transaction, when goods trade for greenbacks— that's up to you. The sites offer useful pages, tutorials, auction aids, and advice, but your actual deal is done offline in a private exchange.

But if these venues aren't involved in the actual transaction, how do they stay in business? Quite well, actually: they charge fees for sellers to list items, just as physical flea markets charge a vendor rent for a fifteen-yard square plot of blacktop. But that's not where the sites make their real profit. The site's big income comes from the commissions they charge sellers based on the final selling price of an auctioned item. It's a nominal percentage of the seller's final take, and it keeps the person-to-person site profitable and happy.

Well, how dare they! If they're not involved in the transaction, why do they feel the right to claim a piece of the spoils? Few people gripe about the listing fees (provided they're reasonable), but the commission is what really gets some people's goat. Now, I'm not an advocate for commission fees, but consider this: how else could you advertise to millions of potential buyers worldwide so inexpensively? Nowhere; not today, anyway. If a reasonable commission is the price for that sort of visibility, then it's one of the cheapest forms of targeted advertising on the planet. I doubt any local show, trade paper, or even television ad would bring the sort of traffic you'll find at these person-to-person auctions. There are literally *millions* of folks out there clamoring to see what's up for bid and who's buying what.

## The Power to Sell

Well, this is a key difference between person-to-person sites and merchant sites. *You* can sell *your* stuff whenever you like. Got a stack of old Spiderman comics? Auction it. Sitting on a collection of coins that you want to get rid of? Auction it. Tired of moving around all those strange gifts of Christmases past (a leg lamp, anyone)? Auction them all. Whatever you've got, there's probably a buyer or three out there who would love to get their hands on it.

Naturally, the benefit to you—besides cleaning out your garage or emptying your attic—is the prospect of making money. Yup, there's gold in that thar Web, and there's nothing to keep you from stepping forward to claim your share. Auctioning your own stuff online is a lot of fun and can be done from the privacy of your own home PC. It's not terribly difficult, and people of all ages (well, almost all ages) are doing it now. Why shouldn't you? So whether you're looking for a cool item or looking to make some cool cash, step on over to the person-to-person sites and see what all the buzz is about.

# Who's Hangin' Around These Auction Sites?

Generally, you'll find people like you and me who are just out for a treasure dig. Rather than travel about town looking for private sales or trudging off to the next collector's show, regular folks have embraced the convenience of looking through a worldwide selection of all kinds of stuff right from their own PCs. And it's the ability to open their own virtual shop that brings them running to these auction sites. Whether they have one item or a hundred, regular people are auctioning their stuff day in and day out. It's a hobby, it's a spare-time thing, and it's fun.

Of course, you'll also find actual shop owners at these auctions. The proprietors of Jack and Jane's Antiques and Oddities might find an expanded customer base when they start offering their items at the auctions. At one time, the Yellow Pages would get small businesses the customer exposure they desired. Today, it's online auctions that attract buyers. Again, since anyone can auction an item online, the overhead for small businesses is practically nil. Some business owners have even gone so far as to close their brick-and-mortar establishments (no more rent, thank you) and have gone exclusively to the online realm to provide their regular income. Why not? With millions of shoppers out there, it makes sense, right? (There are a few issues to consider, though, before you quit your day job. See Chapter 15 for more about that.)

You'll also find bigger businesses using the person-to-person venues. Yes, most often the big boys will sell directly to the merchant auctions and leave it at that. However, it's just as viable for them to tap the "informal" market at the person-to-person sites to scare up some more sales. Hey, good business is wherever you find it.

Expect, though, that most of your encounters at the person-to-person sites will be with private individuals. They've got some stuff to get rid of, or they're looking to buy your stuff. Most person-to-person sites have developed *communities* of regular users, and you'll typically find most people are friendly, courteous, and happy to strike a win-win deal with you.

## I Don't Want Any Trouble, OK?

Nobody wants trouble at these person-to-person sites, but trouble sometimes has a way of sneaking in. Whenever you open a free forum, you also leave the door open to undesirables who want to bend and break the rules. But the auction sites and the auction communities band together to give these no-goodniks the old heave-ho.

The big person-to-person sites have pretty rigorous registration requirements—you'll have to provide a reasonable amount of personal information that will prove you are who you say you are. That works for all registrants, so you can be sure you're dealing with others who are equally on the level. In addition, you'll find that the major sites offer verification methods and controlled ways for registered users to get in touch with one another—but only if usual e-mail communication seems to be failing. A good site will provide a feedback system—a way for buyers and sellers to rate one another based on how well they honor their deals and operate in an honest manner. Further, these sites will provide advice, including ways to contact other organizations that can help you, if you find you're suddenly stuck in a deal gone bad.

**GET A CLUE** Remember, these sites don't usually get involved in helping you sort out your troubles. You're still entering into the old *caveat emptor* arrangement: let the buyer beware.

**DID YOU KNOW?** Several sites offer free insurance (up to a value of $200 to $250) in case you get blatantly ripped off by a shady seller. That's a real bonus and shows that some sites realize how important it is to gain the trust of the using communities.

Don't be surprised if you find the users also getting in the act of policing their favorite auction site. At the good sites, where feedback can be posted, you'll find conscientious users posting the bad news about people who like to deal from the bottom of the deck. The long-time auction-goers have sniffed out most every scam and sham at the auctions and are quick to let others know when some creep is trying to pull a fast one.

**GET A CLUE** Be sure to read Chapter 14 for a complete run-down on the most common auction scams. You'll learn how to spot them and how to avoid them. It's required reading if you want to boost your confidence in the auction spaces.

**IN MY MIND** Please do not become intimidated by the notion that person-to-person auctions are a haven for criminals and rip-off artists. They're not. Just like any other venue, concrete or cyber, there will always be dishonest players. However, the sites that I'll soon show you report that bad deals account for less than 1 percent of their users' transactions. That's minuscule when compared to the thousands and thousands of deals that complete smoothly every day. In all the years I've dealt at online auctions, I've *never* been blindly ripped off. Take heart, be of good cheer, and forget what some of the highly publicized naysayers have been saying.

## Oh, The Places You'll See

The last time I counted, there were well over 200 person-to-person auction sites online. These range from the big players (which you'll soon learn about) to small store-fronts and individuals who are running their own little auctions online. Remember the phone auctions? Well, these private auctions are the same thing, only a Web page or e-mail address has been set up to handle the bidding. Regardless, there's quite a selection of person-to-person auctions out there, and you're free to surf to and through them. However, if you want to learn the game well and find more than enough to keep you busy, I recommend the sites I've reviewed for you in this chapter.

### eBay.com

The discussion of the person-to-person phenomenon should begin at the top, and that is a space occupied by the auction king of the 1990s, eBay. It started in a humble fashion under the name of AuctionWeb. The site's founder, Pierre Omidyar, created AuctionWeb in 1995, responding to a request from his then-girlfriend who wanted a place to buy and sell Pez dispensers (she was an

avid collector of the little candy containers). Pierre created AuctionWeb, and word spread across the Usenet that it was a place to buy and sell stuff while meeting fellow collectors in the process. It was a breakthrough idea and has since evolved into the multibillion-dollar online giant now known as eBay.

**DID YOU KNOW?** Pierre Omidyar has gone from Web master to rich man in only four short years. In August 1999, *Fortune* magazine recognized Omidyar as the fourth-richest man in America under 40 years of age. He is in the impressive company of Michael Dell of Dell Computers (No. 1), Jeff Bezos of Amazon.com (No. 2), Ted Waitt of Gateway Computers (No. 3), and David Filo of Yahoo! (No. 5).

**DID YOU KNOW?** eBay is a publicly offered stock and trades on the NASDAQ board under the symbol *EBAY*. It's been one of the fastest-growing online auction IPO stocks.

## Site Presentation

Well, eBay is synonymous with money, but how well has that money been put to use in developing an amazing Web site? Quite well, I'd say. To look at the site, you might not think it's one of the e-commerce big dogs. The site has a whimsical and cartoony look that inspires users to venture in and enjoy all there is to see and do (see Figure 7-1).

There are a lot of colors, a lot of features, and a lot of visitors. Notice the *Stats* information in Figure 7-1: over 2.5 million items up for bid, over 1,600 item categories, and over 1.5 billion page views (user visits) per month! This place is hoppin', no doubt about it, and it's easy to hop around in, too! You'll find links everywhere in this extensive site, lots of icons, text links, and more. Although it could easily become overwhelming in sheer scope and grandeur, the fun presentation helps users enjoy poking about to see what can be found.

eBay was my first online auction experience, and it's still where I spend most of my time online. It's not perfect, but it's an enjoyable place to be and some great people frequent the site.

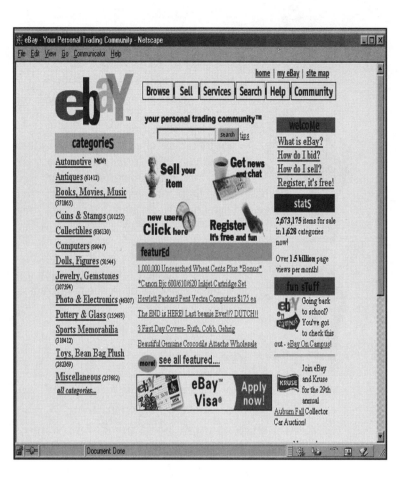

Figure 7-1

Stick around long enough and you'll be calling eBay your home away from home—in the privacy of your own home.

## Site Inventory

This is perhaps the simplest way to describe it: there's *tons* of stuff at eBay. It's what makes eBay the reigning king of online auction sites. Remember those stats I just gave you: more than 2.5 million items are up for bid on eBay at any given time. It's true, and it's all there. This is the place to get reunited with just about anything you're looking for. Thanks to eBay, I've completed collections that have been 20 years in the making and have started new collections with items I never thought I'd own (see Figure 7-2 for a perfect example).

Regardless of what you're looking for, start looking at eBay. I can search for *any* item and probably 80 percent of the time, I find it. If I don't find it right away, chances are it will show up eventually if I keep looking and keep the faith.

Figure 7-2

Incredible! If you're a kit collector, you'll know this rare, Canadian-only model is as hard to find as hen's teeth. I found it on eBay, though.

## Registration

Registration at eBay is a bit of an effort. Although the site is just a venue and disclaims any ownership or liability in deals between traders, it puts one through a couple of hoops and a good amount of legalese to get signed up. In the long run, this policy makes sense—it boosts the proportion of open and honest traders and reduces the proportion of snakes in the grass. You don't have to worry about it right away, though. Just as at other auction sites, looking is always free and requires no registration. But when the time comes to bid (and I'll practically guarantee you'll see something you want to bid on) or to sell some of your curiosities, then a-registr'ing you'll go. Settle into your chair. Here's how it's done.

First, access the eBay registration page by clicking on the *Register—It's free and fun* icon in the center of the home page (refer back to Figure 7-1). Right off the bat, eBay will want to know what country you're from (it's an international trading post). Choose your country and click on the *Begin the registration process now* button at the bottom of the screen.

Hey youngster! eBay is for traders 18 and older. If you're not as tall as the clown at the ride's entrance, you'll need to get Mom, Dad, or Uncle Mort to step in for you.

Why is it an age-controlled community? Well, did you hear about the teenaged kid who bid thousands of dollars on antique furniture? Well, he did, but had no intention of paying. Apparently, he thought it was just a game. And for him, it was: he wasn't of legal age and couldn't be forced to abide by the terms of registration. That's why eBay insists users be of legal age—if a serious problem ever arises, legal action can be taken by either party in the deal. Knowing the ramifications, most users are less likely to pull any nonsense or else they could wind up facing a judge.

From here, registration becomes a three-step process: 1) Complete and submit your initial registration form. 2) Receive your registration confirmation instructions. 3) Confirm your registration.

Step 1 is the usual fare: enter your name, street address, e-mail address, and phone number. After that, you'll find some optional demographic information you can fill in if you like (what's your annual income, how many people live in your house, what's the dog's name).

When you complete and submit this information, eBay will send an e-mail message to you (Step 2). This lets eBay verify your e-mail address *before* you have access to bid or sell at the site. In the e-mail message you receive, you'll get a super secret password that you can use to access the next part of the registration process (Step 3). Go back into the registration screen (or use the hyperlink provided in the e-mail message you'll receive) and complete your registration.

At this third step, you'll use the temporary password as a point of verification, then you'll choose a new password to use for all future bidding and selling. You'll also have the opportunity to choose a user ID (like a nickname or Usenet handle) to identify you rather than using your e-mail address. Then, you're asked to review eBay's User Agreement before you actually sign up. It's a lengthy document that you might like to print and take to the . . . uhh . . . you know . . . room down the hall. It's not riveting reading, but you should always understand what you're signing up for and agreeing to before you join any online auction site.

From start to finish, the whole registration process (excluding the policy review) takes about 15 to 30 minutes on average, a mere drop in the bucket compared to the number of hours you'll spend on eBay afterward.

**IN MY MIND**  OK. So I've been something of a wise guy through this extended registration process. Yes, it's a bit more time-consuming than what you saw at the merchant sites, but there really is a good reason. Remember, these sites allow registered users to *sell* items. The additional information and verification steps are to help ensure everyone who signs up is on the level. Notice that you haven't been required to provide your credit card information, which is a key method used by some merchant sites to look users up to be sure they're playing by the rules. Therefore, expect eBay to want to be more rigorous before they throw open the gates for you.

So, if you're feeling a bit overwhelmed by the whole process, just follow eBay's instructions exactly, and you'll make it through. I'll see you on the other side to show you the different types of auctions and items you can find.

## Auction Formats

eBay offers the two standard auction formats with which you're already quite familiar. However, here they are again:

- **Straight Auctions.** These are the regular ascending-price format. The minimum starting bid is established by the seller, the bidders come (hopefully) and begin bidding, and follow-on bids climb higher and higher using predetermined bid increments (at the person-to-person sites, the bid increments are usually set according to the current high bid, not from a table of $5 or $10 increments as you saw at some of the merchant sites).

- **Dutch Auctions.** Not the "true" Dutch auction, but the '90s online variant where winning bidders pay the lowest successful price achieved at the end of an auction for each of a number of identical items. Beware the Yankee auction mix-up here. Unlike the situation at merchant auction sites, Yankee rules *don't* apply, and it's a confused seller who tries to impose them.

- **Reserve Price Auctions.** This is the auction where the seller has established a lowest price at which the item will be sold, though probably not the minimum starting bid. This is also where that bomb went off within the eBay users' community after eBay stated it would levy a $1 fee for using the reserve price option. Other sites don't charge for this, and the community was none too pleased with eBay's audacious move. eBay quickly reconsidered and revised the charge.

## Site Navigation, Bidding, and Services

The real bonus of eBay is the variety of ways to navigate through it. However, to some folks, that's a bummer, too. If I tell you to click on such-and-such link to get somewhere, someone else will tell you there's a different way to get to the same place. Actually, at eBay there are often multiple paths to take to arrive at the same destination. Why? Well, if you've ever designed or supported a technical environment such as a Web page, it's important to offer users some navigational options. People want easy ways to get here and there depending upon their personal understandings and skill levels. So to keep the variable population happy, sites like eBay give short paths, long paths, and some in between. As you get more and more comfortable with the site, you may find you change the way you use it to best suit your needs.

That said, let me show you a couple of ways to get to all those goods and goodies I've been telling you about. eBay harbors an incredible inventory, so settle into your chair again and get ready to have your eyes widened. Here goes . . .

First, get familiar with the different categories of items. At eBay, there are over 1,600 different item categories (with 1,900 new ones on the way), and you can find out what those are by clicking on the *Categories* banner on the eBay home page (refer to Figure 7-1). Do that and you'll jump to the complete listing of high-level categories and subcategories—see them in Figure 7-3.

Wow! So where does a person start? Well, that's just the beginning. Each subcategory you see in Figure 7-3 includes an even deeper distillation of subcategories; for example: Books, Music, Movies > Movies > Videos, DVD, LaserDiscs. . . . Just keep drilling down until you find the title of something you want.

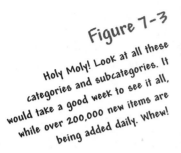

Figure 7-3

Holy Moly! Look at all these categories and subcategories. It would take a good week to see it all, while over 200,000 new items are being added daily. Whew!

**DID YOU KNOW?** The number in parentheses to the right of the category and subcategory titles tells you the number of active auctions under that heading. It's impressive—tens of thousands and sometimes hundreds of thousands of items are offered. Keep an eye on your clock: you'll be staying up way past your bedtime trying to look at them all.

**GET A CLUE** You'll also find a few highlighted items under a *Featured* banner (either at eBay's home page or within the listings of a specific category). Are they the ones eBay picked out as extra special? Nah. Sellers paid some extra money to get up-front advertising for their items, hoping you might see them and bid, bid, bid.

Certainly, in all those categories and subcategories, you'll find something that beckons you to look a little deeper. Click on any subcategory title and drill further in until you find a listing of item titles much like the ones you saw at the merchant sites. When you find that special item you think you'd like to bid on, click on its title and jump to its item details page (see Figure 7-4).

The item details pages you see at eBay provide plenty of information for you, including when the auction started, when it will end, who's selling the item,

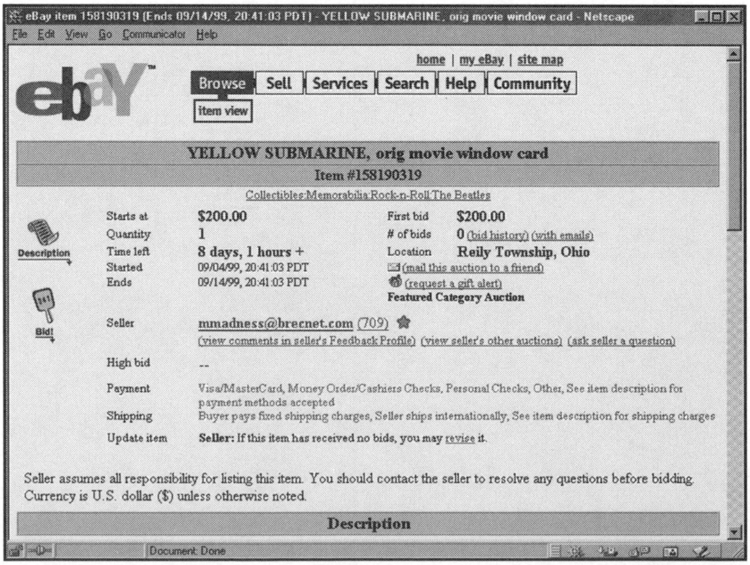

**Figure 7-4**

*This vintage Yellow Submarine movie poster would fill a hole in my collection quite nicely. A sea of holes . . .*

![eBay item details page screenshot showing YELLOW SUBMARINE, orig movie window card, Item #158190319. Collectibles:Memorabilia:Rock-n-Roll:The Beatles. Starts at $200.00, Quantity 1, Time left 8 days, 1 hours +, Started 09/04/99, 20:41:03 PDT, Ends 09/14/99, 20:41:03 PDT. First bid $200.00, # of bids 0, Location Reily Township, Ohio. Seller mmadness@brecnet.com (709). Featured Category Auction.]

who's the high bidder, and what's the current high bid value. Scroll down a bit and you'll see the item description (often including pictures) that the seller hopes will convince you to bid on the item. If you want to bid, click on the little bidder's paddle icon that you see in the left-hand margin of the item details page (refer to Figure 7-4).

Bidding at eBay is a two-step process: first, you enter the dollar amount you want to bid. Your bid has to beat the current high bid by at least the minimum bid increment, and it could be a maximum bid that you'd ever be willing to pay. Plug in that number where eBay prompts you to, and click on the *Review bid* button at the bottom of the screen. The second step—and the second screen—is where you'll enter your eBay user ID and your password. When you've done that and you want to place your bid, click on the *Place bid* button. eBay will zip off and tally your maximum bid amount against any other bidders who've been bidding (or against a seller's reserve price, or both) and will respond with a screen that tells you how you did. If you're lucky, eBay will show that you are now the high bidder. Congratulations!

eBay, just like other auction sites you've already seen, uses a standard proxy bidding system. The proxy system (affectionately known to some as the *eBay elf* ) will bid for you in minimum increments to preserve your high bidder status (provided you got there with your first bid) up to the point that your maximum is reached. After that, it's the outbid outskirts for you. More on that in a moment.

If the auction you're bidding in is a reserve price auction, you'll see that the reserve price is never truly revealed (unless the seller states what it is in the item's description). Bidders will bid on the item, being reminded that they're bidding in a reserve price auction. If their maximum bid meets or passes the established reserve price, the high bid on the item will immediately jump to the seller's reserve (regardless of what the stated minimum bid increment is). When that happens, a *Reserve met* note will appear next to the high bid value on the item details page. If a bidder's bid doesn't meet the reserve, the high bid of the item will increase only by the next minimum bid increment and a note saying *Reserve not yet met* will appear next to the high bid on the bidding page (that might have been what you saw when you placed your first bid).

OK. Now assume that some other bidder comes gunning for high bid status on an item you've tagged for your own. If you're outbid, eBay will send an e-mail message to tell you that you've been officially dethroned, and it's now up to you if you want to bid more to reclaim your prize-to-be. But some bidders will wait until the very final seconds of an auction to deliver what they hope will be a toppling bid, upsetting your claim to the item. It's known as *sniping,* and you'll rarely have any time to get another bid in: eBay won't even have time to send the e-mail message to you before the auction's all over. Y'see, eBay doesn't offer automatic auction extensions. When it's over, it's over. Though it sounds dastardly, sniping at eBay is one of the biggest thrills you'll ever experience—especially if you're the sniper. I'd love to tell you how it works, but then I'd have to kill you.

All right, all right, I'll tell you: briefly, to snipe an auction, you'll need two sessions (browser windows) open. One window will show the item details screen. You can click on the browser's *Refresh* button to redisplay the screen and see the auction clock tick down. In the second screen, you'll be at the same item details screen, but you'll move ahead to enter your bid information, waiting at the second screen where you'll click the *Place bid* button. Don't click on the button until the very last seconds of the auction. This takes skill, timing, and a healthy Internet connection. Some bidders place their final bid within the last few seconds of an auction—doing so prevents another bidder (especially one who's going to be outbid) from having time to place a higher bid. Sniping is a real blast, and it's practically an art form to those who have practiced it well.

**GET A CLUE** If you want even more step-by-step, nitty-gritty details on sniping at eBay, grab a copy of Prima's *Online Auctions at eBay*, written by yours truly. You'll find a chapter's worth of information on the methods and joys of sniping. I like sniping, and I think you will, too.

Now, if you're fuzzy on how eBay works, you'll be thrilled to find it offers an excellent amount of help, services, and other user-friendly goodies. First, notice the main navigation toolbar at the top of every eBay screen (refer to Figure 7-4, for example). It's a great way to get around the site. Each selection on that toolbar leads you to a submenu of choices (like the one in Figure 7-3). Of particular note for eBay newcomers is the *Help* toolbar: it will lead you to tutorials, FAQs, and a bunch more informational pages that help you get cozy with the eBay environment.

Just above the main navigation toolbar is the mini navigation toolbar, which includes *Home* (the eBay home page), *My eBay* (a personal page I'll describe soon), and *Site map*. It's the site map that you'll find particularly useful—it's loaded with links to just about everywhere in the site. In fact, there are so many navigational links at eBay that you should make a conscious effort to check them all out. You won't be disappointed.

## After the Auction Ends

So when all bids have been entered and any snipers have delivered their blows, hopefully you're still standing as high bidder. If so, eBay will notify both you and the seller that the auction is over and that you two should arrange the actual exchange. You'll be given each other's e-mail addresses, and you should start the dialog flowing to close the deal. This is the part where many folks get nervous—dealing with a complete stranger. However, just use a professional style when communicating, be prompt to respond, and get that deal done quickly.

Most sellers will specify the type of payment they're willing to accept: personal check, money order, cashier's check, credit card, and so on. That's usually stated in the item details page, and you should be sure to review the seller's terms (including postage costs—don't forget those) before you place a bid. If you don't like the terms, don't bid. When the auction ends and you're the winner, you pay for the item (buyer pays first) and the seller ships it to you. You'll be happy to know that 99.9 percent of all deals close without a hitch.

 **GET A CLUE** Since closing an auction at a person-to-person site can be somewhat intimidating, you'll be happy to know that the details of making end-of-auction contact and arranging for the exchange of goods are in Chapters 11 and 12. See Chapter 12 for a full explanation of paying for items and closing the deal. For the purposes of this chapter, I'll keep the discussion focused on the key functions and features of the sites.

## Selling at eBay

For a lot of folks, this is a bigger lure than all the neat items up for grabs. If you are searching for a sales opportunity, eBay is one of the best new bets. eBay boasts a registered user base of 5.6 million people. They've all come to eBay looking for treasure, and you might have just what they're looking for. The real plus about selling at eBay is that you'll be doing it in an auction environment where bidders become entranced by the auction and will often fight to the bitter end to emerge victorious. Sellers smell good profits in this venue.

If you have something you want to sell, click on the *Sell your item* link in the middle of the home page (refer to Figure 7-1); it guides you to a form where you enter the details of whatever it is you'd like to offer to the hungry bidding populace. The item listing form leads you through the simple process of getting your item up for all to see, and even allows you to plug in some dandy HTML (HyperText Markup Language) code to give your auction a truly eye-catching look.

It does cost to sell an item, of course. (That's how eBay's staying in the black, remember?) Listing your item can cost as little as 25 cents, or go on up past $100, depending on the number of extras you'd like to attach (such as bold titles, icons, featured status, and so on). When the auction ends, provided there's a winning bidder, eBay will charge the seller a *final value fee*—a commission—that is a percentage of the final price. Be sure you fully understand all fee policies before you list your item. To get the skinny on selling costs, click on *Help* from the main navigation toolbar, then *Seller's Guide,* then *Fees.*

And for sellers who are a bit unsure about the whole auctioning process or how to best close a deal with a winning bidder, eBay offers a generous helping of assistance that you'll find under the *Help* selection of the main navigation toolbar.

## Additional Site Features

So many features await you inside eBay that I can't possibly list them all here. However, here are some that I think will be of immediate use to you:

- **Search Tools.** eBay has plenty to offer in the area of search tools. On practically every eBay page, you'll find a search window located in the upper-right-hand area. If some item pops into your mind, pop its name or description in the search field—chances are you'll find something you're looking for much faster than scanning through the item categories. Also, use the *Search* selection from the main navigation toolbar at the top of every eBay page—that sends you to a special search page where you can search for items by description, seller ID, bidder ID, current price, and more. Get familiar with eBay's search tools, and you'll make the most of each visit.

- **SafeHarbor.** As eBay describes it, this is the site's "full service customer support and educational resource." To you, that means SafeHarbor is home port to many a wary (and weary) wannabe auction-goer who still isn't sure how safe online trading really is. Therefore, this umbrella of user services strives to make trading on eBay safer and less worrisome to bidders and sellers. This includes resources like eBay's highly touted Feedback Forum, buyer's insurance program, Legal Buddy (a program designed to keep bootleg booty away from befuddled bidders), online escrow (bringing in an intermediary to coordinate high-dollar exchanges), and more. You'll find a link to eBay's SafeHarbor services at the bottom of eBay's home page.

- **Feedback Forum.** This is one of the cornerstones of the SafeHarbor program. It's where eBay users flock to share the good news and bad news about one another. It's why you'll strive to do the best trading you can, working hard to earn a well-respected feedback profile. It's also where you can go to learn more about the other sellers and bidders you might rub elbows with. Whenever you see a user ID at the site, you'll see a number in parentheses alongside it. That number is the user's feedback profile rating. Click the number to read the comments other users have posted. This was eBay's first user-safety program, instituted only two months after the site went live. You can learn more about the Feedback Forum via the SafeHarbor link and from the site map as well.

- **My eBay.** It's not only *my* eBay, it can be yours, too. My eBay is a useful auction tracking page where you can monitor your bidding and selling, as well as the fees you owe the site. Though there are several other ways to find this sort of information on the site, My eBay is your command center to see just where you've been and where you're going. Most users consider this the best tool the site offers. Because of its popularity, My eBay has a link in the mini navigation toolbar you'll see at the top of every eBay page.

■ **News and Announcements.** Wanna keep abreast of the latest goings on at eBay? Want to know when the next scheduled maintenance period will be (when the site goes down for regular backups and checkups)? Want to hear what eBay's top dogs are saying about (or in response) to the latest goings on at the site, good or bad? Then you'll want to visit the News and Announcements boards. Access them via the site map. You'll be glad you did.

■ **Chat Rooms.** If you're looking for some auction yik-yak, look to the many different eBay chat rooms. Besides chats devoted to discussing eBay features and online trading in general, you'll also find many "category-specific" chat rooms where collectors and enthusiasts discuss the hobbies and passions near and dear to their hearts. Grab a virtual latte and join in.

 GET A CLUE  The features I've had room to mention are great, but there's much more to see. Make the effort to travel the site. Launch from the *Site map* or *Help* links to get to everything you wanted to know and more.

## AuctionGuy Rates This Site . . .

On the scale of 1 to 5, eBay gets a 5.

eBay earns exceptionally high marks because it dared to venture where no others had gone before. eBay blazed a trail of online auctioning that others would soon follow. Though many other auction sites have tried to unravel and upset eBay's leadership in the auction market, none has yet succeeded. In market branding, eBay was the first to plant the flag and is the site the most often comes to mind when people think online auctions.

eBay has worked hard over the years not only to present a great auction site but a great philosophy as well. eBay was first to proclaim that online traders are good and honest people, deserving a safe and cheery place to meet and exchange their goods. This core philosophy is what attracted so many folks early in eBay's short history and established the framework for what would be a community of users, strong in their passions as well as in their belief in fair and honest play. For me, this has been and continues to be the strongest draw to the site.

And eBay has a ton of stuff. As I briefly noted, eBay is the place that put me in touch with a lot of items I never dreamed I'd ever own, and I've made many new friends throughout the adventure. eBay's helped me learn more about the things I collect and the true market value of those things. As large as eBay is, both in number of goods and number of customers, I believe it serves as a useful barometer for properly valuing items. To collectors, that's a real plus.

But as big as eBay is, it's also suffering some growing pains. When Meg Whitman took the post of CEO at eBay (fresh from high-seated stints at Hasbro and Disney), eBay seemed to go corporate. The community immediately felt a change in style, and many have contested the direction in which site seems to be going. eBay's size was already an obstacle to users' getting helpful one-on-one attention from site administrators. With a new corporate feel, site administrators now seem to toe a line of canned statements and responses. If you're just at the site for the goods and don't have much interest in how it develops, you'll probably never notice. But ask any of the old-timers who've been using the site since day one, and they'll give you an earful.

As a long-time user of eBay (as both buyer and seller), I share the concern that others have expressed about the site. In the battle of Internet titans, eBay's moves often appear to be aimed more at winning a corporate war (mainly against Amazon.com) than caring for and feeding its own infantry (the users). The result is a customer service approach that doesn't leave the loyal customers feeling really satisfied. Though I've awarded five fistfuls to eBay at this time, I'll be keeping pulse on the site's potential drift away from its roots—the community.

However, I applaud the site for some great features, great online documentation, and obvious concerns over site security. Most important, I give a standing ovation to the user community I have come to know so well. They're a terrific group of 5.6 million folks, and you'll feel their warmth when you get involved in the action. This is a great site. Try it, and you'll see what I mean.

GET A CLUE
Though I've talked at length about eBay here, you might still feel a bit lost or uncertain about the site. That's OK because it's a big site, and conducting person-to-person exchanges involves a wide range of variations and nuances. It would take a whole volume devoted specifically to eBay to properly describe it all, so I'll direct you to Appendix A of this book for a terrific resource that gets into all the nitty-gritty details of this mammoth auction site. Take a look.

## Yahoo! Auctions

Now here's a site that seems to have the Midas touch (gold, not mufflers). Yahoo! is one of the premiere Internet portals and has been for a number of years. Presenting itself in an informal and engaging manner, Yahoo! has drawn in Net surfers from all walks of life. It has offered a wide variety of free services such as e-mail, messaging services (pager notifications), chat clubs, online maps, and much more. Why not auctions?

That's just what Yahoo! did—launch auctions. But Yahoo! did it with its own personal touch and flair. As with its other user services, Yahoo! made its auctions *free*. That is, anyone who wants to sell at Yahoo! Auctions can do so for free: no listing fees or final sales commissions.

Yahoo! gave its auction site terrific visibility, right near the top of its highly visited home page (**www.yahoo.com**). If you want to expand your use of Yahoo! services or have yet to travel there, make a stop at the auctions page.

DID YOU KNOW?
Yahoo! is a publicly offered stock and trades on the NASDAQ board under the symbol *YHOO*.

## Site Presentation

Whether or not you've been to Yahoo! before, I'm practically sure you'll like the site design. It's a lot of fun and easy to use. Amazingly, Yahoo! has learned to deliver a plethora of goodies and services without the clutter that would leave you feeling lost. No, Yahoo! delivers links in an easy-to-find and easy-to-use

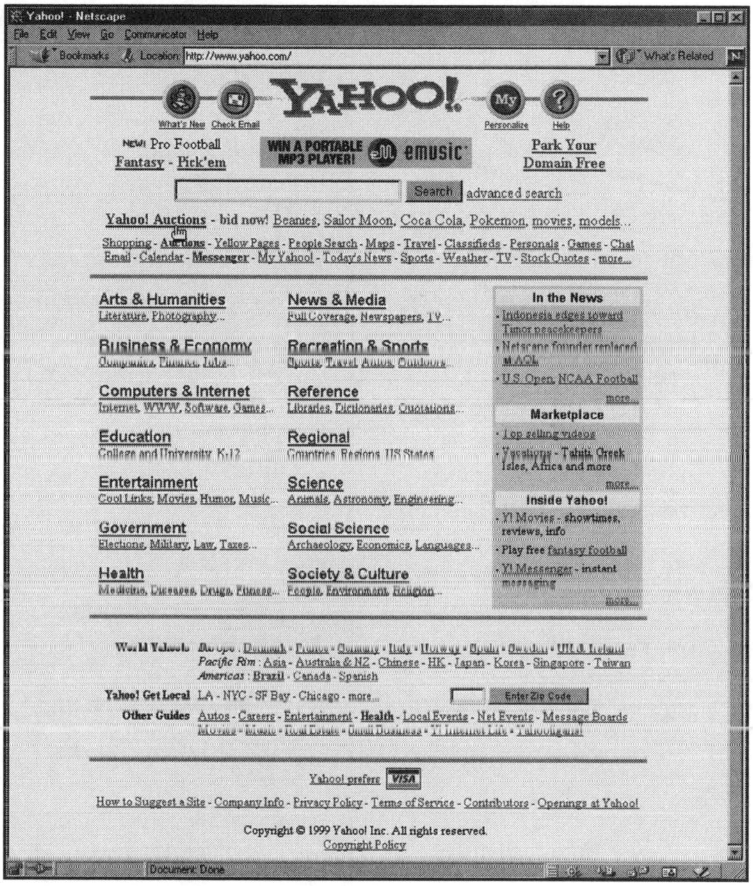

Figure 7-5

Stop off at www.yahoo.com to see one of the best Internet portal sites on the World Wide Web. Click on Yahoo! Auctions to get to the bidding and selling fun.

manner, with enough flash and personality that they'll draw you in to trying something you might otherwise skip over.

When you visit Yahoo! Auctions, you're greeted with a look and feel that mirrors the home page, with many easy-to-read links right at your fingertips (see Figure 7-6). Item categories are right in front of you in the main display area as opposed to being tucked away in some side column. In addition, you can quickly see the parenthetical statistics of just how many items are to be found within each major category.

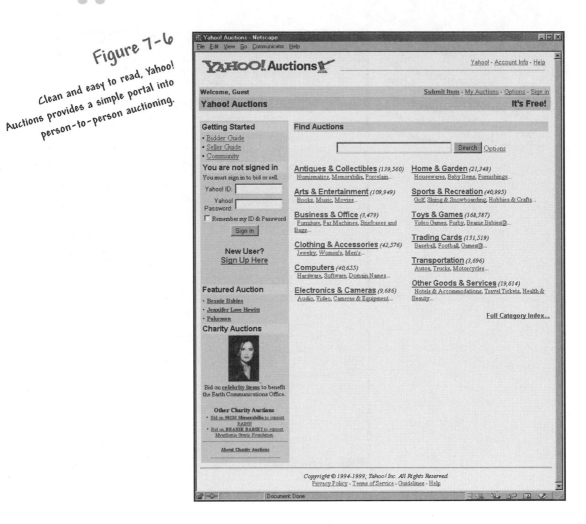

*Figure 7-6*

*Clean and easy to read, Yahoo! Auctions provides a simple portal into person-to-person auctioning.*

In the left column of the home page, you'll find informational links in the *Getting Started* column. You'll also find a quick *Sign in* field to let Yahoo! know who you are so the site can get your account dialed up and ready to use.

## Site Inventory

Well, it's no eBay, but Yahoo! does boast an impressive 500,000 items up for bid. A quick look at the category listings shows you that there's much to be seen on Yahoo's auction block. For you antique and collectibles shoppers, you'll find that's where Yahoo! seems to queue up most items. To the person-to-person auction-going crowd, Yahoo! is the second-best place online to find and sell stuff. Because of that community endorsement, chances are good that you'll find something you'll like.

Don't let the reduced number of category titles (when compared to eBay) discourage you. Yahoo's done a great job of distilling items into fewer logical buckets than eBay. For shoppers, that makes your search a bit easier when you decide to stroll the category aisles.

## Registration

The cool thing about registering for Yahoo! Auctions is that you might already *be* registered. If you use any Yahoo! services now, it's just a matter of signing in and jumping into the auctions. If you're new to Yahoo!, all you need is to register on the Yahoo! Auctions home page using the link *Sign Up Here* (refer to Figure 7-6).

When you register at Yahoo!, you'll be able to use all the Yahoo! free services, many of which work in conjunction with the auction site (I'll review a few of those in the "Features" section a bit later). To register, just choose a clever Yahoo! ID, a password, and a current e-mail address. Then supply the usual personal information (name, address, and so on), and click on *Submit this form* at the bottom.

WARNING! I sense there are duplicates among us! You might need to take a few tries at creating a usable Yahoo! ID. The ID you want could already be taken. Be creative and keep trying.

If you plan to sell at Yahoo!, you'll need to provide credit card information as a method of properly identifying yourself. By this time, that's not anything new. Also, some bidders might be required to have credit card information on file: an option to sellers is to require that all bidders with low feedback ratings have credit card information on file at Yahoo! in order to place valid bids. It's one of the ways Yahoo! keeps the auction environment safe for all users. Yahoo! never divulges the information to anyone, though.

IN MY MIND

You might think it somewhat prejudicial for sellers to require users with low feedback to register their credit card before being able to bid. Actually, it's a clever remedy to a problem that has arisen in the online auction circles: some bad users could get booted out of an auction site for misbehavior, only to traipse over to another auction site and start up the same nonsense there. Yahoo! makes the *Minimum Bidder Rating* method available to sellers only if they choose to use it. However, it does protect sellers from having to work with creeps who were previously run out of another auction town. That's not to say Sleazy Sam won't show up at Yahoo! (or any other auction) and be able to ruffle some feathers, but he has had to provide a bit more information that could filter him out if credit fraud is his favorite poison pastime.

If you're new to Yahoo! Auctions (but not a creep), just be patient with the process. It could come back to serve you if and when you decide to begin selling.

## Auction Formats

- **Straight Auctions.** The usual ascending price auctions you'll come to know and love.

- **Reserve Price Auctions.** The lowest-selling-price auctions you'll either love or hate.

- **Buy Price Auctions.** A new auction variant at Yahoo! In some auctions, sellers will start up a regular straight auction, but will also post an immediate "buy price." With this, any bidder could decide to forego the usual tit-for-tat bidding and pay the seller's stated buy price right away, thus ending the auction with one fell swoop. Of course, the auction is still open for regular ascending price bidding and could still end successfully even if the buy price is never met. It's a neat variation, I think.

## Site Navigation, Bidding, and Services

All you need to do is take a look at the Yahoo! Auctions home page (refer to Figure 7-6), and you'll see how clearly the site is laid out. Just click on a category or subcategory and start your eyes working. You can click on the pictures you see or click on various item titles to jump into the item details. The Yahoo! item details pages are much less cluttered than those at eBay (see Figure 7-7).

Figure 7-7

The absence of visual treats on this page might make it look a bit bland at first glance, but it's extremely easy to read and use.

Figure 7-7

The absence of visual treats on this page might make it look a bit bland at first glance, but it's extremely easy to read and use.

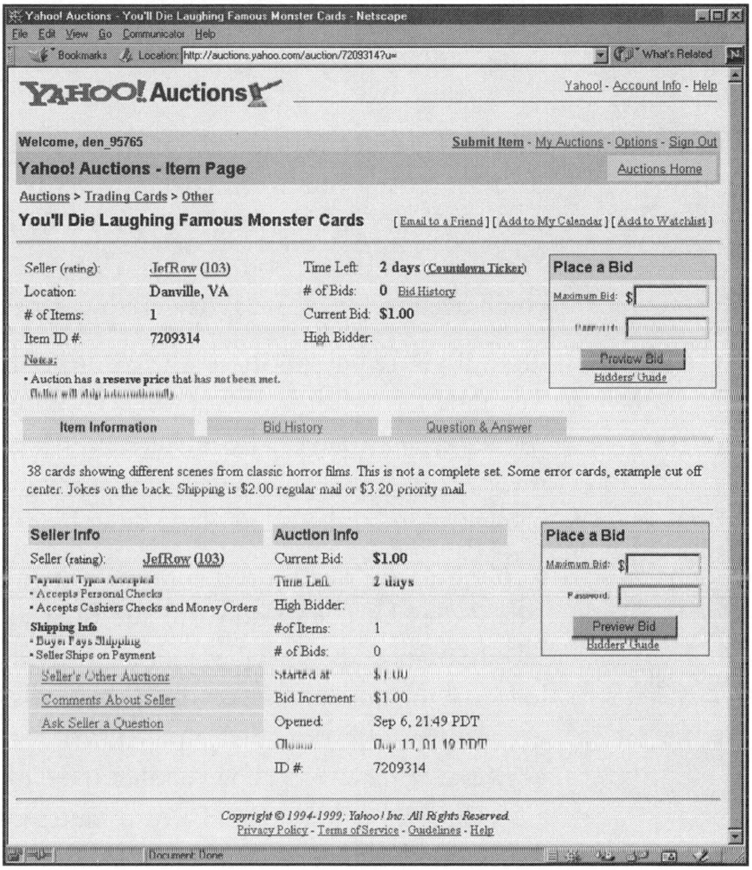

All the information you need is right in front of you when you view a Yahoo! Auction item details page. In the upper area, you'll learn about the item and its seller as well as what the current high bid is and time remaining in the auction. In the lower portion of the page, you'll find the seller's terms and conditions of the auction. The bidding area is just to the right. To stake your claim just enter your maximum bid amount (Yahoo! also has a proxy bidding system) and your Yahoo! password.

GET
A
CLUE
If you haven't yet signed in on Yahoo! to let the site know who you are, the bid-ding area will be replaced with a sign-in area. So get signed in and get bidding!

Enter your bid and your password, then click on the *Preview Bid* button. In the next screen, you have a chance to verify your bid amount and, if all looks well, click on *Place this bid*. The proxy system goes to work (in case there were other bidders before you), and you'll find out if you're the high bidder or if you'll need to bid again. Proxy bidding works just like it does at eBay.

Now, if you're outbid, that's where other Yahoo! services come into play. The free Yahoo! Messenger service will send immediate alerts to your downloaded Messenger software (it's free at Yahoo!). It can send e-mail alerts, or it can send messages to your alpha-numeric pager if you prefer. If you've been outbid, get back into the game and let those other bidders know you mean business.

At Yahoo!, the auction can end one of two ways. It can have a "hard close" where the clock ticks down to the final moment and the auction ends as scheduled, regardless of who's bidding (that's how eBay works and where snipers love to hang out). A note on the item details page will read "Auction does not get automatically extended" in the *Notes* section if the seller chose this option. However, Yahoo! also allows a seller to enable automatic auction extensions, extending the auction's end five minutes every time someone places a bid within the final five minutes of the auction. Those auctions can go on and on, and sellers love it when that happens. Unlike at eBay, you can't count on sniping a Yahoo! auction. A lot of Yahoo! auctions use the automatic bid extension process.

## After the Auction Ends

So when the auction finally comes to a close, whether by snipe or bidder endurance, it's time to settle up. Yahoo! Auctions, like eBay, doesn't get in the middle of the deal. The seller and high bidder are notified via e-mail, and it's up to them to work out the exchange. At practically all person-to-person auctions sites, that's the modus operandi. You needn't worry about deals with strangers. It happens thousands of times each day, and if it were truly a bad

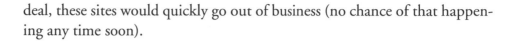

deal, these sites would quickly go out of business (no chance of that happening any time soon).

## Selling at Yahoo! Auctions

Yahoo! has certainly embraced the seller. There are so many features, options, and choices that it makes the site a definite draw to those who are looking for a good place to unload some stuff.

First, adding items is quite simple through the Yahoo! Auction's *Submit Item* link found at the top of every Yahoo! Auctions page. If you haven't done so already, you'll be asked to provide your credit card number before you can proceed. Once that's done, it's off to the listing page.

 **WARNING!** Disable defensive circuits! Registering at Yahoo! is free; the credit card information is just a security step to protect the community from ne'er-do-wells. Credit card information will be immediately verified against the personal information you've already entered. If you're on the up and up, you have nothing to worry about and your credit card won't be charged for anything during this step.

Just enter your item title, description (no HTML here, though), your sales and shipping terms, and your price and auction duration desires. After that, it's off to the preferences, where you can specify a *Minimum Bidder Rating, Auto Extension, Early Close* (allowing you to close the auction early if you choose), *Reserve Price,* and *Buy Price.* Two more interesting options are the *Closing Time* specifications, where you decide which hour of the day you'd like to see your auction end, and the *Auto Resubmit,* where you specify how many times you'd like to have this auction automatically resubmitted in case your item doesn't sell.

Yahoo! also provides a great photo upload feature to help you easily insert images in your auction listing. Yahoo! allows you up to three images direct from your PC to Yahoo!'s servers for your special auction. What could be simpler?

Remember that selling is fee-free at Yahoo! Auctions. In addition to all the other bonus preferences, it's a great environment for folks who want to take up the gavel and offer their goodies to the Yahoo! bidders.

## Additional Site Features

- **Auction Alerts.** These allow you to receive automatic notification whenever a new auction shows up that might be of interest to you. Just tell the auction alert messenger what keywords you're looking for, and it will do the sleuthing while you do something else. Access auction alerts from the *Options* link at the top right-hand corner of the Yahoo! auction pages.

- **My Auctions.** This is where you'll go to see what you've been up to lately. It shows you open auctions you're tracking, those in which you're actively bidding, those in which you're selling, and a history of closed auctions in which you were the winner. It's a great repository that helps you keep track of where you've been and where you're going, auctionwise.

- **Watchlist.** The watchlist is a feature you invoke at an auction's item details page. If there's an auction that interests you (whether you've bid yet or not), add it to your watchlist. You'll be able to track when bids are made and when the seller makes any changes.

- **Customize Winning E-Mails.** Here's a real time-saver. When the auction ends, both seller and high bidder receive "end of auction" e-mail messages. However, at Yahoo! Auctions, sellers can customize those messages to also include friendly greetings, payment instructions, or whatever. That way, when the high bidder receives the end-of-auction message, the seller's terms are right there as well.

- **Bidder Blacklist.** Here's one for potential controversy. If you've been shammed or shafted by some nasty bidder, you can automatically *blacklist* that bidder from participating in any of your future auctions. Talk about control! To access the blacklist function, click on the *Options* link at the upper right-hand corner of the Yahoo! Auctions screen, then follow on to the link labeled *Blacklist.* Just enter the user ID of the bad bidder you want to keep out of your auction backyard.

There are actually so many more features that you really need to take the time to review them from within Yahoo! Auctions *Auctions Help* pages. You'll be glad you did.

## AuctionGuy Rates This Site . . .

On the scale of 1 to 5, Yahoo! Auctions gets a 4.

Yahoo! Auctions gets high praise for the number of features and added extras to the site. Yahoo! practically invented online gadgets and hasn't skimped much in its auction realm.

The site is well-presented and easy to use. That's a real bonus to newcomers. The inventory is nicely categorized and is not so fragmented that it would ever be difficult to zoom in on an item.

Inventory is another of Yahoo's perks. There's over 500,000 items to wade through, and you're pretty certain to find something you like. Much of the stuff is somewhat common, though. You'll find some rare treasures, but the real "hen's teeth" usually gravitate to eBay, not Yahoo!

Lots of seller bennies here, the biggest being the free listings. I especially admire the Blacklist feature. Other sites might find that too controversial to implement, but Yahoo! has stepped forward to call it like it sees it. Hats off for that bold move and raspberries to the nay-sayers.

The area where Yahoo! Auctions falls short, though, is in the area of community and user loyalty. Though it has a feedback rating system and some message boards, you'll find usage of these features is limited. That signifies a certain amount of apathy or even mistrust among the users. This situation certainly isn't helped by unresponsive customer support. Yahoo! Auctions needs to focus on these important areas if it truly wants to take a bite out of eBay's apple.

In addition, the help function could use some reorganizing. True, there's quite a bit of online instruction, but it's not always clear how to get to the information you seek. Many useful help links are hidden within other help links. A site map approach to its help features would be a definite improvement.

However, it's a good site and one you should bookmark. I have faith that Yahoo! will address the areas of concern, and I believe it will be the likeliest site to give eBay a run for its money.

## Amazon.com Auctions

Well, from one battle camp to the other, this is currently eBay's biggest contender for the person-to-person auction reign. Amazon.com is one the most recognized names in online retailing among U.S. adults. It has found incredible success in online bookselling, quickly branching into music, movies, gifts, and drugs (the legal ones). Amazon strives to be online shoppers' single port of call for anything they might need or want, so it was inevitable that Amazon would venture into the online auction realm.

Amazon.com Auctions launched on March 20, 1999, starting with a group of core "charter merchants" who were on hand to make the initial auction offerings. It's a person-to-person experience, though the startup was more like *small business*-to-person. Amazon decided to attract the charter merchant involvement so it could go live with a backlog of auctionable items already on hand. Soon after, Amazon.com Auctions quickly attracted private individuals who wanted to explore other auction venues besides eBay. Today, Amazon.com features more than 100,000 daily auctions—nowhere near eBay's 2.5 million, but still plenty to look at.

## Site Presentation

Amazon is known for its clean site presentation. It has developed a consistent look throughout its different product "departments" and has extended that design into its auction arm.

When you visit **www.amazon.com**, you'll find a simple-to-use tab strip across the top of the page (you're probably quite used to those by now). Near the right end of the tab strip is a selection named *Auctions;* click on it, and you'll land at the Amazon.com Auctions home page (see Figure 7-8).

At first glance, the Amazon auctions might seem a bit lackluster and unattended. Not so. There's a lot of activity going on at this site, but you're not overwhelmed by it the moment you arrive at the doorstep. You can see the different item categories in the site—they're listed in the left-hand column of the home page. And using the familiar tabs, you can easily jump from

Figure 7-8

Amazon.com Auctions gives you a clear and intuitive route into person-to-person auctioning.

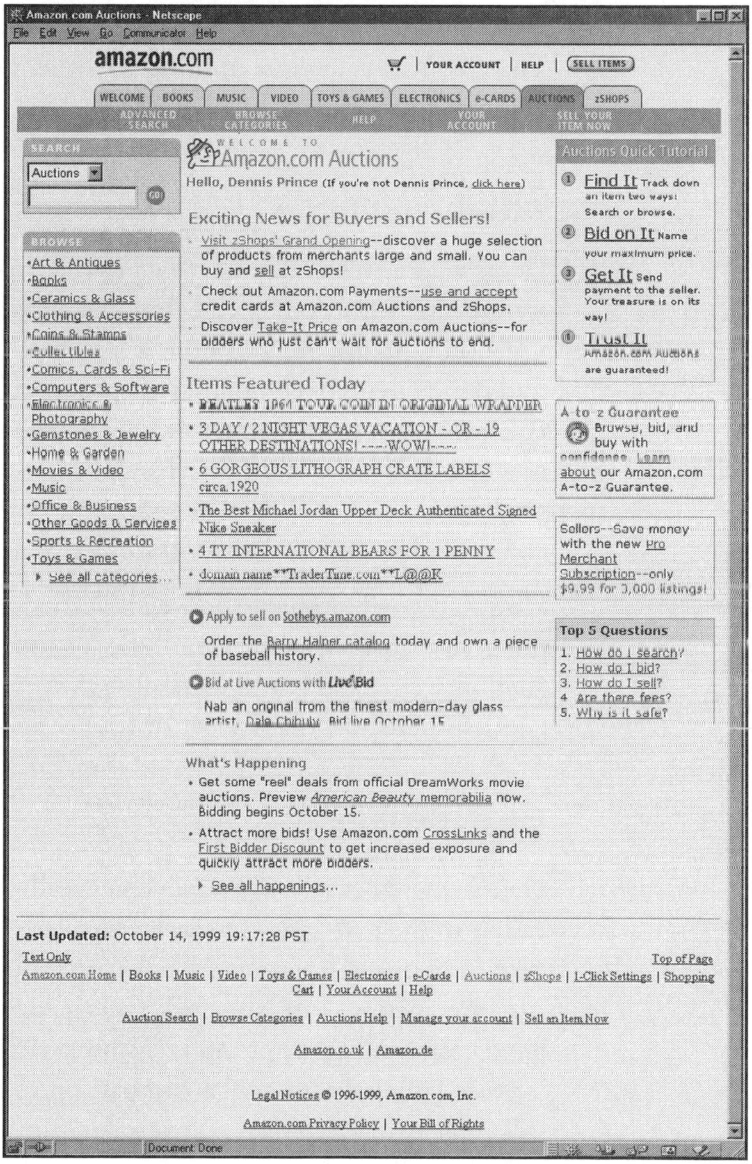

bidding to selling to retail buying and back with a simple click of the mouse. That reduces your time hunting for other areas of the site you mih›Ù suddenly want to visit.

## Site Inventory

Here's where even Amazon's huge presence in e-tailing can't make up for a paltry showing when compared to top-dog eBay. Amazon auctions do offer a large selection of items, but you won't see a lot of wild variety at this site. Mostly, I find trendy items or common types of collectibles and antiques (baseball cards, Pokémon, diecast cars, and so on). The real rarities are rare at Amazon. But, much as with some of the merchant auctions I introduced to you, navigating a smaller site might be an easier task for those who aren't looking for hen's teeth and don't have time to look under every stone in the riverbed.

However, you'll probably do well if you're looking for books, software, computer accessories, electronics, music, or movies. Amazon's still young in the auction scene, and it will certainly grow its inventory over time, but there's enough there now that it's worth your time to visit.

## Registration

Here's where Amazon auctions scores really big. Its registration is one of the easiest in the person-to-person marketplace. In fact, if you've ever bought an item from one of Amazon's retail departments, you're already registered! When Amazon auctions first launched, it bragged about having over 8 million registered users—all of the previous customers in Amazon's vast database. Though it wasn't an apples-to-apples comparison to eBay's then 2.6 million users, it still rang true that every previous Amazon customer was also considered a bidder or seller in good standing.

GET A CLUE   Hey, Amazonians: even though you've shopped the site before, you'll still want to establish an auction nickname (alias) for yourself. That way, you can be identified in the auctionplace without freely divulging your e-mail address. Read on, and you'll see how to grab your own handle.

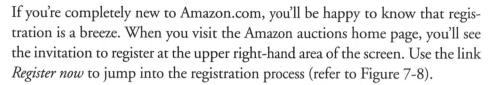

If you're completely new to Amazon.com, you'll be happy to know that registration is a breeze. When you visit the Amazon auctions home page, you'll see the invitation to register at the upper right-hand area of the screen. Use the link *Register now* to jump into the registration process (refer to Figure 7-8).

To begin, provide your name, e-mail address, and a password of your choice. Click on the *Sign in using our secure server* button for a secure entry into the next page of registration. On the second page, you'll need to enter your credit card information and billing address. What!? Does it cost to register at Amazon auctions? No, but Amazon uses your credit card and billing information to verify you're you. It's the site's answer to keeping the auction streets free of ill-intentioned interlopers.

DID YOU KNOW? Amazon contends that none of its now 10 million registered users have ever been defrauded by having their credit card information permanently on file. I'll admit, the worst that's ever happened to me is that *I've* made unauthorized purchases at the site, evident when the bill arrived.

So if you're still with me, get that credit card information entered and click on the *Submit* button. Amazon's little cyber-elves contact your card issuer to verify that everything's A-OK. The final screen you'll see is where you're asked to enter an auction nickname for yourself. Keep it simple and something you wouldn't be embarrassed to have your mother see. Then, read the Amazon auctions *Participation Agreement* (it's a doozy) and click on the *I Accept* button.

Welcome. What would you like to bid on first?

GET A CLUE By the way, upon completing your registration, Amazon will call you by name. (see the "Hello Dennis..." line in Figure 7-8?) How'd it do that? Simple—it gave me a cookie and will give you one too, if you accept it. Having been a long-time Amazon customer, I accepted their cookie long ago and find it has helped my speed up my shopping excursions at the site.

## Auction Formats

At Amazon.com Auctions, you'll find the usual formats available, but you'll also find a new twist that combines the styles of the auction with those of the early-bird sale. Added to that, another auction feature includes *live* auctions that you can watch and join in right on your PC's monitor. Read on.

- **Straight Auctions.** Nothing really new here, except the name. Amazon calls these "standard auctions." These are the familiar ascending price auctions. Bid high and bid often.

- **Dutch Auctions.** Again, the usual online auction flavor of Dutch auctioning where the winning bidders pay only the lowest successful price.

- **Reserve Price Auctions.** Same here, as well. The reserve price in an Amazon auction can be set by sellers who want to recoup their investment but don't want to scare off potential bidders with a high minimum starting bid.

- **First Bidder Discount Auctions.** And here's the twist: have you ever seen an auction that rewards the first bidder simply for being first? Nope, me neither, but at Amazon auctions, sellers can indicate whether their auctions will provide a 10 percent discount to the first bidder to place a successful bid. That means if the first bidder stays in the running and eventually wins, the seller has agreed that the first bidder will receive an automatic 10 percent deduction on the final high bid price. This is a great draw to encourage bidding, and it allows the first bidders to potentially bid 10 percent more than they normally would, anticipating the discount to come.

- **LiveBid.** If it's the "real" auction experience you're looking for, then this recent acquisition of Amazon's might fit the bill. Amazon bought up LiveBid.com in 1999 and features a link to the LiveBid site right from the Amazon.com Auctions home page. LiveBid is a Seattle-based auction firm that patented an Internet broadcast program allowing bidders to step into the bidding parlor from their PCs. Using RealPlayer streaming video and audio software, bidders can listen, view, and bid in real-time auctions. The auctions are hosted by a variety of qualified auction houses, and a LiveBid administrator is on hand to broadcast and monitor the online bidders' activities. Click on the LiveBid link to learn more. Note that your

Amazon.com registration won't carry over. All bidders must register to use LiveBid and must also be approved by the auction house conducting a particular auction.

## Site Navigation, Bidding, and Services

Site navigation is a snap, since Amazon presents all of its Web pages in a clean and easy-to-follow format. Click on a category that interests you and drill into the listings. You'll find a variety of images for featured auctions, or you can peruse the listing titles as you like. There's also a search window you can use to enter specific keywords to help you find that special something.

**GET A CLUE** Don't be surprised if your key word search turns up a bunch of items that don't seem to fit the bill. Amazon's simple search engine searches item titles *and* item descriptions for the words you entered. Use the *Advanced Search* (you'll find the link in the tab strip at the top of the page) and you can limit your searches to title only, and specify other criteria such as category, auction status, item location, and end date.

However you do it, find an item you like (I imagine you're getting quite good at this by now), and click on it to see the item details screen (see Figure 7-9).

The item details screen immediately shows who's selling the item, who's high bidder, when the auction closes, and the current high bid price. Amazon's item screen has the bidding window conveniently located just to the right of the item information. Enter your high bid amount for this item and click on the *Bid Now!* button. After that, you'll jump to another simple screen that displays your user ID, your current bid amount, and your maximum bid amount (in case you're bidding higher than the minimum and invoking Amazon's proxy bidding system, called *Bid-Click*). All that's left to do is click on the *Confirm Your Bid!* button and you're done.

If you're outbid at Amazon, the site will jump to your rescue with the standard outbid notification sent to you via e-mail. Amazon, like Yahoo!, uses automatic auction extensions—a bid within the last ten minutes of the auction will extend the auction for another ten-minute period. That gives the outbid bidder a chance to bid more and gives the seller something to grin about.

P A R T

Figure 7-9

Amazon gives you all the pertinent details of an auction in progress in a cleanly presented item details screen. Plus, this Martian Spy Girl's just the kind of woman to take home for Mom to meet.

## After the Auction Ends

When the bidding's over and the dust has settled, perhaps you'll emerge victorious. If so, good for you. The site now takes the familiar person-to-person route of delivering e-mail notification to both seller and high bidder. From there, the seller contacts the high bidder to arrange payment and shipment of the item. Remember, Amazon started with a group of 100 "charter merchants;" you'll still find many merchants conducting auctions at Amazon, and the person you deal with might be a representative of a small business or even a large business. Regardless, the seller will let you know the method of payment, so get out your money and get ready to bring home your new prize.

**GET A CLUE**   Remember, when dealing with private individuals, you might not have as many payment options available to use. If you're not able to use a credit card to make the purchase, you should be able to opt for money orders or cashier's checks with no problem. See Chapter 12 for more detail of the ways to pay.

## Selling at Amazon.com Auctions

Just as at the other person-to-person sites I've already shown you, selling at Amazon.com Auctions is simple. Just click on the *Sell Your Item Now* selection from the tab strip on any Amazon auctions page, and you're off to carve your piece of the market. You'll enter the usual information that describes your item and your terms during the auction. The description is open for you to enter HTML code that will jazz up the look of your auction. Follow the simple on-screen instructions, and you'll soon have your item in front of Amazon's 12 million potential bidders. Amazon does charge selling fees. Visit the *Are there fees?* link from within the Auction Help pages for the full scoop.

GET A CLUE

Psst. Looking for more ways to sell at Amazon.com? Take a look into Amazon's *zShops.* If ever you wanted to open your own online store with virtually no over-head or headaches, zShops are a venue where you can sell items at a fixed price. You list it, someone buys it, you collect your money, ship the item, and you're done. It's still person-to-person trading, but without the duration of an auction. zShops are new and need some time to catch on, but they're definitely worth watching and even testing with the things you're ready to sell now. If you're interested and want to learn more about selling at Amazon's zShops, click on the *zShop* tab on the Amazon.com tab strip.

## Additional Site Features

- **Auctions Guarantee.** Amazon was the first to implement auction insur-ance, providing up to $250 reimbursement to sellers who never received items they paid for or if the item that showed up was significantly different from what was advertised. At Amazon, the site managers implemented a "few questions asked" policy, striving to make an unfortunate auction out-come less sticky for the buyer. There is no deductible to pay, either.

- **Bulk Loader.** Gonna list items till the cows come home? Amazon's Bulk Loader will give you a hand. If you're deft with spreadsheet programs (such as Microsoft's Excel), you can enter all of your item details in a spreadsheet and then ship it off to Amazon for bulk loading. Rather than spending the time to list potentially hundreds of items one at a time, you can let the Bulk Loader do the work for you, leaving you more time to count your money. For full details, visit Amazon's *Seller's Guide* within the *Auction Help* pages.

- **Auction Advertisements.** This is a nice little freebie. Whenever customers search Amazon's retail pages for items, any auctions that match the search criterion will also show up. Who knows, someone searching for recent pa-perbacks of Edgar Allen Poe's works might jump at the chance to nab the original editions you have up for auction. Cool.

- **Feedback.** Amazon lets you reward others with good referrals, and they can reward you. Just as at other sites, feedback earns points for your feed-back rating and lets the rest of the community know who's who.

- **My Auctions.** Amazon also provides a personalized auction page where you can round up the details of what you're bidding on, what you've won, what you're selling, and what others are saying about you in your feedback profile.

- **Customer Support.** At Amazon, customer service *is* a feature, largely because it's handled so expertly. Amazon has always gained high marks for customer service in retail ventures, and the auctions are no exception. Amazon offers a toll-free customer support number to help with your auction-specific questions. If e-mail's your thing, you'll be pleased to know that all e-mail queries are answered personally by Amazon's support staff. Yes, Amazon shows that *support can be beautiful.*

 ## AuctionGuy Rates This Site . . .

On the scale of 1 to 5, Amazon.com Auctions gets a 3.

Hey, AuctionGuy, that's a little harsh, isn't it? After all, you were singing so many praises about the site and its fun features. Why not a higher praise?

Amazon.com is a fine auction site, and it's worth visiting on a regular basis. The safety and support can be felt immediately upon entering the pages, and that's a real plus for new players. However, Amazon still has an uphill road to climb when it comes to inventory. There's a lot to see, but it just doesn't compare to what you'll find at eBay or even Yahoo! This can largely be attributed to overcatering to buyers and undercatering to sellers. Amazon needs to spend some time providing more useful services to sellers—after all, without them, there are no auctions.

Amazon does get high marks for the simple site design. It's easy to navigate, and it's quite reliable. Site security is truly well done, and I've never had any qualms over dealing at Amazon's sites (retail or auction). Customer service, as I mentioned before, is premiere.

The final observation on Amazon is that it is clearly bent on upsetting eBay. In the quest for eBay's crown, Amazon gives you the feeling that all the moves and acquisitions are directed *at eBay* rather than executed *for the customers.* And, by that philosophy, you'll find Amazon.com Auctions is weak when it comes to a sense of community. All in all, though, it's still a good site and a place where you'll find some interesting items in a safe bidding and selling environment.

## Hey! Is That All?

Obviously, there are a great many more person-to-person sites out there, but I promised I'd boil down the sites to give you the best places to start out with or settle down at. With these three sites—eBay, Yahoo! Auctions and Amazon.com Auctions—I've shown you where you can find literally millions of items up for auction and where you'll find as many, or more, bidders anxious to see what you might have to sell. With that, I expect you'll have your hands full for a while.

There are other good person-to-person sites out there, and I invite you to inspect the runners-up in Chapter 19. What you've seen here, though, are the sites that best embody the spirit of person-to-person trading online. Obviously, I've only scratched the surface of what these sites have to offer, but you now have a springboard to these sites and can get moving all the quicker. Explore these sites: that's the fun of person-to-person auctioning. Around every link there's something new popping up. More important, the more you wander about these auctions—not just in bidding or selling—the more you'll get a feel for the sites' community values. Just as you might shop for a neighborhood when you shop for a home, so you should also shop for a community when you shop for auction sites. eBay is still has the best community, but it's also been around the longest. The other sites I mention in this chapter (and Chapter 19) have the same potential. But that's for you to judge.

## Voices and Choices

Before wrapping up this tour of the person-to-person sites, I want to leave you with one additional morsel: your voice can be heard online. Not to say someone's necessarily going to hear you speak out of turn, but the person-to-person sites are particularly attuned to what their communities think about online auctioning.

If ever you've been frustrated at an establishment and have complained about service or store policies only to be handed some meaningless *Customer Response Card* that the store manager will throw away once the suggestion box fills up, then you'll be glad to find something different at the person-to-person auction sites.

In my opinion, these sites *really need* your involvement and approval. Though the sites get really big and preoccupied with promoting themselves, I maintain that it all comes back to the users. Without active users, the sites will become ghost towns that look great but stand empty most of the time. Recall the reserve auction policy that eBay attempted to implement. It didn't go off anywhere close to what was planned because the using community virtually exploded in protest and outrage. eBay's message boards filled up, alternate auction forums were all a-buzz, and even many of the online news sites were covering the incredible mobilization of an auction community that cried "Foul!"

Though these sites are large and you might think one user is just a drop in the bucket, it's a comfort to know that there are others who share the same joys, disappointments, or questions as you do when your favorite person-to-person site seems to be drifting out of touch with its foundation of users. I believe these sites have nearly perfected the mechanics of online auctioning. Now the true winners will be those who recognize how their bread is buttered and will reach out to the buyers, sellers, and lookers to truly meet their needs.

CHAPTER 8

# The Elite Few

So far, you've seen some pretty innovative stuff at these online auction sites. Surely with all the online bidding and selling going on at auction sites and online retail sites it could appears that many of the world's physical establishments are on the verge of extinction. And what does this obvious endorsement of online auctions mean to those real-world auction mainstays like Sotheby's, Christie's, and the other high-end houses that laid the foundations for auctioning and built on it for hundreds of years? Are these auction icons about to kiss the wrecking ball? Hardly.

As the adage goes, *"Old age and treachery will win over youth and agility every time."* Well, the auction elders are not exactly treacherous, but they do possess several lifetimes' worth of experience. Auctioneering has been a respected profession for hundreds of years. Auctioneers, auction houses, and certified appraisers have seen it all, and then some. It's not plausible to think their services would simply become obsolete at the appearance of a new technological flavor of their lifetime profession.

But does this mean the traditional auction houses are going to remain in the physical world, no more than mildly curious about these online auction thingamajigs? Don't bet on it. Traditional auctioneers are quite in tune with technological advances—doing so keeps them sharp and broadens their ability to draw interest and bolster a bottom-line profit.

But can you teach an old dog a new trick? If keeping an industry healthy and strong in earnings is involved, you'll quickly find that this dog can learn. Traditional auction houses have seen the online auction opportunity and have embraced and harnessed it themselves. But see for yourself.

It's time to fluff up your ascot and straighten your cummerbund. You're now venturing into the land where the millions you'll encounter refer to bidding dollars as opposed to numbers of items for sale. This is the big time.

## Traditional Sights

Internet or not, the traditional auction houses have done well and will continue to do so with their long-held adherence to high-end artwork, antiques, and collectibles. These sites have made their names (and fortunes) by bringing forward items of specific interest to the discriminating collector and investor.

You probably won't find a Partridge Family lunchbox or talking Herman Munster doll at these houses. No, these are the places where you'll find more significant pieces, such as the works of Rembrandt and da Vinci, exquisite furnishings and decor from the 19th century, and Impressionist paintings.

Of course, you'll also find collectibles and memorabilia, but these will be truly unique and notable items such as a Honus Wagner baseball card from 1910 or Clark Gable's Oscar for Best Actor for his role in *It Happened One Night*.

The high bids are as impressive as the items put on the auction block. Consider these auction results:

- Vincent van Gogh's *Portrait of Dr. Gachet*—$82.5 million
- Pablo Picasso's *Le Rêve*—$48 million
- Walt Disney's *The Orphan Benefit*—$286,000

This is just a small sampling of some of the record holders that Christie's auction house has managed. You can see, though, that the stakes get pretty high, and it's usually society's high rollers that will take home such treasures.

When old world meets new world: Leonardo da Vinci's manuscript, *Codex Hammer,* was sold for $30.8 million to software mogul—geek Bill Gates. Hope he's not planning to upgrade it.

# Untraditional Sites

So now the auction aficionados have made the jump into the Internet world. Their sites, you'll find, present a nice blend of old-world auctioneering with new wave Web designs. But more than that, the traditional auction houses and the auctioneers that have worked at them are sought after in this new market. Sought by whom? Well, it seems the online auction biggies are looking for involvement and partnership with the flagship auction experts.

With so much concern about fraud and the need for educated authentication, online sites have been turning to the long-service auctioneers who know the real thing from a real fake. Though sites like eBay have begun to promote third-party authentication services (such as the International Society of Appraisers), the issue of trust has prompted many sites to go back to the "fathers of the auction" for history, guidance, and even teamwork.

In early 1999, eBay acquired San Francisco auction house Butterfield & Butterfield in an effort to branch into higher-end auctions without having to grow the trust and respect of the upper-end bidders the way they would have if they'd chosen to go it alone. The highly-respected auction house (and its clientele, they hope) cost eBay $260 million.

Not to be outdone, Amazon.com soon after announced an online partnership with traditional auction house Sotheby's. Obviously, this quest for the master house's experience and participation means these old dogs aren't anywhere near ready to be put out to kennel.

So does this mean you should jump into the traditional auction houses' sites? Well, before you think about scoring a Renoir for your family room, be sure you understand a few differences about the master auctions.

## The Price of Participation

First of all, don't expect that you'll grab dollar-day bargains at the traditional auction houses. That's not what they're about. These houses realize they have a reputation of being only for the "upper crust," so they encourage new bidders by assuring them that a large majority of their items sell for less than $5,000. I don't know about you, but I've yet to spend that much for *any* item at an auction. I guess I'm not much of an upper cruster—more like a soggy center. Anyway, remember that these aren't sites where you can grab a van Gogh for cheap while nobody's looking.

But the more important thing to remember about the traditional houses is that *buyers* pay a commission, too. Yes! If you win at the high-end houses, expect to pay anywhere between 10 to 15 percent commission on top of the final value of your purchase. It's a premium you pay for the privilege of bidding on such rare and unique items. I won't say whether that's good or bad. It's just a fact.

GET A CLUE
Hey! Don't get pushed out of shape. The buyer's commission applies in the physical auction house and isn't just a Net punishment. If you're not willing to pay that commission, then you're probably not ready to bid for higher stakes.

So if this is your cup of tea, then take a look at the new Web presence of a few of the auction big boys.

IN MY MIND
Even if you don't think you'll be bidding at high-end auction houses, I still encourage you to visit these sites. You can learn quite a bit about auctions' heritage and see how this centuries-old business is embracing and migrating to the World Wide Web. More importantly, you'll have the opportunity to learn about this facet of online auctioning. If you're truly serious about understanding online auctions, you should strive to learn all venues in the industry. That's my outlook, anyway.

## Sotheby's

So the place to start is the grand house—the one that set the terms of understanding and participation in auctioning for modern culture. If you recall from Chapter 1, Sotheby's was established back in 1744. A London book-seller named Samuel Baker established the auction as a new way for sellers and buyers to come together for the pricing and selling of works of "polite literature." When Baker died in 1778, the auction (a huge success) was carried on by Baker's nephew, John Sotheby. By 1917, Sotheby's business was of such volume that it needed to relocate, settling on its current home on New Bond Street in London. With business still on the upswing, Sotheby's moved into auctioning fine art and, in 1964, opened its first international business place in America. Since that time, Sotheby's has opened, and is currently operating, over 100 international offices the world over.

Today, Sotheby's has found the Internet, a sort of third dimension to its international market. Sotheby's actually announced its online presence back in January 1999. At that time, it earmarked more than $25 million for development and staffing of its Web venture, bringing its brand of auctioning to online collectors and investors. To see what's going on at Sotheby's online, visit **www.sothebys.com**. You'll find a nicely designed page awaiting you (see Figure 8-1).

I must tell you that, as this book goes to press, Sotheby's has yet to begin its online bidding. What?! Have I been pulling your leg all this time? No. Sotheby's *will* be introducing online bidding in the form of its collaborative site with Amazon.com at **www.sothebys.amazon.com**. The official press release states that the site will be online some time in 1999 (though as of September, this still hasn't come to pass). But don't bail out yet. If you are interested in Sotheby's auctions, you'll still find out how to participate today by reviewing their Web site. Read along, and I'll show you.

## Site Presentation

A nice site, indeed, and very friendly. Though you might expect an auction giant like Sotheby's to be somewhat stuffy and presumptuous, you'll be pleased to learn that the site designers have taken a down-to-earth approach to explain their business and how to participate in its auctions. You'll find plenty of links to take you to items of interest and an extremely good dose of site information, history, and educational content that teaches all visitors more

Figure 8-1

When you visit Sotheby's online, be ready for a treat in upper-class bidding and selling.

about auctions at the iconic auction house. Sotheby's even jokes that some visitors are apt to exclaim, *"But I don't have a chauffeured limo or a diamond choker for my poodle!"* The site then goes on to assure you don't have to be a millionaire to visit Sotheby's. Nice touch.

Look again at Figure 8-1, and you'll see how clean and organized the Sotheby's home page is. It's easy to find the links to get where you want to go or to strike off on an exploration to learn more about upscale auctioning.

**IN MY MIND** Here's where Sotheby's site immediately impresses me: notice the advertising of the Barry Halper baseball memorabilia collection and see how the current site design uses nostalgic images of the early days of apple-pie sportsmanship. This, in my opinion, is a well-designed presentation that could bring in many non-regulars. The site is making its appeal to, perhaps, the regular sports enthusiasts out there, encouraging them to come in and learn what Sotheby's is all about. If the site only caters to the "rich and famous," then it will miss an incredible opportunity to expand its clientele. It's refreshing to see that Sotheby's is not "exclusive." Good show, Sotheby's!

## Auction Lots

At a house like Sotheby's, you'll be previewing *auction lots* as opposed to searching through an inventory of *stuff*. The presentation is much more formal than what you've seen previously, but it needn't be intimidating. Look again at the site home page, and you'll see a heading mid-page titled *Collecting*. Below that, you'll find a link to *Collecting Depts*. Click on that to see the different categories of items that will be available in upcoming auction lots.

Though you might have thought you'd only find 19th-century relics, fine and historic works of art, or Fabergé eggs, you might be surprised to find other items, such as collectible autos and motorcycles, rock 'n' roll memorabilia, and comic books. It's true: Sotheby's *does* cater to a wide range of collectible tastes, but these are the *really* hard-to-find goods.

If you'd like to know what's coming to the auction block, click on the *Auction Schedule* link under the *Auctions* heading on the home page. Take the time to look around. You'll be amazed at what you'll find.

**DID YOU KNOW?** Sotheby's managed the auction of John Lennon's psychedelic Rolls-Royce. It sold for $2.3 million. Imagine.

In traditional fashion, Sotheby's prepares an auction catalogue that showcases the items coming up for bid. Each catalogue features full descriptions and illustrations of items coming to the auction block. Catalogues also include names and phone numbers of Sotheby's specialists who can help answer questions about particular items. You can purchase catalogues individually or as an annual subscription. Just click on the *Catalogues* link on the home page to learn more. You'll also find that catalogue text is available online, though Sotheby's warns it might not be as complete or up to date as the final published catalogue.

Also by tradition, Sotheby's holds auction exhibitions prior to the actual auction. This is where prospective bidders take a personal look at items to help determine if and how much to bid when the auctioneer steps up to the podium. Naturally, you might find it difficult to actually attend the exhibitions, which is why the catalogue and inquiries to Sotheby's specialists will be so valuable to you.

## Bidding at Sotheby's

I've already tipped you off that Sotheby's isn't ready to receive online bids as of this writing. However, its Web site still has plenty of information that *will* get you into the bidding at auctions held regularly around the world.

If you can't attend the actual auction—registering for your little bidding paddle and the whole business—you can still bid in an auction by absentee rules. If you see something you must have and want to bid on it, Sotheby's can assign a representative to bid for you. Each auction catalogue contains an *Absentee Bid Form* that you can fill out and mail or fax to Sotheby's offices. This kind of bidding is much like online bidding using a proxy system: you'll state the item you want and your maximum bid price. The Sotheby's representative will bid on your behalf in minimum increments until your maximum bid is reached. Who knows? Maybe you'll be a winner. If so, you'll be awarded the item at the high bid price, plus buyer's premium and sales tax.

**IN MY MIND** Remember, Sotheby's has more than 100 locations around the world. If you ever have a chance to attend a live auction, do it. I've never attended one, but having studied auctions for so long, I really feel the tug to experience a traditional auction firsthand. It would be a real education and great fun. Who knows, perhaps I could sneak away with one of Picasso's napkin doodles . . . .

## Additional Services

First and foremost, know that whatever you bid on at Sotheby's is fully authenticated and strictly graded. No bogus merchandise here. If you think you want to step into high-dollar, highly coveted pieces of significance, then a house like Sotheby's is there for you with a reputation you can trust. Sotheby's boasts that its staff of 200 experts can accurately represent items from over 65 collecting categories. From Rembrandt to Rockwell, from Mozart to Madonna, Sotheby's will give you the straight story on the items that have caught your eye.

Sotheby's is also in the business of appraisals. If you have items of high value and want to get a fair market assessment, the Sotheby's experts promise to help you. You'll receive a detailed description of your item, including artist or maker, date and location of origin, and the medium used. Sotheby's states that each appraisal will be professionally bound with a signed affidavit that is accepted by the Internal Revenue Service, tax professionals, and insurance companies. Don't wing it yourself if you have a valuable piece; check into Sotheby's to see what its people can do for you. Of course, appraisals do carry a fee based on the type and quantity of items you're inquiring about.

And if those treasures you own have begun to show their age, Sotheby's also provides professional restoration services. Though many might argue that restoration diminishes the value of an item (a line of thought that claims any alteration of an item's historic wear is near-falsification), proper restoration can help preserve a rare item for generations to come. Left uncared for, rare and historic items can literally disintegrate over time. Sotheby's professionals can halt the ravages of time and preserve your item in a way that will help it endure where otherwise it might wither away.

Sotheby's offers many more services, and if you're interested in this type of collecting, visit the site and learn more of what they offer.

 ## AuctionGuy Rates This Site . . .

On the scale of 1 to 5, Sotheby's gets a 4.

Even though it doesn't yet offer online bidding? Sure, because what it does offer is an incredible wealth of information and history. I have been pleased to visit this site frequently to see what the masters are up to, how they'll be plotting their move to the Internet, and how prepared they are to embrace the huge online bidding populace. On each visit, I've found the site to be visually appealing, educational, and intriguing.

Clearly, I'm no high roller, and I'm not in a position to drop millions of dollars on rare art or a psychedelic Rolls. However, the goings-on at Sotheby's are of great interest. It's amazing how much is paid for some items and who's paying those prices. Don't feel like some street urchin peering in through the window—Sotheby's invites all comers to see, learn, and participate if they're of a mind to.

I'll be paying close attention as the Sotheby's-Amazon partner site comes online. Maybe that's when I'll get my first opportunity to bid at the regal house of riches. But I still think a pilgrimage to an actual auction is required to give any serious auction-goer (online or otherwise) an appreciation for this incredible industry.

## Christie's

Christie's is another of the founding auction houses that has helped form the modern understanding of traditional auctioning. Christie's also began operation in London, in 1766. Founder James Christie set out to launch the first fine art auction house (remember that Sotheby's initially focused on literature), and Christie's soon developed a reputation as being an upper-class salesroom for the finest art available. Christie extended the use of his auction house to local artists, inviting them to exhibit their works there.

Christie's has enjoyed a very successful run of more than 230 years, and is known the world over for its fine art auctions while also having diversified its expertise and offerings to over 80 different collectibles categories. Included are fine art, wine, stamps, and even sunken cargo. Christie's is another auction house that can offer truly rare and unique items of curiosity and significance.

In its Web presence, Christie's reaches out to potential auction-goers the world over. Its site represents its rich heritage while also educating visitors on the fine practice of auctioning. When you're ready to visit Christie's online, go to **www.christies.com**.

## Site Presentation

The Christie's site is regal in design but comprehensible in its content. The designers have properly balanced the site to convey the richness of the auction house without delivering a message that might seem exclusive or snobbish.

In fact, much like Sotheby's, Christie's site design also makes it clear that the auction house is not stuck in the 18th or 19th centuries in either its offerings or appeal. Figure 8-2 shows that, as of this writing, Christie's is celebrating the importance of current cultural events and personalities.

## Auction Lots

Christie's sponsors auctions throughout the year that are held at its various sales rooms around the world. Along the top and bottom banners of the Christie's home page, visitors will find a selection of links that easily guide even the novice user through the site to tour all that Christie's has to offer.

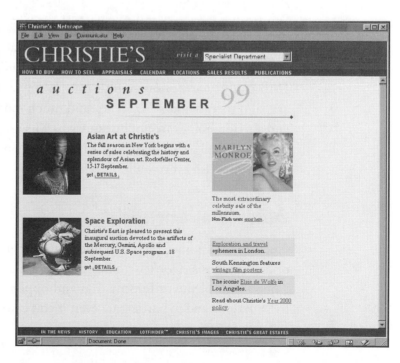

Figure 8-2

Christie's site features significant collectibles items while also recognizing the value of more current pieces of cultural value.

If you want to see what's coming up for auction soon, click on the *Calendar* link in the top banner of the Christie's home page.

GET
A
CLUE

If there's a certain kind of collectible you're most interested in, click on the *Specialist Department* down arrow at the top of the page. The drop-down list will reveal the different categories of treasures you can inspect.

If there's something specific you're interested in finding, use Christie's *Lotfinder* function, an auction search you can use to see if a specific item or type or item will be coming up soon for auction. With Lotfinder, you can search for items using key words that describe the artist, medium, dimensions, or price of the item you're looking for. You can also limit your search by price and auction location.

But Lotfinder is more than just a search engine. It's also an automatic auction agent that will retain your search criteria and search Christie's catalogues (per your specifications), contacting you via e-mail or fax when an item matching your criteria is found. There is a subscription price for this service, but it frees you from having to continually scour the site yourself.

And what kinds of items might you find for auction at Christie's? Well, with over 80 categories of items, you'll be able to find things like Impressionist and 19th-century art, photographs, musical instruments, animation and comic art, film memorabilia, Asian art, and much more. As you can see, these high-end auction houses are not just stuffy parlors offering esoteric items that appeal only to a small sector of society. There's pretty much something for every taste (if not quite for every wallet) up for auction.

## Bidding at Christie's

Christie's is another high-end auction site that's online but doesn't sponsor online auctions. Don't wrinkle your nose and take the next hyperlink out. There's still plenty of information and opportunity to learn about Christie's live auctions and to participate even if you can't attend an auction of interest.

Like Sotheby's, Christie's offers online information about items in upcoming auctions. You can purchase auction catalogues and contact Christie's experts to learn more about items to be auctioned. Christie's sponsors pre-auction exhibitions where potential bidders are welcome to carefully inspect each item up for auction. Remember, if you can't attend the exhibition, the house experts are available via phone to answer your specific questions.

If you can attend an auction, that's preferable. If you can't, you can register for absentee bidding. Christie's supports proxy bidding by which a Christie's representative will bid on your behalf in minimum increments until your maximum authorized bid amount has been reached. Your absentee bid can be mailed to the auction house and will be used as your bidding instructions.

Christie's also invites distant bidders to phone in their bids. That's right, Christie's can call you on the phone when the item you're interested in comes up for bid. Working with a Christie's representative, your bids can be relayed to the auctioneer while the auction is actually under way. Truly the next best thing to being there.

If you participate in and win an auction at Christie's, you'll be required to pay your high bid price, plus a buyer's commission fee (10 to 15 percent of the final price), plus local taxes and possibly other fees. The Christie's catalogue will specify all applicable fees. Be sure you understand them before you participate in an auction.

## Additional Services

At Christie's, you can also contract for expert appraisals and advisory services, purchase books about different collectible interests, learn about and possibly participate in luxury real estate auctions (Christie's Great Estates), and even enroll in courses to learn the art of collecting and auctioning from the Christie's staff of experts.

## AuctionGuy Rates This Site . . .

On the scale of 1 to 5, Christie's also gets a 4.

Again, another well-presented site that imparts a sense of history and tradition to visitors. The site is simple to navigate and understand, and the information is presented so as to be of interest to anyone who decides to take the tour.

The site offers a down-to-earth attitude similar to Sotheby's, though Sotheby's employs a bit more comforting humor. However, Christie's is carefully designed to not scare off anyone who's curious about the *other* great auction house.

I enjoy visiting Christie's site because of its welcoming design and the wealth of knowledge to be gained. I've yet to bid in a Christie's auction, though some of the vintage movie memorabilia has been tempting. But whether you bid or not, Christie's is an important site to visit to further enrich any auction-goer's knowledge and understanding of auction style and history.

## Butterfield & Butterfield

The next soon-to-be online auction of high-end items is Butterfield & Butterfield. Based and founded in San Francisco by William Butterfield, this auction house started operations back in 1865. At that time, it operated as a business centered on providing supplies to ships anchoring in San Francisco Bay. The business was quite successful and as the city grew, so did Butterfield's. The company's success spurred the offering of fine art and furnishings, and Butterfield's soon became known as the West Coast's auction house of choice for fine collectibles. It continued to serve the public's desires for unique items, increasing its range of offerings with each successive year.

In 1989, Butterfield & Butterfield opened a second auction gallery in Los Angeles and has more recently expanded into the Midwestern region of the United States. In May 1998, Butterfield & Butterfield announced a merger

with historic auction house Dunning's of Illinois, forming the new auction venture Butterfield and Dunning.

But Butterfield & Butterfield doesn't operate only on its native soil. The prominent auction house also has international offices located in Munich, Paris, London, and Brussels. It currently serves a buying clientele more than 450,000 strong.

So, with a long history of success and notoriety, Butterfield & Butterfield expanded again, this time to the World Wide Web. Its online presence further spreads the word to collectors all across the Internet that Butterfield & Butterfield is an auction house you simply must visit if you're interested in finding and bidding on high-value items of distinction. If you're ready to visit Butterfield's online auction house, go to **www.butterfields.com**.

## Site Presentation

Of the high-end sites I've visited, I think I appreciate the Butterfield & Butterfield design the most. Take a look at the home page shown in Figure 8-3.

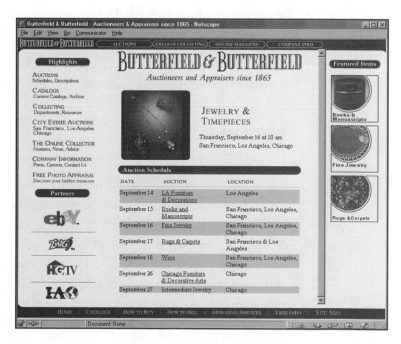

Figure 8-3

The Butterfield & Butterfield site is a pleasure to visit and is easy and fun to tour.

This, too, is another clean site, but the combination of graphics, easy-to-find links, and intuitive organization makes Butterfield & Butterfield's site an enjoyable visit. You'll find a good selection of links around the site in the top and bottom banners, including a useful *Site Map* link (I always appreciate those when they're done well).

Much as at Sotheby's and Christie's, you'll find great information and historical facts at Butterfield & Butterfield. You'll be able to quickly learn the house charter, areas of expertise, and special features that provide for a well-rounded auction experience.

Look at Figure 8-3 again, and you'll see a side column that links to Butterfield & Butterfield partners. Preeminently, you'll notice the eBay logo (remember that eBay purchased this San Francisco auction giant for $260 million). Notice the second link to Zing.com, an online venture specializing in digital photography and the development of an online community of members who create and share online photo albums with family and friends. Clearly, Butterfield & Butterfield is poised for a significant Net presence.

Notice, then, the partner link to HGTV (cable TV's Home & Garden Television). Experts from Butterfield & Butterfield are featured on the channel's series of programs where appraisals are made of a variety of rare and curious items.

Finally, you'll see the link to International Auctioneers, billed as the largest network of international marketing experts in the auction industry.

## Auction Lots

Look back at Figure 8-3, and you'll see the top banner link, *Areas of Collecting*. Click on that and you'll jump to a new page that explains a bit more about Butterfield & Butterfield's operation and also provides a healthy list of item categories. You'll find links to such areas as Books & Manuscripts, Coins & Stamps, Furniture & Decorative Arts, Arms & Armor, Jewelry & Timepieces, and more. Butterfield & Butterfield hosts over 150 major auctions annually and provides full descriptions of all items coming up for auction either online or through printed catalogues.

## Bidding at Butterfield & Butterfield

By now you're probably a bit suspicious about these high-end auction houses and whether you really can bid for items online. At Butterfield & Butterfield, you'll find once again that you can't bid online—not yet, anyway. Remember the acquisition by eBay, and bear in mind that these two auction giants have plans to offer online auction offerings from the regal house in the very near future.

But, as with the other two sites you've just learned about, lack of online bidding doesn't prevent you from participating in one of Butterfield & Butterfield's auctions. On the Web site, you'll find the usual instructions that explain how you can view items either online or in catalogues you can purchase. Then, when you find an item you'd like to bid on—and assuming you can't attend the auction in person—you can register for absentee bidding though one of Butterfield & Butterfield's representatives. As usual, there's a proxy bidding system that allows your bid to be increased incrementally until your maximum authorized bid amount has been reached. And, as at the other high-end auction houses, buyers pay a premium that will be added to the final high bid price.

## Additional Services

Butterfield & Butterfield also offers appraisal services for your rare items. If you feel you have an item that might do well at the auction, the appraisal fee is often refundable. If satisfied with the valuation of your item, you can elect to consign it to Butterfield & Butterfield for auction. There's also a free photo appraisal in which you submit photos of your item (either by regular mail or e-mail) along with an appraisal form you'll find online. The Butterfield's experts will evaluate your item with no obligation for you to consign it. Click on the *Appraisal Services* link at the bottom of the Butterfield's & Butterfield's home page to learn more about these services.

Butterfield & Butterfield's site is also rich in feature stories about collecting and collectibles. You can learn much just from reading what the site experts have to say about different types of items that show up for bid at auction. Butterfield & Butterfield also offers a free online magazine that has even more feature articles about certain collectibles, artists, museums, and expert Q & A sessions.

## AuctionGuy Rates This Site . . .

On the scale of 1 to 5, Butterfield & Butterfield gets a 5.

I gave Butterfield & Butterfield a higher rating simply because I like the carefully balanced blend of information, history, and site presentation. It's a friendly place to visit, and it doesn't attempt to overwhelm or intimidate you in any way.

This site makes the top list of high-end auction sites in that it offers a large selection of auctionable items year-round. Collectors of rare and curious items will not be let down when they visit this site. Newcomers are definitely welcome and are schooled in the ways of high-end auctions.

Butterfield & Butterfield further promotes the fact that high-value auctions don't have to be feared or avoided by the common collector. Stop by and see what's coming up for auction. Even if you're only there to browse, it will be time well spent.

## Biddington's

If you've reached the conclusion that high-end auctioning simply isn't conducted online yet, I'm ready to throw a curve at you. There's one more high-end auction site I want to show you, and you'll be pleased to know that this *is* a site where you can cast your bids from your PC today.

Biddington's describes itself as an "upmarket" auction host, bringing a variety of fine art, textiles, antiques, and rare tribal art to bidders in cyberspace. Biddington's conducts online auctions on a continual basis, but it acts more like a consignor than a venue. At Biddington's, sellers are invited to register and list their items for auction to any prospective bidders. However, once the auction is over and a winning bidder has been announced, Biddington's actually manages the trade in that it acts the role of online escrow provider. The buyer sends payment to Biddington's, at which point Biddington's informs the seller that payment has been received and the item should be shipped. After the buyer receives and accepts the item, Biddington's releases payment to the seller, less a commission. For other auction sites I've shown you, the financial intermediary service was elective and managed by a third party not affiliated with the actual auction site.

If you want to try your hand at bidding on upscale items online and like the idea that this site gets involved to help manage the exchange, go to **www.biddingtons.com** and get started.

## Site Presentation

Well, the items you'll find at this site are definitely high-end, but the site itself is rather low-end. It's not necessarily a *bad* site, but site design was not high on the priority list of the site developers. Maybe that's not important to you since it's the rare treasures you're after, not a breathtaking Web site. If so, you'll be satisfied with Biddington's site (see Figure 8-4).

The site is easy to navigate, and you'll find many active hyperlinks spread throughout. Take the time to traverse the *virtual tour*—you'll find a link at the bottom of the home page. It's not an image-laden journey: the tour is presented in a textual manner that guides you through Biddington's virtual auction house. There are plenty of links in the tour that allow you to veer off and learn more about a specific site feature or policy. At the end of the tour, you'll find links to the different categories of items available for auction.

## Auction Lots

Unfortunately, there isn't lots to see at Biddington's. What you do find is intriguing, though. This is a site that will appeal to collectors of contemporary and tribal art. There are many different categories for "potential" auctionable items, but you'll find the greatest selection in the *Art Auctions* listing. Still, don't pooh-pooh this site; a truly rare item you're looking for just might show up here.

## Bidding at Biddington's

As promised, Biddington's is an upscale site where you *can* bid online. First, you'll need to register. The Biddington's registry requires you provide your

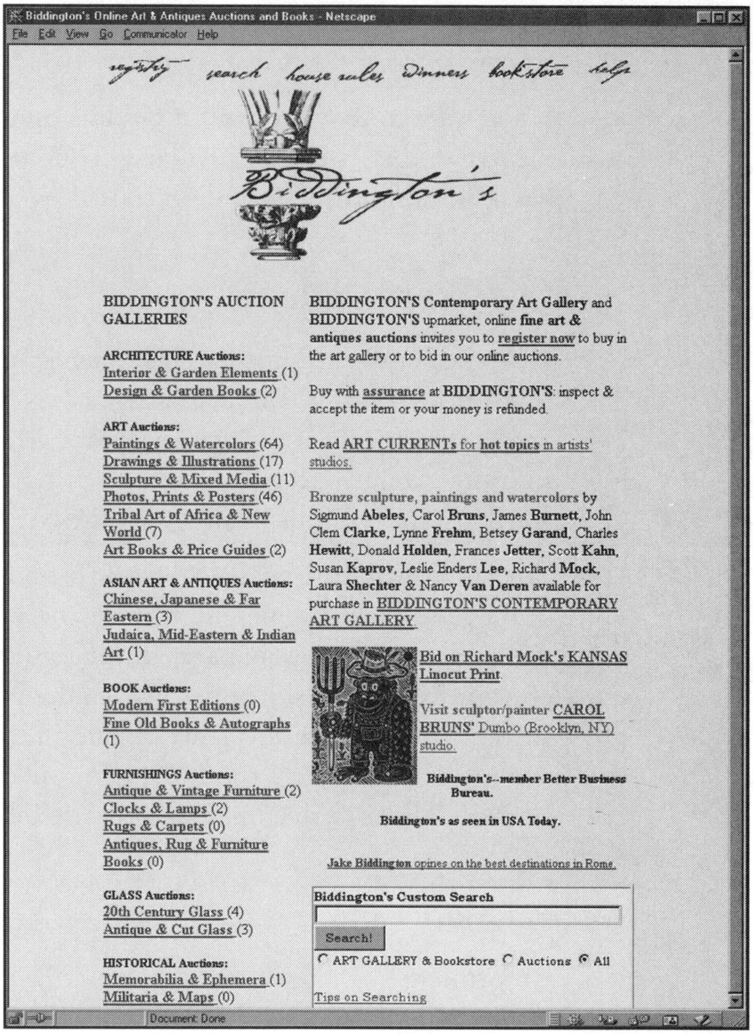

Figure 8-4

Biddington's offers online auctions for the more cultured bidder. The site's not a thing of beauty, but there are some compelling items inside.

Figure 8-4

Biddington's offers online auctions for the more cultured bidder. The site's not a thing of beauty, but there are some compelling items inside.

personal information (name, address, telephone number, e-mail address). Next, you select the type of payment you'll submit if and when you win at the auction. Biddington's currently only accepts payment in the form of a check, money order, or wire transfer. Though you might think it inconvenient that you can't use a credit card at Biddington's, the policy does mean that you avoid any concerns about your credit card information being stored on the site.

DID
YOU
KNOW?
At Biddington's, you'll identify yourself to other bidders by way of your chosen *epithet*. Oh my. No "nicknames" here, and clever monikers like *kittykat, barfy,* or *imtoosexy* would undoubtedly be inappropriate. Yes, you have stepped up in society when you bid at Biddington's.

Once you've registered, it's off to the auctions. Use the item categories you see on the Biddington's home page to drill into an area of interest to you. When you find something you like, click on its title to get to the item details. Bidding is as simple as entering your epithet, password, and bid amount (you can enter a maximum bid using Biddington's *Auto-Bid* proxy bidding system). You also have the option of not bidding but adding the item to your *Auction Watch,* Biddington's system that lets those who are interested track the progress of a specific auction.

If you're outbid in an auction, Biddington's can send an e-mail notification to you. If you win the auction, you'll be notified by Biddington's of your final price, at which point Biddington's will step in as exchange intermediary as I described earlier. It's a twist to what you've seen in earlier discussions, but it does lend a bit more security to the exchange without the need to involve a third-party escrow service.

GET
A
CLUE
At Biddington's, buyers *do not* pay a buyer's premium or any other winning commission. That's a pleasant change.

## AuctionGuy Rates This Site . . .

On the scale of 1 to 5, Biddington's gets a 3.

I like the fact that Biddington's has emerged as an upscale auction site that actually accepts bids online. That in itself will help to forge a path for the historic auction houses to fully migrate to this sort of electronic auctioning for high-value items.

Biddington's site, though, appears to lessen its own credibility. While flashy sites are no indication of a site's contents, Biddington's design is far too simplistic (dare I say, amateurish?) for many potential bidders to actually stay and participate. That, inevitably, will reduce the amount of traffic from serious bidders and sellers.

When site traffic is low, selection is also low while minimum bid prices are typically high. To make up for a lack of bidders, sellers often price their items quite high in case they only attract a single bid. However, those high prices usually scare away would-be bidders. Granted, these are upscale items, and they are due their proper value. However, for an auction to be successful, there has to be a large enough bidding population to properly establish accurate item valuation.

That said, I don't consider Biddington's an inferior site. True, it's not up to par with the high-end sites described earlier in the chapter, but it still offers some unique items that otherwise might not be available to collectors. The fact that Biddington's auctions are online and have been for some time is a credit to its established presence. As this is relatively uncharted territory for high-end auctioneers, Biddington's site brings more opportunity to buyers and sellers of fine items to the Web.

## The Final Hammer

Clearly, I'm not one who bids at these traditional auction houses, nor am I currently collecting the sort of rare and significant items to be found there. However, as a student of "the auction," I find the traditional, upscale auctions to be highly important to the online auction community. Their heritage and history is what has defined the format for the auction sites you're most familiar with on the Internet. However, auctioneering is a whole new world for these new online auction companies—and the Net-bidders who frequent them—and it's understanding traditional auctioning that helps everyone further emulate and establish online auction methods. Without the traditional houses, the current online sites would hardly exist as they do today.

Again, even if you don't plan to bid, I encourage you to frequent the high-end auction sites. Learn more about how they work and how they differ from sites like Onsale and eBay. Chances are, you'll see the current online auction giants further model themselves after the old masters.

C H A P T E R 9

# Charity Auctions

Well, what kind of auction book would this be if it didn't show you a few of the *other* types of traditional auctions? Probably the second thing to come to mind after the posh English auction houses are charity auctions. These are the auctions that raise money for ongoing medical research, disaster relief, preservation of local arts, or to help keep Big Bird on the air.

Charity auctions have historically been successful—the pull of the charity encourages bidders to bid higher. *"C'mon, this is for charity. Bid till it hurts."* In response, bidders usually raise their stakes, knowing that their money will help a needy cause. And online auctions are the perfect staging area for charity auctions. No longer confined to a geographic region or local television station's broadcasting range, charitable auctions on the Internet reach more altruistic donors and bidders than ever before.

## What's It All About?

At their core, charity auctions (and other fundraising activities) have a need for some sort of monetary assistance or relief. An organization pulls together volunteers, donors, and sponsors to stage an event. The event attracts attendees, shoppers, or whomever—the ones whose monetary participation raise the needed funds. The biggest problem facing such philanthropic endeavors is overhead—the cost to develop, coordinate, advertise, and execute the function. Overhead costs have long plagued charitable efforts and have effectively eaten away at the final amount left available to donate. The Internet, though, has changed all that.

A Web site or Web event is quite low in cost compared to the normal physical events. Think of the facilities that need to be rented and staffed for a charity event. Think of the catering involved (someone's gotta feed that bank of phone volunteers). Think of the cleanup afterward. It all costs money and usually takes a big bite out of the event's bottom line.

But if it's not an event that's going to be the fundraising vehicle, then what? There's the usual direct-mail method, which costs money for printing and distributing mailers. How about telephone solicitations? Those are expensive to establish and staff, plus recipients are often unsure whether the person asking for a donation is truly affiliated with a viable cause and sometimes unwilling to listen long enough to find out what the cause is. Or consider the door-to-door method. These days, that's getting a bit dicey, too.

Online, though, many of the overhead expenses and donor worries disappear. Advertising is infinitely easier, thanks to partnerships with mega-sites and search engines (perform a search on *charity auctions,* and you'll see how many are going on right now). Staging the event can be managed by a small team of coordinators and Web developers. Potential donors can fully review the organization's site and determine if it's on the level or on the take. A well-designed site will provide all pertinent information and government filings of proof of viability that can be reviewed by site visitors through a series of mouse clicks. But, most important, the reach of an Internet charity far surpasses that of a physical event or solicitation.

GET A CLUE
If you're involved in a charitable organization, it's not necessarily best to abandon traditional fundraising methods. Many folks today still aren't online. However, any organization should advertise its Web presence or e-mail address on all the literature that it distributes via direct mail or at fundraising events.

Next, consider the duration of getting the message out—a charitable event or ongoing cause represented on the Internet can be seen 24 hours a day, 7 days a week, 365 days a year. These efforts are no longer bound by a finite amount of handbills to be distributed, operating hours of a physical site, or live people-power required to answer basic questions about the mission of the event. Donations, sponsorships, and participation can be solicited and managed online through published forms and automated e-mail response routines.

**IN MY MIND**

When I consider the immediacy of the Internet, I think of the whimsical bidding at some of the other sites. You can bid whenever the urge strikes. For a charitable cause, you can *give* whenever the urge strikes. I can only imagine how many potential donations are lost at "normal" charitable events due to the logistics of contacting the event staff, possibly traveling to the event's site, and so on. Online, just as you can shop and bid in the convenience of your own home, so you can also help a good cause in a single mouse click. That's pretty powerful.

## Who Gets the Money?

This is always the ultimate question. How do participants know their money is *really* going to the needy cause and not lining the pockets of some embezzler? How much of the money raised is actually translated into funding or aid? And, by the way, which charity am I supporting here?

Naturally, you'll need to do a bit of homework. If you're currently involved in the ongoing support of a charitable (nonprofit) organization, you're probably quite aware of how it collects and allocates donated funds, goods, and services. But if you're new to giving and want to be sure your donations get to the right place, hit the Web.

You can start by performing an Internet search on the name of the organization you want to help support. Chances are, you'll find a related Web site that explains the organization's charter and means of providing assistance. If the organization operates or participates in charitable auctions, you'll learn where those auctions are being conducted.

**DID YOU KNOW?**

All nonprofit charitable organizations are required to have a 501(c)(3) (Recognition for Tax Exemption) form on file with the Internal Revenue Service. Any good charity hosting an auction site will verify this status for the organizations that are represented at the auction site.

# How Can I Help?

You don't have to actually participate in an auction to help a charity of your choice. Many nonprofit organizations with an Internet presence can take your donations online as well. Most nonprofit sites are set up to take advantage of the fundraising potential of online donations, and have provided secure pages where credit card donations can be made.

If you wish to donate on a regular basis (perhaps monthly contributions), some sites make it easy. They invite you to authorize recurring charges against your credit card, so the donation will show up on your bill and provide a durable receipt for your tax records.

But back to the auctions. Many sites actively invite donation of items that can be auctioned with proceeds benefiting the recipient charity. Individuals or larger companies can donate goods for auction. If you think you're interested in bidding or donating for charitable causes, take a look at a few online auction sites where your efforts really go to work.

## WebCharity.com

This is probably one of the best-known charity auction sites online today. Launched in July 1998, WebCharity acts as an auction host site for charities and nonprofit organizations. They provide a sort of self-service venue for the creation and operation of charity auctions.

WebCharity will sponsor individuals and organizations, allowing them to operate charity auctions or sell items for fixed prices in the WebCharity Online Thrift Shop. WebCharity verifies the exempt status of applicant organizations, then turns them loose to manage their fundraising events on the Web site.

If you want to donate to one of the registered WebCharity organizations but don't have cash, simply fill out a WebCharity donation form for items you wish to donate in the name of a particular organization. When you fill out the donation form, you're actually creating an auction listing in which you'll describe the item and minimum bid price. After the auction, WebCharity handles collection of the high bid value and then tells you where you should ship the item. The organization you specified will receive 100 percent of the auction's proceeds.

Figure 9-1

WebCharity.com offers a variety of fundraising services and opportunities at its Web site.

WebCharity...Where the World Comes to Give. Online Auctions and Virtual Thrift Shop to Benefit Chari - Netscape

File Edit View Go Communicator Help

WEBCharity
Where the World Comes To Give

Held August 13 - 29 at

**WEBCharity.com** ™
Where the World Comes to Give

| SHOPPING | DONATING | FUNDRAISING | EVERYTHING ELSE |

*Get a Great Buy With the Proceeds Going to a Good Cause*

Please Join Our Mailing List: |your email address    | Add Me! | Thrift Shop Contest! Win up to $500 for your nonprofit organization! Click here.

**Charity Auctions**

- The Majors Collection by Tico Torres
- Broadway For Autism

**What's Hot!**

Our Thrift Shop is Now Open! Thrift Shop Contest! Win up to $500 for your nonprofit organization! Click here for contest details.

Join Us! Over 600 nonprofit organizations have seen the benefits of being WebCharity members. There is no cost or obligation to join, but you must be a 501 (c)(3). Click here to add your organization.

Over $150,000 Raised! Turn your in-kind gifts into cash using our Virtual Thrift Shop or host an online Charity Auction Event to raise funds. It's easy!

**Auction & Thrift Shop Items For Sale!**

| Antiques (6) | Collectibles (60) | Home & Business (6) | Services (1) |
|---|---|---|---|
| Ancient World | Advertising | | Accounting |
| Books, Manuscripts & Paper | Art (15) | Appliances (1) | Automotive |
| Bottles & Glassware (1) | Autographs (3) | Baby | Children |
| Ceramics, China, Pottery & Porcelain (4) | Beanies, Bears, & Plush (1) | Bath | Computer |
| Crafts & Folk Arts | Books & Magazines (3) | Farm | Construction |
| Dolls | China | Food | Counseling |
| Furniture & Rugs | Clothing | Furniture & Rugs | Education |
| General (post-1900) | Coins | Garden | Financial |
| General (pre-1900) | Comics | Kitchen (5) | Health |
| Glass (1) | Dolls | Machinery & Manufacturing | Legal |
| | Figures | Other | Maintenance |

Document: Done

**GET A CLUE** Great news! Since WebCharity manages receipt of payment from high bidders, that opens the opportunity for bidders to pay using a credit card. One study reported that people who purchase using credit cards typically spend more than twice as much as they would if they were purchasing with cash. That translates to more funds being raised. Also, since WebCharity is managing collection of payment, you won't need to concern yourself with worries of receiving bad checks or any other form of bogus payment.

Since WebCharity hosts donation auctions and thrift sales, you could find all sorts of things to bid on or buy. Visit the site at **www.webcharity.com** (see Figure 9-1), and take a look through the item categories on the home page. Unfortunately, the inventory can vary in volume. If you don't see much activity going on at the site, consider supporting one of the member organizations and doing some donating and auctioning of your own, helping out a good cause in the process.

## Universal Studios Charity Auctions

So when shoppers' interest isn't fully philanthropic, how do you raise large donations for worthy causes? Enlist Hollywood, that's how. Celebrity auctions are another mainstay of fundraising, and just about anyone becomes a high-bidding auction-goer when they discover unique tinsel-town pieces on the auction block.

You'll find a bunch of celebrity auctions being staged at physical locations (especially in California), but if you want to bid on real Hollywood memorabilia online, you'll want to make a beeline to Universal Studios' Real Hollywood Online Auction (see Figure 9-2).

Just as at the traditional auction houses, you could have the chance to bid on rare and one-of-a-kind items from some of the biggest names. You won't find Seurat, van Gogh, or da Vinci at Universal's auctions, but you might find Schwarzenegger, Van Damme, or DiCaprio. At Universal auctions, bidders are treated to original props, wardrobe, autographs, and promotional merchandise.

As you might expect, the philanthropic mission of any Hollywood auction is to promote the film industry and assist individuals in their endeavors in the motion picture field. Specifically, a portion of the proceeds from Universal auctions goes to the Women in Film foundation, committed to providing more opportunity in Hollywood for women in front of and behind the camera lens.

Universal auctions run at various dates, usually for a period of two weeks. Register at the site, and start bidding when the auctions officially open. At the end of the auction, if you're the winner, Universal will automatically charge your credit card (which you provide when you register) for your high bid

Figure 9-2

How would you like to own Barbra Streisand's throw pillows or Cher's Versace jumpsuit? You can, if you bid high enough at Universal's Real Hollywood Online Auction.

value plus a 10 percent buyer's premium. It could get a bit pricey, but where else can you find prop tools from *Starship Troopers* used for the bug autopsy scenes? Yumm.

## TheBroadcaster.com Hollywood Auction

Still with Tinsel Town in your sights, travel off to **www.thebroadcaster.com/ AUCTION.html**. TheBroadcaster.com is a Web site operated by the Broadcasting Training Program. The mission is to assist minority college graduates with training and eventual job placement in radio and television broadcasting. Selected applicants are placed in radio or television stations for free training, and then, once trained, are provided job placement assistance. As a nonprofit

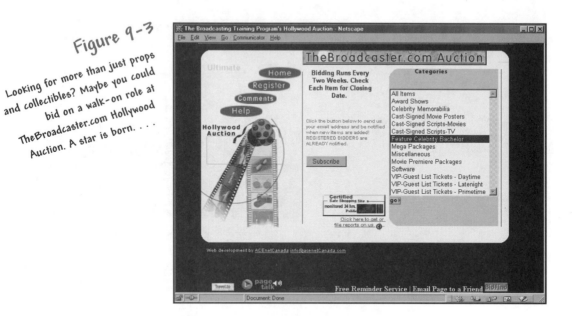

Figure 9-3

Looking for more than just props and collectibles? Maybe you could bid on a walk-on role at TheBroadcaster.com Hollywood Auction. A star is born. . . .

organization with ties to all sorts of media outlets, the Broadcasting Training Program is in a strong position to sponsor online Hollywood auctions.

Of particular interest at TheBroadcaster.com Hollywood Auction are the types of items you can bid on. Not only will you find celebrity autographs and Hollywood memorabilia, you can also win movie premiere packages, and even walk-on roles in theatrical and television productions. Go for it.

## Charity Auctions at Other Sites

If charity auctions are of particular interest to you, don't forget to visit some of the auction sites I showed you in the preceding chapter. Person-to-person sites have been quite active in raising awareness and money for charitable organizations. Here's a couple of familiar faces that are doing their part to fight the good fight:

- **eBay.** Due to the size of its registered user base, it's the perfect environment for charitable causes. eBay sponsors the auctions of Rosie O'Donnell, who regularly auctions celebrity guest items, autographs, and even some of her own Beanie Babies. All proceeds of Rosie's auctions go to the For All Kids

Foundation, an organization that helps foster the intellectual, social, and cultural growth of at-risk and underprivileged kids across the country. Tune in to Rosie's television show, and you'll hear her speak of her eBay auctions on a regular basis.

*People Magazine* has also been active on eBay, selling celebrity autographs to raise money for charitable donations. Even actor-director Ron Howard has hosted auctions to raise money for worthy causes. Learn more about Rosie, *People Magazine,* and other high-profile charity auctions by choosing the *Cool Features* link on eBay's home page.

Further, eBay has developed the eBay Foundation, which awards grants to organizations and efforts that are committed to building communities and the skills of individuals within them. Learn more about the eBay Foundation by choosing the *About eBay* link at the bottom of the eBay home page.

- **Yahoo! Auctions.** At Yahoo! charitable organizations are invited to list celebrity items or special collectibles whose proceeds will be donated to worthy causes. As always, listing at Yahoo! Auctions is free. Charitable organizations are asked to create a Yahoo! user ID that identifies the organization (such as *habitatforhumanity*). Space permitting, charity auctions can get home page advertising for all Yahoo! Auction visitors to see.

## AuctionGuy Rates These Sites . . .

On the scale of 1 to 5, *all* charity auctions get a 5.

I can't think of a better way to harness the fundraising and giving potential of people than in the online forum. And, for any site that has the potential to attract millions of Web-surfers in the name of helping others, that earns high praise in my book.

You'll see lots of variety in the charity auction sites—the ones I've mentioned here as well as others you might find in your own online travels. Remember that low cost, low overhead, and high return on investment is what these sites (and the charities they represent) are all about. These might not be the most whiz-bang auction sites you'll visit, but that shouldn't keep you from visiting and bidding.

So do something good for yourself and something even better for someone else: visit a charity Web site, and see if there's anything you might like. The folks on the other end will be glad you stopped by, and so will you.

C H A P T E R 10

# Specialty Auctions

Have you seen enough? Though I've sifted out only those auction sites I consider the best, you still might want a break about now. After all, with the variety I've shown you in the past several chapters, what could possibly be left? Believe it or not, there's still more to be seen. Back on your feet—this will be the last area to tour, then you can take a break—I promise.

You've seen the merchants with all the great new, refurbished, and overstock goodies. You've seen the person-to-person sites with their selection of general goods where you can find almost anything imaginable. You've seen the high-end sites where some of the most valuable and unique items are paraded about. You've even seen some great sites that benefit charitable organizations. But you still haven't seen the *specialists*. There are auction sites on the Web that cater to specific collectors and enthusiasts. Therefore, the tour's not complete without a visit to the *niche sites*.

## What's the Story?

If you've spent any time surfing the Internet, you'll know that any sort of hobby, interest, or passion has probably been translated into Web space. If it's something you like, your friends like, or anybody else likes well enough to generate any sort of group activity or income, expect to find it on the Web.

After all, that's the beauty of the Internet: people have an open space to talk about what interests them, network with others who share the interest, and develop an educational and economical repository to assist others new to the interest or those who might want to understand more about it.

So with all the hubbub about auctions, it makes sense that folks who have specific interests would create a unique sales forum that caters to those interests. Therefore, the specialty auction has sprung forth.

## Is Smaller Better?

Many auction goers and auction analysts wonder if the small sites can compete in the shadow of the auction biggies. It's hard to argue that the big sites get most of the attention. When auction heavies like Amazon.com Auctions and Yahoo! Auctions are struggling for increased bidder and seller participation, how can a little site focused on a single commodity expect to have any drawing power?

Well, don't be too quick to drive the nail in the coffin for those smaller sites. A site that deals only in sports memorabilia, for instance, will know its market and can alter itself specifically to serve the sports enthusiast's needs. Whereas the big sites rarely succeed at being all things to all people, a site that is devoted to a single interest (including logical spin-off interests) will know its audience better, do a better job keeping up with developments in the commodity market, and be able to work hand-in-hand with its community to provide exactly what the users want. Enthusiasts who have found a specialty site that focuses on their hobby, interest, or collectible know they can visit the site and find the items they really want to see without having to navigate through an online morass of other categories and listings. Besides users finding what they want quickly, sellers at these sites also find what they want quickly: enthusiastic buyers. Sellers who choose specialty sites don't often reach millions of bidders, but the bidders who do visit are more likely to bid on the sellers' items, since that's the kind of stuff the site is all about.

In some cases, the focused sites offer what the big sites can't: expertise, authentication, and customer service. Consider each of these attributes and how the specialty site can sometimes run circles around the online behemoths:

- **Expertise.** It can be difficult and often frustrating when you query a seller at a big auction site, inquiring about an item up for sale, only to find out the seller doesn't really know much about the item. This isn't true of all sellers at the big sites, but some offer a wide variety of items to match the variety of categories and tastes of the big site bidders. So when you're looking for a specific answer to a specific question about that vintage Les Paul, you hope you're hooking up with an expert who knows guitars and not some bloke who picked it up cheap at a consignment store. If ever you have a question about the items up for bid at a specialty site, you're almost guaranteed to get an informed answer from someone who knows their stuff and knows about the stuff that's up for auction. Sometimes the bigger sites just can't provide this kind of knowledge base.

- **Authentication.** Many of the specialty sites maintain that the experts who are running the site can monitor the wares that are put up on the block, closing down any auctions that might be misleading or fraudulent and confirming the authenticity of the items being offered. For wary bidders, this is a real bonus—it frees them from much of the worry of being duped in an auction purchase.

- **Customer Service.** Many of the specialty sites offer telephone assistance and rapid response to e-mail inquiries. Since the site is focused on the needs of the specific collector or enthusiast, it can respond appropriately to most queries without having to dish out a multitude of "form responses" to potentially millions of requesters.

## Does a Smaller Site Equal Smaller Profit?

Actually, no. At many of the specialty sites, you can expect to see some lively trading and occasionally some substantial prices. For the most part, though, you'll find seasoned collectors paying fair-market prices for the items up for bid. The specialty sites draw folks who know what they're shopping for and are usually well attuned to the market value of the commodity. Sure, you'll see some super deals at these sites—and you'll see some runaway auctions that inspire lively bidding battles, too. But the norm falls somewhere in between, maintaining an environment that is typically active and exciting, translating to steady business for the auction site.

## Do You Deserve Special Treatment?

Well of course you do. If you're an honest, well-intentioned buyer or seller, you deserve the special treatment that a specialty site can offer. These sites, knowing they're going up against the Goliaths of the online auction world, work hard to earn the trust and respect of the community they're striving to develop. These sites often keep tabs on what sorts of items are presented for auction, are actively monitoring their communities to ensure only fair and honest trading is taking place, and are focused on providing the kind of information the community wants and needs to make the most of the shared passion. Knowing they're smaller is what keeps these sites working hard for you, and for you that's great news.

## AuctionGuy's Top Ten Specialty Auctions

By this point, you've probably gotten quite comfortable with what makes an auction good and what features and policies you should look for at an auction site. Remember, to get the best auction experience, be clear about how the auction site works, what auction types it supports, and what bidder and seller tools it provides. Be on the lookout for an easy-to-understand and easy-to-navigate site, and you'll usually have a better time and be in the company of more bidders and sellers.

So without further ado, AuctionGuy presents the following 10 specialty sites. They have an assortment of qualities that make for a good auction coupled with the benefit of specialization, making sites that focus on the auction-going experience for the discriminating enthusiast.

## Collecting Nation

Right out of the chute I'll tell you about a specialty site that's actually a con-glomeration of many different specialty sites all rolled into one—*that's* the specialty of Collecting Nation (**www.collectingnation.com**). Millions and millions of people love to collect, and an innovative site that specializes in collectors' interests while also diversifying the types of collections it promotes is special enough for me (see Figure 10-1).

Collecting Nation acts as a portal to many specialty sites that serve collectible interests from porcelain dolls to Pokémon, from teddy bears to Beanie Babies

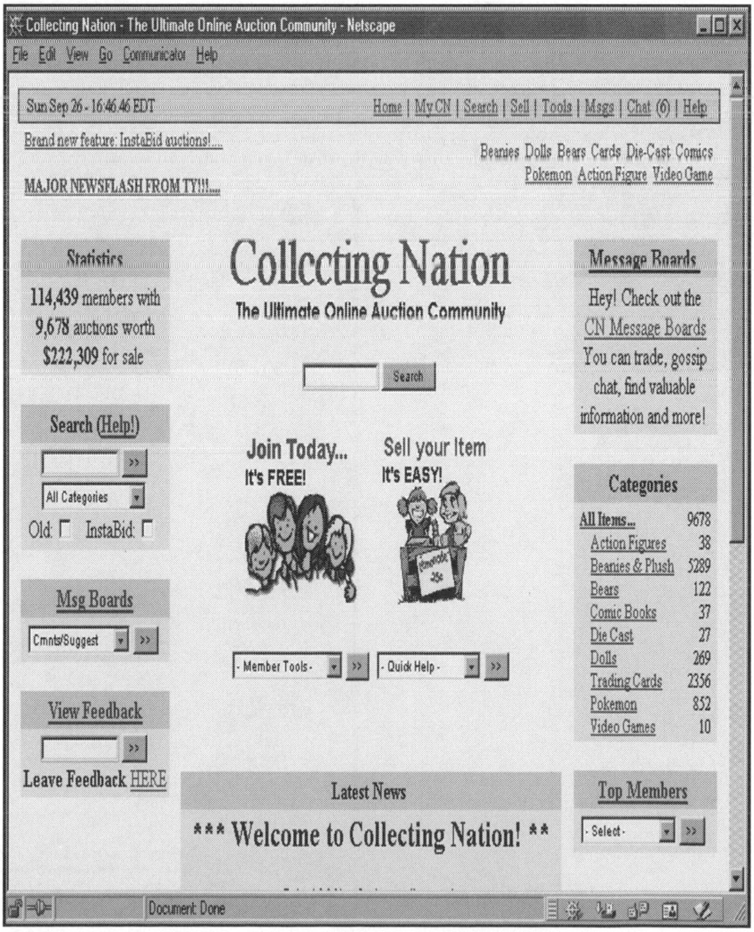

**Figure 10-1**

Looking to improve your national interest . . . in collectibles? Go to Collecting Nation.

(more on those next). Collecting Nation hosts many special "nations" where collectors with a particular passion can go to bid, trade, chat, and learn from one another. The site is relatively easy to navigate, but it is a bit lackluster in design. However, be prepared to find a decent selection of items in the different categories, and perhaps a category that you'll soon call home.

## Beanie Nation

So you may have guessed that Beanie Nation (**www.beanienation.com**) is one of the "nations" under the Collecting Nation umbrella, but it is also

Figure 10-2

Beanie Nation is perhaps the most popular of the nations accessible through the Collecting Nation portal. Visit it, and you'll see why.

regarded as the Number 1 Beanie Baby auction site online today (according to BeanieTop50.com). Therefore, knowing there is a huge population of Beanie collectors out there, don't waste any time—get to this site immediately (see Figure 10-2). Though it still suffers slightly from the overall Collecting Nation affliction of bland design, the content makes that an insignificant concern. If you love Beanies, go to Beanie Nation *now!*

## Just Glass

Approaching its second anniversary as of this writing, Just Glass (**www. justglass.com**) is an excellent example of a specialty auction site (see Figure 10-3). You'll find *just glass* and nothing else. Whether you collect carnival glass, Depression glass, kitchen glass, or even paperweights, Just Glass is a site that is clear in its mission.

The site offers a wide assortment of items in a well-developed listing of glass categories. You'll find chat boards and features that explain more about this site's love of all things glass.

## WineBid

Looking for a special wine for a special occasion? Have an extensive wine collection that needs a few holes filled? If you're looking to rub elbows and bid among some fine wine connoisseurs, then WineBid (**www.winebid.com**) is your online cellar (see Figure 10-4). Don't expect to find grocery store fare here. At WineBid, you'll see some of the finest, aged premium wines being managed by a site that delivers auction offerings every two weeks.

WineBid is proud of the fact that all of its inventory (owned or consigned) is inspected by wine experts to verify accuracy and all lots are stored in temperature-controlled facilities. The site charges a 12.5 percent commission for both buyers and sellers. That seems a bit lofty to me, but WineBid maintains that's one of the best commission rates in the wine industry. (And I guess *somebody's* gotta pay for all that inspection and storage!) Also expect each lot to carry a reserve price that is kept confidential throughout the course of the auction.

**Figure 10-3**

*Just Glass is where glass collectors can get together to talk about and deal in their passion without fear of breaking anything.*

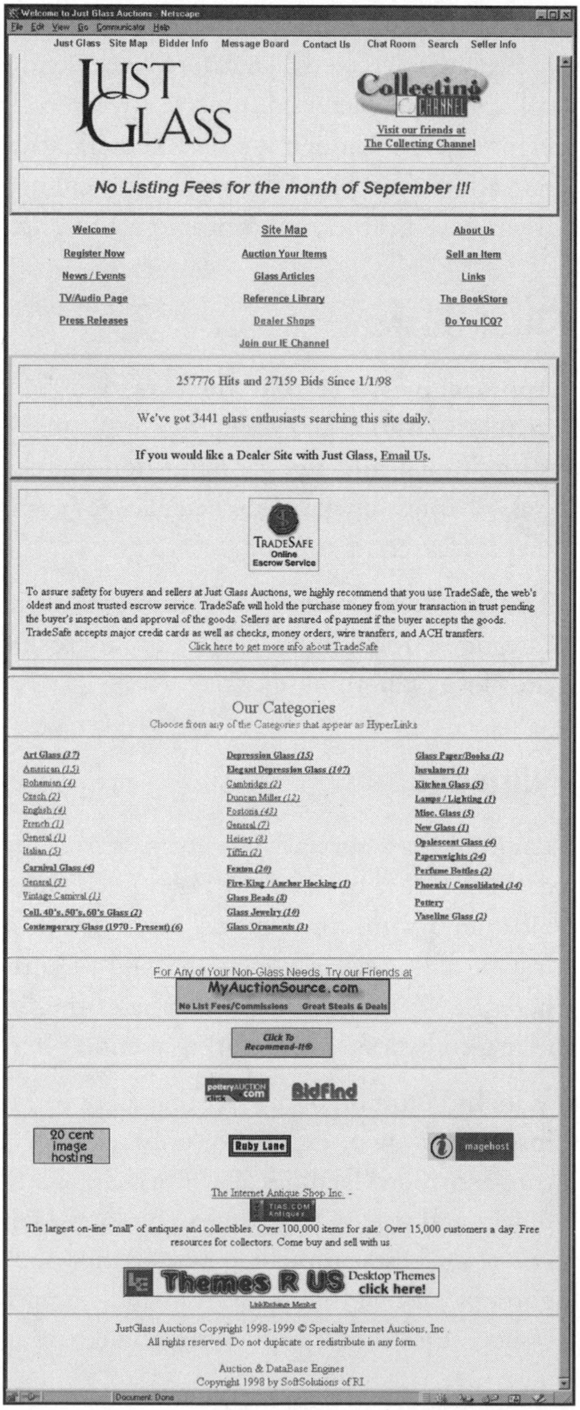

**Figure 10-4**
*Whether it's Chardonnay, a fine Port, or just about anything in between, WineBid is the best wine auction online today.*

If you're looking for a *spirited* auction and can appreciate the majesty of a vintage wine, WineBid is where you'll want to cast your next bid.

## Collectors Universe

Though this site might seem more general on the surface, it is actually another portal to an excellent variety of specialized collector's auction sites. Much like Collecting Nation, Collectors Universe (**www.collectors.com**) presents a good range of specialty sites in a useful front site that helps visitors navigate to their area of choice (see Figure 10-5). Don't forget to drop by the extensive *Resources* area, where you can find a terrific library of related feature articles. In the spirit of serving the specialized communities, Collector's Universe offers visitors many well-written articles that speak directly to their assorted fields of interest. There are 49 "universes," each geared to a specific major collectible market.

Figure 10-5

What are you collecting? Check Collectors.com for a portal to the specialty site that focuses on your collectible passion.

Figure 10-6

StampAuctions is the kind of specialty site philatelists have been longing for, but no longer.

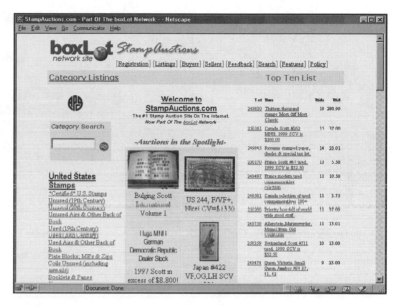

## StampAuctions

If you have a feeling about philately, then here's a site that focuses on all things stamp collectors love. This site is actually underwritten by BoxLot, another of the general auction sites. There's nothing general about StampAuctions (**www.stampauctions.com**), though—it's all stamps. The site has a nice presentation, and you'll find some comprehensive category listings that should put you in touch with the stamps missing from your collection.

## Tickets.com

Is Tina in town, but you've got no tickets? Is Pavarotti about to pass by, and you'll be left weeping through opera glasses? Is your favorite ball team about to take the field but the stadium's sold out? Don't fret—Tickets.com (**http://auction.tickets.com**) has come along to help ticket seekers and ticket sellers come together without all those messy allegations of scalping (see Figure 10-7). This is a nice site that's easy to navigate. A great feature is the ability to search for tickets by geographic area of the event. And if you've got tickets for the big show but the babysitter's going to be out of town, then you can sell your tickets online to make sure they go to an appreciative fan.

Figure 10-7

This site is just the ticket for buyers
and sellers of tix to music, museum,
and sporting events.

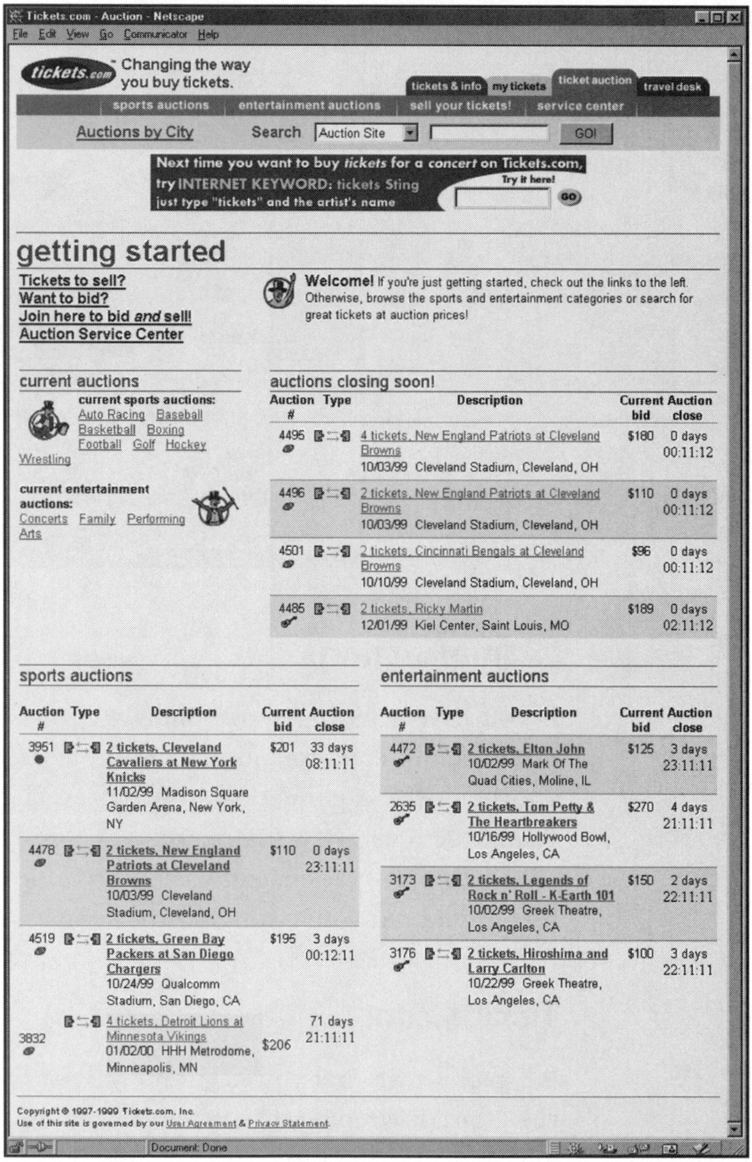

## Magic Auction

It's not just a cute name, and it's no illusion—this is a site that's devoted to the mystical, the mysterious, and the wonders of sleight of hand (see Figure 10-8). Magic Auction (**www.magicauction.com**) is a site that auctions all sorts of magic supplies, books, videos, vintage posters, and other peculiarities of prestidigitation. Magic Auction holds weekly auctions that end every Wednesday. If you're a hankering Houdini or a closet Copperfield, peek behind the curtain to see who's bidding and who's selling at Magic Auction. They even have their own site genie—*Zim zalabim!*

*Figure 10-8*

*If you have an interest in magic and illusion, be sure to see Magic Auction before all the great deals disappear. Poof!*

WELCOME TO

Magic Auction

TO CONTACT US

EMAIL - cwshop@nfis.com

THE PLACE FOR MAGICIANS TO BUY
OR SELL MAGIC AND ILLUSIONS

VISIT ANY AUCTION BELOW - NOW IN PROGRESS
ALL AUCTIONS END EVERY
WEDNESDAY 10:00 PM EASTERN TIME

| PREOWNED ILLUSIONS (8 PAGES) | STAGE & PLATFORM (3 PAGES) | MAGIC BOOKS (3 PAGES) | MAGIC VIDEOS (2 PAGES) |
| PREOWNED ILLUSIONS (Located outside USA) | MAGIC TABLES | CLOSE UP MAGIC (3 PAGES) | CARD MAGIC (2 PAGES) |
| STAGE & ILLUSION LIGHTS, SOUND ETC. | DOVE MAGIC | MENTAL MAGIC | COIN MAGIC |
| SILK & FLOWER MAGIC | MAGIC UTILITIES | COMEDY & KID SHOW | POSTERS |
| MAGIC JEWELRY | MAGIC SETS | VENTRILOQUISM | COLLECTORS MAGIC |
| UNDER CONSTRUCTION | HOW TO SELL YOUR MAGIC | HOW TO PLACE A BID | UNDER CONSTRUCTION |

## Pottery Auction

The clay man cometh . . . to Pottery Auction (**www.potteryauction.com**). Here's a specialty site that simply oozes with passion from its founder and CEO, Barry Brooks. By his own admission, Brooks is a "pottery nut" who loves well-turned (or otherwise formed) pottery art. His site has a well-executed design and is easy to navigate. Take some time to look over the site's policies—Brooks is big on authentication and honest business. That, in itself, is a beacon to all pottery lovers who are looking for a safe place to trade their favorite pottery items.

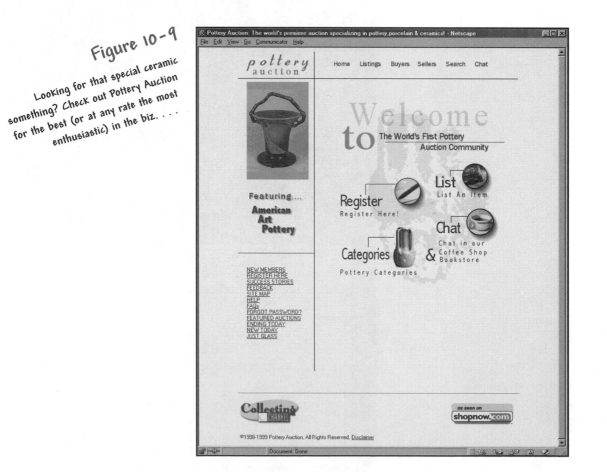

Figure 10-9

Looking for that special ceramic something? Check out Pottery Auction for the best (or at any rate the most enthusiastic) in the biz. . . .

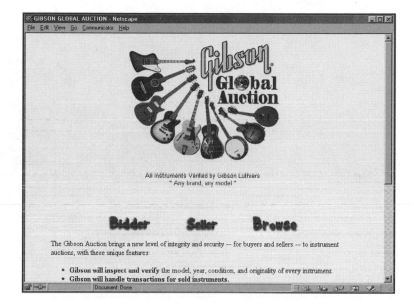

## Gibson Global Auction

Here's a site that really rocks. Whether you're looking for a new axe to wield at your band's next gig, or you're looking for a nice acoustic to play softly at the park, check out the wide variety of top-notch guitars available at Gibson Global Auction (**http://auction.gibson.com**)—and don't forget the banjos for all your foggy mountain breakdowns.

Gibson offers great services such as inspection and verification of all instruments sold at the site. It also manages the transaction on-site, too. Commissions are a bit steep, but the inventory you'll find will be music to your eyes.

## Bonus Site!—URLMerchant

This bonus 11th site is offered just because of its unique commodity: Internet domain names. In case you haven't heard, domain names are worth big bucks to whoever owns them. URLMerchant (**www.urlmerchant.com**) specializes in domain names that can have big potential with netizens. Think of sites like

Figure 10-11

URLMerchant is where you can bid on and buy the next big domain name.

www.buy.com, www.dictionary.com, and www.books.com. Those are site names that are easily remembered and are thus apt to capture the attention (and business) of Net surfers. Therefore, URLMerchant offers other potential site names that could be on the tips of Net goers' tongues in the very near future. Often the name is worth a bundle, and often the current name owner can make a bundle selling the name. That's what URLMerchant is all about.

## Hey AuctionGuy! There's Still So Many More!

You bet there's more, and maybe I've missed some of the sites that cater to your field of interest. I could never expect to detain everybody long enough to go over *all* of the sites out there. You're quite adept now at sifting through the sites yourself and should feel comfortable striking out to find the site that best serves your tastes.

# Part III

## After the Gavel

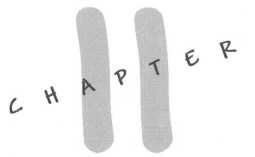
# When the Auction Ends

All good things must come to an end. Hopefully, when the good thing is an auction that closes, you've either bagged a great find, dealt a great deal—from one side or the other—or pocketed a decent profit. Whether you're buying or selling, the end of the auction marks the beginning of even more activity.

Not necessarily on your part, though. If you buy something at a merchant auction, you won't have to do a thing: the site will charge your credit card for your win and then arrange to ship your merchandise. Just like catalog shopping—all you have to do is open the box. And if you're a merchant selling at one of those sites, you probably have a whole staff (or at least a set of procedures) devoted to that sort of thing.

So this chapter is mainly about the person-to-person venues. There, the end of the auction is when many auction goers (buyers and sellers alike) get a bit anxious about closing the deal with a complete stranger who might be living across the state, across the country, or across the ocean. But never fear. These transactions happen every day, and you can perform them with ease just like everyone else.

# Keeping Track of Your Auctions

After the auction closes, you'll want to quickly assess your income or outlay. The key to your auction financial success is keeping track of monies coming and going. Don't expect the person on the other end to keep track of this stuff for you—your mother's not out there looking after you, and you run the risk of error if you let someone else call the shots for you.

Keeping track of auctions is really no big deal provided you stay with it from the outset. Whether buying or selling, you'll find several tools right at your fingertips at most auction sites, plus there are a few simple things you can do to keep your own auction records. Take a look at what buyers and sellers can and should do to keep track of their auction activity.

## Buyers

At the key auction sites I described in Part II, you'll find some variation of a *My Auction* tool. Essentially, these are auction organizers that pull data of your activity from the auction site's database. These tools show you which auctions you've bid in, which you've won, and which are still in progress. Some of the better tools also provide a running tally of how much money you've thrown on the table during the course of your bidding.

 **WARNING!** Danger, Diamond Jim! Those $20, $40, and $80 bids can add up faster than you can shout, *"I've won!"* If you're still new to online bidding and are working with a finite amount of funds, keep track of your bids at every auction site you use. It'll be a real eye-popper to find out you've committed a cool grand and the sellers are eager for you to pay up.

Take a look, then, at what I've recently been up to at eBay. That site offers the *My eBay* auction management tool. It provides the useful facts (or sobering truth) of your auction comings and goings (see Figure 11-1).

Each auction site offers a similar tool: Amazon.com Auctions has *Your Auctions*; Yahoo! Auctions has *My Auctions*; Onsale has *Bids, Orders, & Shipments*.

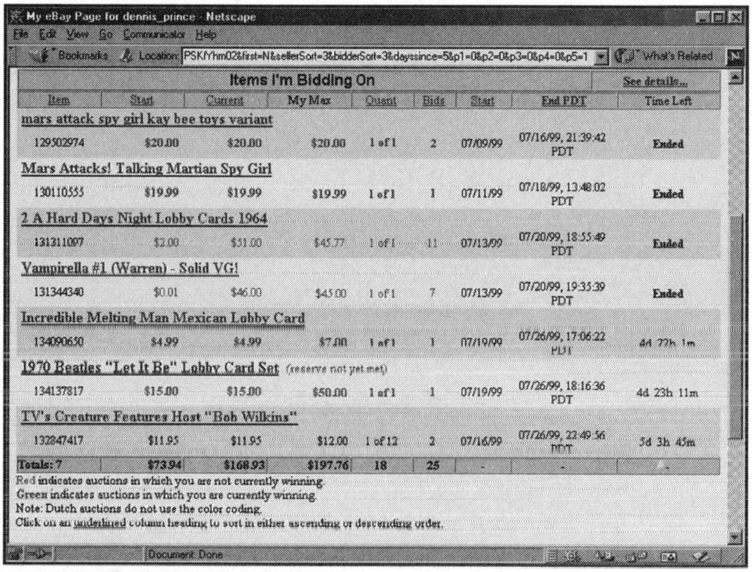

Figure 11-1

Be it exciting or sobering, a site's auction management tools give you the facts of how your bidding is adding up.

You get the idea. These tools help you quickly assess—or remind yourself of—how much you've been bidding out there. Remember, it's easy to click the mouse all hours of the night, so find out if you've been missing too much sleep. You'll usually find these tools listed on a home page tab strip, side column, or within the site map. Find them and use them.

You can also use the site search tools to get a quick look at what you've been buying. The person-to-person sites most often let you search on a bidder's user ID. Naturally, you would enter your own ID and decide if you want to view current bids or closed bids (I recommend both). The search results show where you've been throwing your ID around.

If this isn't enough for you, you can also do a bit of your own record keeping. I like to keep a spreadsheet of my bidding activity, just in case a site's server is unavailable or doesn't provide *all* the information I'd like to have regarding items I've bid on. Take a look at the end of this chapter and you'll find a model for your own personalized bidding activity tracker. Call it overcautious, but I always keep a few vital details just in case I need to refer back to a particular deal a month or more after the fact. What kinds of extra information? Well, how 'bout these:

- Seller's surname
- Seller's e-mail address
- Seller's street address
- Postage and insurance I paid
- Date I was notified by the seller
- Date I sent my payment
- Date seller shipped item (if communicated)
- Date I received the item

Sheesh! That sure seems like a lot to keep track of when you're only buying. Maybe, but what if an item you buy never arrives, or you've forgotten about it entirely (not a stretch of the imagination if you buy a lot of stuff at the auctions)? What if you've lost the contact information for the seller, and it's been more than a month or so by the time you remember about the purchase? This kind of information might come to your rescue someday.

**WARNING!** Attention bidders! Most auction sites only keep closed auction data available for a period of 30 days. After that, you'll have a difficult time retrieving the data you might want or need.

**GET A CLUE** For you businesspeople and resellers out there, these are the kind of records you'll need to keep if you plan to claim any of your auction purchases as business expenses or store inventory (for resale). You'll need full records of item costs including any postage, handling, and insurance you paid. This kind of data will become your ripcord when you find yourself in a dead fall in the tax auditor's office. Of course, check with your tax adviser in case you'll need even more details come tax time.

## Sellers

If you're at a site where you'll be selling your own stuff, then you especially need to keep good records. Remember, the seller is in the so-called driver's seat when it comes time to close the auction. Sellers especially need to have all the accurate details of their auctions.

Again, the auction management tools you'll find at various auction sites also help sellers keep track of their activities. Figure 11-2 shows the same *My eBay* tool (I've been spending most of my time there lately), only this time it has information on the auctions I've been hosting.

These tools work well for sellers, and the sites often have search capabilities for sellers to look up their auction standings on the fly, but this clearly isn't enough information to constitute good sales records. So it's off to an alternate form of record keeping once again.

**Figure 11-2**

When I'm the auctioneer, auction management tools help me keep track of my auctions and help me prepare for end-of-auction action.

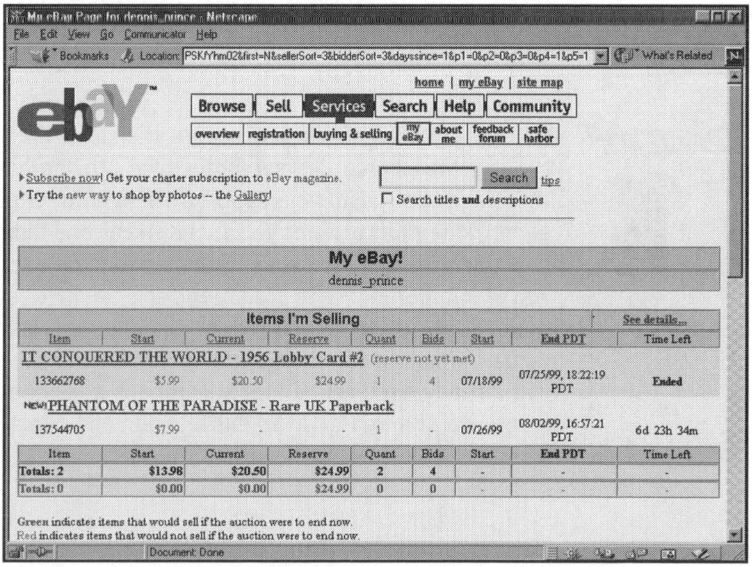

When I sell, I use a spreadsheet to keep track of all the item details the site tools provide, but I also keep track of a few other key elements:

- High bidder's surname

- High bidder's street address or post office box

- Date bidder was notified about payment

- Date bidder responded that payment is being sent

- Date payment was received

- Method of payment (money order, personal check, or whatever)

- Insurance requested?

- Date item shipped

- Shipping method and tracking number (if any)

Again, this might seem like a lot of information to track and store, but if ever something goes awry (especially when beyond a month's time of the actual exchange) you'll wish you had this information. It will help you recreate the transaction and guide you through problem resolution in case you need to get in touch with the buyer or if the buyer gets in touch with you regarding an oversight or dispute.

 **IN MY MIND**   Actually, this sort of record keeping is more than just a C.Y.A. effort. In the past, these records have helped me provide better customer service and establish better customer rapport. Having many repeat customers (those who are interested in the kinds of items you auction) is a good thing. When you can recognize individual customers personally (aside from their auction user IDs), you show your customers that you remember them and are organized enough to recall how the previous exchange with them went. Often, a good repeat customer will get little perks from me, the most welcome being waiving the personal check clearance period (for reasonable amounts) if I've already established that someone is a trusted customer. Folks really respond well when you can treat them in this manner, and it makes for better auction relations.

**WARNING!** All warm fuzzies aside, understand that you might need this sort of information to work out a disputed buyer claim. If a buyer contacts you weeks or months after you believed the exchange had ended, claiming the item never arrived, you'll be scrambling to get the facts of how, when, and where you shipped the item. I've headed off potential conflicts many times with buyers who, far from being dishonest, simply lost track of the items I shipped. Believe it or not, one fellow confessed that the item I sent to him had mysteriously found its way under his sofa. Glad I was prepared with the facts or we could've been feuding about that one until spring cleaning finally rolled around.

## Basic End-of-Auction Rules & Etiquette

Now let me explain how to get the ball rolling when the auction ends. Whether you're buyer or seller, there are some basic understandings among auction goers concerning the exchange of goods for money. Begin, then, with these general philosophies, guidelines, and *"rules of engagement"* when kicking off the end-of-auction transaction at a person-to-person site.

- **Be responsive.** If you're buying, don't keep a seller guessing whether you intend to honor your bid or when payment might arrive. Be prepared to respond quickly when the seller contacts you requesting payment. Don't let the seller's message go unanswered or (worse yet) unread. Hop to it, and let that seller know you're ready and anxious to close the deal. If you're selling, let the buyer know that you've received payment and when you'll be shipping the item. Remember that buyers take a leap of faith when they send their money out there, hoping there's an Honest John or Jane at the other end. Lots of communication on both ends can eliminate lots of mix-ups and hassles. Communication is *king* in online auction transactions. *Hail to the king!*

- **Be punctual.** This is much like the previous point, only with money and goods instead of talk. Buyers should pay promptly and help both themselves and the seller close the deal as quickly and cleanly as possible. You'll both be happier, and you'll be less likely to be bumped from winning bidder status by sending payment in an expeditious fashion. Equally, sellers should ship promptly and do so when they say they will. Like expectant parents waiting for the stork to arrive, buyers are eager to receive their package of joy; try not to keep them waiting longer than necessary.

- **Be flexible.** Chances are you're not dealing with a business. It helps to show some understanding when dealing with a private individual, both when you're waiting for an item to be shipped to you and when you're waiting to receive a buyer's payment. As long as the deal hasn't gotten out of hand or seemingly been disregarded at the other end, understand that life goes on regardless of auctions, and little bumps and slowdowns occasionally arise. Keep the lines of friendly communication open, and provide an honest explanation if the exchange has been unexpectedly delayed.

- **Be polite and professional.** Nothing helps a deal go better than a dose of good manners. The respect you give will usually be reciprocated. It's as simple as that and applies to buyers and sellers equally.

GET A CLUE    Remember, these tips won't necessarily apply at a merchant site or a high-end site. Read those sites' rules before you bid, though, just so there are no surprises.

If you think this all sounds like common sense, you're right. But if it's common sense, why write it down? Well, in my experience, the thrill of the auction can often obscure common sense and reasonable expectations. It's terrific that sellers are excited about their auction income and buyers are thrilled with their auction winnings, but don't forget that you're still dealing with people through all of this—regular people like you and me. They're not all Web developers, professional merchants, or even heartless crooks. These are folks drawn to the auctions just as you are, and by and large they're doing their best to make it a good experience. Brush up on your manners and set realistic expectations. Most likely, you'll make a friend or two in the process.

## Notification

So when it's all over, who's got the ball? Is it the buyer, the seller, or someone else you haven't yet met? This is an area where some folks get kind of shy—Mom always said don't talk to strangers. But, using some methods you can rely on to work in most every exchange, you'll be yakking it up and successfully communicating with other auction goers in no time.

So who breaks the ice? Usually, it's the auction site. If you'll recall from the site reviews in Part II, I explained how most sites will automatically generate and distribute end-of-auction e-mail messages to the seller and high bidder.

**GET A CLUE**   Remember, if you've been bidding and winning at merchant sites, the end-of-auction message you receive will usually also bring your billing and shipping invoice. The site has already charged your credit card, and your package is probably well on its way by the time you read your e-mail.

In the person-to-person scenario, the end-of-auction e-mail message notifies buyer and seller of the final bid price and provides each party with the other's e-mail address so they can finish the deal.

Though the auction site has officially opened the notification process, the close of the deal hasn't truly begun until the seller and buyer start communicating. The seller needs to spring into action and contact the high bidder to arrange for payment and shipment of the auctioned item. This should be done quickly (within no more than 72 hours of the auction's close, but preferably within 24 hours) to establish the high bidder's trust and confidence. The bidder is going to be eager to get the prize and will be anxiously awaiting information about how and where to send payment. Therefore, a good seller who's been tracking the auction closely will anticipate the auction's end and will be poised to begin the final transaction.

OK, all you sellers out there: here's where you make your first impression on the buyer about the kind of businessperson you'll be. Fast and friendly, punctual and professional, the initial end-of-auction notification *you* send will set the tone for the rest of the deal. Comb your hair, straighten your collar, and put your best foot forward. Customer service counts here and, if you do well, your customers will most likely feel confident about bidding on other items that you may be auctioning.

But what about the buyers? Don't they have rules to follow at the point of end-of-auction notification? Sometimes yes, and sometimes no. Most often, the buyer will need to sit tight and await payment instructions. The best piece of advice I can give buyers is to *be patient*. Though you're probably still strutting about the house, proud as a peacock about your auction win and anxious to get your item, you'll need to keep in mind that the seller might have other customers to serve.

Some buyers will jump the gun and e-mail the seller the moment the auction has ended and they have been declared victorious. Though this isn't grossly wrong, it is indicative of an overzealous buyer or a general auction newbie. Give the seller the customary 72 hours to notify you of your win. If, however, three days pass and you've yet to hear from the seller, then it's perfectly acceptable to inquire about sending payment and receiving the item.

## Your Key to Successful Communication

So the auction's ended, and both buyer and seller are poised to begin talking. What you say and how you say it is just as important as your punctuality. Don't scoff—many people are concerned about what to put in an e-mail message and how to be sure it's read with the intended tone.

The best, and safest, bet is to adopt a professional style: simple, clear, and direct. If you're a seller who needs to notify a buyer that payment is due, try something like this:

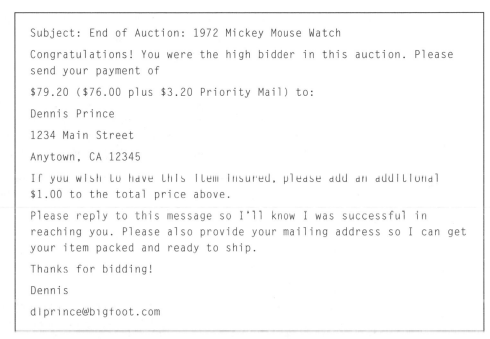

Subject: End of Auction: 1972 Mickey Mouse Watch

Congratulations! You were the high bidder in this auction. Please send your payment of

$79.20 ($76.00 plus $3.20 Priority Mail) to:

Dennis Prince

1234 Main Street

Anytown, CA 12345

If you wish to have this item insured, please add an additional $1.00 to the total price above.

Please reply to this message so I'll know I was successful in reaching you. Please also provide your mailing address so I can get your item packed and ready to ship.

Thanks for bidding!

Dennis

dlprince@bigfoot.com

See? No big deal and no fancy language. It's a simple, direct statement of the facts and your expectations. The addition of *Congratulations* and *Thanks for bidding* add a friendliness to the message and help the bidder feel good about bidding on your item and more secure that a friendly exchange will occur. But at the core of the message, it is clear how much the item will cost (with all postage and insurance fees) and where the payment should be sent. Some sellers will even add an additional line such as

Payment should be received within 10 days of this notice to maintain high-bidder privilege.

This is really up to the seller, but buyers shouldn't be offended if they're given such a policy to follow. Sellers need to quickly close up their auction exchanges, and they don't have much time for chasing down slow-to-pay bidders. In some cases, bidders will even try to wiggle out of the deal entirely (known as *deadbeat bidders*). A seller who has inventory to move needs a reasonable

amount of time to know if the buyer's going to make good on the bid or if the item should be awarded to the next-highest bidder (or possibly put up for auction again).

**IN MY MIND** Some folks think a seller who states such a policy is being unreasonable. Actually, sales policy is up to the seller to establish at person-to-person auctions. Provided that sellers agree to sell at the winning bid price, they're pretty much left to their own policies regarding how they want their trades to go.

Of course, this doesn't give the seller carte blanche to make up bizarre rules or add a bunch of exploitative fees (handling, storage, transport, and so on). Sellers who operate that way often feel a hit in the form of reduced business. But the seller *does* have to draw some line of sales and shipping policy.

The best bet is for a seller to clearly state sales policies right in the auction ads and for buyers to be sure they fully understand and agree to those policies *before they bid*. A bid is an acceptance of the seller's policies.

To tie this one up, a seller who imposes unreasonable policies without having previously stated them is probably in for a disgruntled buyer and bad business on the auction site. Just adopt and adhere to a standard set of reasonable rules, and all will be fine.

## Post-Auction Prep Work

Just a few more notes about post-auction activity. When the auction's over and you've made contact with the other party, you'll need to take some actions to help the deal go smoothly.

If you dealt at a merchant site, be sure your credit card has plenty of "buying power" left in it. Also, if your card has recently been renewed, be sure to update your account data at the merchant site (the site will get a "transaction denied" response from your card issuer otherwise—not good). And if you're dealing at a site where you're going to send money in some form, be sure you're financially prepared to do so. Actually, you'll want to be sure of your financial solvency before you ever place a bid, but especially when the auction's ended and it's time to pay the piper. Be ready to send that payment out the moment you hear from the current proprietor of your newfound treasure.

If you're a seller and the buyer has indicated that payment is on the way, get to work prepping that item for shipment. Don't wait until the payment arrives (or worse, let it sit around for a few days) to start pulling together shipping supplies and packing the item up. And definitely be sure to make note of the buyer's shipping address when the payment arrives if you don't already have it nailed down. (In your spiffy spreadsheet, maybe?) If you're even slightly over-burdened or otherwise disorganized, that buyer's shipping address can often disappear without a trace—another reason I request it in my end-of-auction notification e-mail.

So get your house in order, be ready for the end of the auction, then get ready for the big exchange . . . coming up in Chapter 12.

## Bidding Activity—Vital Details

Seller's surname: _____

Seller's e-mail address: _____

Seller's street address: _____

Postage and insurance I paid: _____

Date I was notified by the seller: _____

Date I sent my payment: _____

Date seller shipped item: _____

Date I received the item: _____

Additional information: _____

_____

_____

_____

_____

_____

## Bidding Activity—Vital Details

Seller's surname: _____

Seller's e-mail address: _____

Seller's street address: _____

Postage and insurance I paid: _____

Date I was notified by the seller: _____

Date I sent my payment: _____

Date seller shipped item: _____

Date I received the item: _____

Additional information: _____

_____

_____

_____

_____

_____

_____

# Money, Merchandise, and the Mail Carrier

So now you're on to it—paying for stuff, shipping stuff, or waiting for stuff to arrive. Though the auctions sometimes seem like a twist on PC gaming, it's real business going on out there. Once the cyberplay has ended, the real world takes over. For those less experienced in long-distance dealing, this part of the auction can be a bit perplexing and possibly perturbing, but only the first couple of times around. Get a few experiences under your belt, and you'll be singing the praises of online auctioning, mail order, and customer satisfaction, guaranteed.

## Which Comes First?

The usual question at this stage of the deal is "which comes first—the money or the merchandise?" Does the buyer first send the payment, or does the seller first send the item or neither or both or what? Ooh, yes. Trust becomes a key factor at this critical stage in the exchange. If you were paying attention in Chapter 11, you'll see that I clued you in to the way things normally flow at this point: the buyer pays first.

Sure, this could be cause for apprehension. The buyer and seller are usually strangers to one another. How can a buyer be sure that the seller won't abscond with the payment and disappear without a trace? Trust. In the post-auction notification courting, the buyer and seller politely size each other up, determining through professionalism, punctuality, and overall attitude whether either can be counted on to complete the exchange quickly and fairly. But even before that, bidders and sellers are encouraged (and I encourage you, too) to check out each other's feedback on those person-to-person auction sites. There, you'll find some pretty telling commentary regarding whether said auction-goer is on the level or on the take. And if either party has any doubt, it's a good idea to communicate before the auction is scheduled to end. In that way, both will have some idea of the other person's commitment and style. Don't be overwhelmed, though. These exchanges go off without any trouble 99.9 percent of the time. You'll just need to exercise some good old-fashioned trust and faith, preferably based on a foundation of testimonies found in the other person's auction feedback profile.

**WARNING!** *Negative! If I'm planning on sending in excess of several hundred dollars or whatever, I'm not prepared to throw that up to the winds of chance.* Fair enough. There are ways to conduct a high-dollar deal with private individuals where you both can get the comfort and security you both deserve. That information will be coming up a bit later in this chapter.

Remember, at the merchant sites and some other venues, your credit card will be on file and will be automatically charged upon the completion of the auction. There's nothing else for you to do but wait for your item to arrive (as well as your credit card bill, don't forget about that). But if you're going the person-to-person route, the standard rule is that the buyer always prepays.

For the seller, your biggest responsibility at this time is to provide as much comfort and assurance to the trusting buyer as you can; that is, if you hope to build a good rapport with this and other potential bidders at the online auctions. Your good communication at the end of the auction served as the solid foundation upon which you'll quickly complete a successful transaction.

As seller, don't be lulled into thinking that just because you hold the item and can set terms of payment, a buyer will simply roll over for you. Understand that many buyers are also sellers (and vice versa), and most know how the deal should work. If a seller acts lazy, unfairly, or otherwise less than satisfactory,

you can bet the buyer will have something to say about it—and will usually go ahead and say it loud and long in the site's feedback area.

So, although the buyer is expected to pay first in an auction exchange, both sides should actually be progressing at an even pace (paying, packing, communicating) to ensure the transaction goes through smoothly.

## How Would You Like to Pay Today?

So if you're the buyer, you're going to be paying up front for your goodies. The next question is *how* will you pay? There are several ways to make your payment, each of which can match the unique circumstances of the particular auction (price, location, familiarity with the seller, and so on).

As I've already said, the seller can largely control the method of payment they'll accept. That should clearly be stated in the seller's auction listing before the auction even begins. Remember, if you don't like the seller's terms, don't bid. But, assuming the seller posted reasonable terms, move ahead and prepare to pay.

**GET A CLUE** OK, OK. What *are* "reasonable terms"? Glad you asked. Online auctioning, having gone on for many years now, has developed some basic rules and guidelines, written and unwritten. In regard to terms of payment at the person-to-person venues, here's the sort of thing you should encounter:

Buyer will pre-pay, plus postage. Buyer will be responsible for additional insurance costs, if insurance is requested. For payment made via money order or cashier's check, item will ship within 24 hours of payment receipt. Personal checks gladly accepted, but must wait 10 days to clear before item is shipped.

There are variations, but these are generally the kind of payment terms you should expect to encounter. There's more discussion of each payment option, plus some additional options, coming up in this chapter.

Although the seller can dictate the terms of payment they're willing to accept, that shouldn't mean the buyer is without options. Wise sellers leave buyers several payment types to choose from. So as a buyer, here's a few things you should consider when you decide how you'll be paying today:

- **Who are you dealing with?** Always check the seller's feedback rating and get a feel for this person during the post-auction (or preferably the pre-auction) communication. See what others have said about this seller and use your own gut instinct when you begin talking. Your level of trust can drive which form of acceptable payment you'll choose.

- **How much are you paying?** Of course, the total cost of the item you've won will help determine how you'll be paying. If you're forking over less than $20, you're apt to be relatively flexible in the way you'll pay. If you're paying into the hundreds or higher, you'll want to find a method that will protect your outlay and even protect the seller from any mishaps—a good seller can be unjustly accused of wrong-doing when a high-value money order gets lost in the mail. You'll learn how to best protect your payment in the upcoming discussion.

- **What's most convenient and economical for you?** Why not? As a buyer, you're trying to keep your final costs down and avoid jumping through hoops to get that payment out. Remember, you're already on the hook to pay for postage costs. Any other add-ons just drive up your outlay and can often turn a great deal into a mediocre deal after the final tally. Personal checks are free, and you can write them at your kitchen table. Money orders usually cost a dollar or two, and you'll need to go to the post office, grocery store, convenience store, or wherever to get them. Don't forget that you'll need to pay cash (real dollars or debit card) to get one—you can't write a check for a money order. Cashier's checks can sometimes cost up to $5 and are typically only offered at banks or other financial institutions. Credit card payments might incur a charge fee (from the seller, not the issuer—the issuer charges the seller, who may turn around and look to get the money back from you) but they are convenient to use, provided you understand who's at the other end—a private individual with a merchant account, a small business, or what? Weigh these costs and conveniences with the level of payment protection you need, and choose whichever method you find safest, easiest, and most economical.

- **Is the payment traceable or recoverable?** This will actually be covered in the next section of this chapter, but it's definitely worth mentioning here. The biggest issue is often not the payment itself but the tracing of the

mailing of the payment. If you are at all uncertain about the safe delivery or receipt of your payment, register your letter so that a signature is required of the seller upon receipt. A seller who signs for your letter and then tries to skip town with your moolah has just committed major mail fraud. Bad ju-ju, friends.

■ **Is this an international transaction?** Expect that at person-to-person venues, you can easily and frequently engage in a transaction across countries. It's nothing to be feared or avoided (for either buyers or sellers). The usual payment for international deals is with an International Money Order. These are available at your local post office and usually cost around $3. Some international buyers send cash to the U.S. for their auction purchases. Cash is *not* a very safe method, for obvious reasons. However, if you're a seller and an international buyer does send cash, give that transaction the highest priority and lots of communication to be sure you're never accused of having taken the money and run.

## Protecting Your Payment

The different methods of payment all have their own advantages and disadvantages. Here's a brief look at how protected you are in each scenario.

## Cash

Well, I'll get this one out of the way right now. Cash is the single most unprotected way to pay. With cash, you have no recourse to trace your money, and it can be easily misplaced at the seller's end. (*"Oh, sorry dear. I needed a few dollars for groceries so I picked up that twenty on the counter. Was it for something special?"*) My advice: don't use cash. If you receive cash, ship that item quickly and track it every step of the way.

**IN MY MIND** *Hey AuctionGuy, what if I'm only spending a few bucks? Why can't I just grab some bills from my wallet and send them out?* Well, you can, and if you feel secure with the seller or don't mind risking a few bucks, then go ahead. But it's just as easy to send a personal check. Of course, this is only *my* advice. In all transactions, the final judgment and decision is yours.

## Personal Checks

For items of reasonable price (less than $50), you should feel comfortable using a personal check. You can trace clearance of your check through your bank or in your bank statement. The seller needs to endorse your check before it can be deposited, so you'll have proof positive that payment was received. If a check truly gets lost in the mail, both buyer and seller can agree the buyer should stop payment on the misdirected mail and arrange for another attempt.

Personal checks are the most-used method of payment among buyers. For them, it's much like paying a bill. Of course, buyers need to understand that sellers will wait for the check to clear before shipping the item. Among buyers, this is generally understood. If ever a buyer's check bounces, for whatever reason, the buyer had better be prepared to do some quick apologies and reimburse the seller not only for the price of the item but also the returned check charge the bank slapped on the rubber remittance.

## Money Orders and Cashier's Checks

For sellers, these are probably the most-preferred methods of payment. Why? Since money orders and cashier's checks need to be bought with cash (or the virtual equivalent), they're truly money in the bank. Money orders and cashier's checks don't bounce, and a seller can confidently ship an item immediately upon receipt of this sort of payment. That's good news for the buyer: the item arrives quicker. It's good news for the seller: the transaction is completed quicker. It's just good all around.

For the buyer's protection, money orders have unique check numbers that can be traced by the issuer, and they are printed (stamped) so the payable value can't be altered in any way. But what about the seller—can a money order or cashier's check be fraudulent? Unless the buyer has an elaborate basement process for printing counterfeits, probably not. The buyer can't cancel a money order or cashier's check after the fact. The only way a buyer can receive funds back for these checks is if the original check is returned to the point of issue. Therefore, the seller can't be ripped off for shipping an item before depositing the check.

# Credit Card Payment

Clearly, if you're bidding at merchant sites or some other "managed payment" sites (those that handle payment for items won), your credit card is usually how payment will be managed. At person-to-person sites, you'll encounter small business owners (antique dealers, collectible shops, or whatever) who have a business license and established merchant account for acceptance of credit card payment. Private individuals can sometimes accept credit cards, but those transactions have to be processed through credit establishments. Since statistics reveal that buyers tend to spend more than double of what they originally budgeted if they can pay via credit card, consider using the online and offline businesses that enable private individuals to safely and securely process credit card transactions (such as Billpoint.com or CCNow.com). Many auction sites are also working to establish on-site services or partnership services that allow sellers and buyers to easily and securely manage credit card payments without having to independently source out a third-party business.

But for the matter at hand, using a credit card is a good news/bad news sort of thing. We all know how credit card numbers can be used illegally by the kid swiping carbon slips from the checkout stand trash, or how phone solicitors can fraudulently obtain credit card numbers from the people they call. Buyers should understand who they're dealing with before providing a credit card number. However, credit card issuers are excellent about intervening when a charge dispute comes into play. Most often, card holders can request the issuer work with the "merchant" who billed the card, unraveling any funny business that could be going on. Credit card fraud is also serious stuff.

Buyers should expect a seller will process a credit card payment prior to sending the merchandise. It only takes a few minutes in most cases, and the seller will quickly determine if the card information provided is accurate. But to the buyer's benefit, many card issuers also provide additional *buyer's protection policies*—such things as replacing damaged goods or automatically extending manufacturer warranties (usually only available when purchasing from a merchant site that offers manufacturer's warranties on the items it sells).

All in all, credit card payments are convenient for buyers and the sellers who choose to accept them. Just keep an eye on the bill the same way you keep an eye on your auction site bidding.  It adds up fast.

## Escrow Services

Escrow is a terrific way to manage high-dollar purchases at person-to-person auction sites. Recall that Giant Insect kit I showed you in Chapter 7 (Figure 7-2). Well, that was one 'spensive item, and the seller and I agreed to use the online escrow service, *i-Escrow*, to manage the deal. Though I had no reason to distrust the seller, an item like that was almost too good to be true. I felt the extra protection was reasonable.

In a nutshell, an escrow works like this:

1.  The buyer and seller establish an online escrow transaction at an escrow site (i-Escrow and TradeSafe are the biggest names today).

2.  The buyer and seller agree on the terms of the escrow (who pays postage, who pays escrow commission, how long the item inspection period will be).

3.  The buyer sends the high bid payment to the escrow service (using check, money order, or credit card).

4.  The escrow service lets the seller know the buyer's payment is now in the escrow trust.

5.  The seller sends the auctioned item *directly* to the buyer by means of traceable delivery (USPS registered, UPS, or whatever).

6.  The seller provides the shipment tracking number to the escrow service for the item shipped.

7.  The buyer receives the item and accepts it, if satisfied, within the stated inspection period time window (usually two days).

8.  Upon buyer's acceptance, the escrow service releases the buyer's payment to the seller.

Yes, there is a commission to pay for using an escrow service (usually in the neighborhood of 3 percent to 5 percent of the item value). Though no one's looking for more cost add-ons to the auction, when you climb into the big dollars, it might be good (and relatively cheap) insurance.

The real benefit of escrow is that the buyer gets a reasonable period of time to inspect the item to be sure it matches its description at the auction. If it's genuine, everything's fine; if it's bogus, bail out. Buyers can reject an item and arrange to return it (in the same condition received) to get their money back out of the escrow account.

For the seller, escrow protects against a buyer's damaging or swapping an item received and then dishonestly returning it "as received" to the seller for a refund. The seller is also protected from a dishonest buyer who receives an item but contends it never arrived. The package tracking system determines when the item arrived and who signed for it. If a buyer is delinquent in releasing payment to the seller, the escrow service automatically releases funds to the seller once the agreed inspection period has elapsed.

Escrow really works. It requires a little extra effort and will likely add an extra week to the transaction. However, having used it several times, I've been pleased with the outcome when working through high-value exchanges.

WARNING! Be aware that some escrow users, sellers in particular, have complained of slow payment from the escrow providers. Apparently, sometimes the escrow site tends to dilly-dally a bit when getting that payment out. Check with the escrow service before you decide to open an escrow transaction. Contact their customer service to clarify how quickly a seller can expect to receive a released payment and what penalties the escrow site will absorb if the payment is delayed for any reason.

IN MY MIND   I've yet to be disappointed by an escrow service, but I can't deny the testimony I've heard from others who have been less than dazzled by the outcome. Having done some investigation of my own, I've learned the escrow services have heard the customer complaints and are working hard to provide premiere service. If ever you're dissatisfied with such a service, let 'em know. They need your endorsement, your support, and your business. Without it, they're sunk.

Oh, and by the way, that Giant Insect transaction went off just fine for both seller and buyer. The item was exactly what I'd been looking for. The seller was pleased to have learned about escrow services and now adds them to his list of payment methods.

## Does Anyone Still Use COD?

How many times have you heard on TV, "*No CODs allowed*?" That's because most businesses want your money up front. In all my years of buying and selling at auctions, I've yet to use COD (cash on delivery). Like escrow, COD carries a usage cost that needs to be negotiated between the buyer and seller. As with an escrow, the buyer has to pay someone before getting hold of the goods, but will be assured that the goods do exist (or at least the package containing them does). In this case, the buyer pays the package carrier and the carrier, in turn, reimburses the seller for the item. Contrary to popular belief, using COD *does not* allow a buyer to inspect an item before paying the carrier. The carrier will demand payment *before* handing the item over. COD isn't particularly bad, but it's rare to see it used any more.

## Speaking of Payment . . .

By the way, how's the communication going? Remember the sensitivity of the payment process. This is no time to get lax in your two-way communication. Both buyer and seller could get anxious during the "money stage" of the transaction, so a good dialog is necessary to keep both minds at ease. The buyer should clearly communicate when payment has been sent. Something simple and direct like this:

```
Subject: Payment sent: 1972 Mickey Mouse Watch

Hi Dennis!

Just wanted to let you know my payment of $79.20 is on the way in
the form of a money order. Please let me know when you receive it
and when you'll be shipping the watch to me.

Thanks!

Mark Mallard

makrmaldrill@buyer.net
```

A simple e-mail message like this lets a seller know you're holding up your end of the bargain and are committed to completing the deal quickly and smoothly.

At the same time, you're also setting the expectation that you'll be notified when your payment is received and when the item will be shipped, putting the ball back in the seller's court to hold up their end of the deal as expeditiously as you have. So when the seller receives payment, it's their turn to keep the dialog alive:

```
Subject: Payment received: 1972 Mickey Mouse Watch

Hi Mark!

I received your payment today. Thanks for sending it so quickly.
Since you've paid with a money order, I'll be able to ship the
watch out to you with tomorrow's mail. It will be traveling via
USPS Priority Mail.

Thanks for helping this exchange to run smoothly. I hope you'll be
pleased with the watch. Please let me know when it arrives.

Hope we can do business again soon.

Best,

Dennis Prince

dlprince@bigfoot.com
```

More good dialog here. The buyer is assured that payment arrived safely, and the seller is ready to ship the item. It's important (though often overlooked) to let the buyer know how the item will be shipped. Some carriers have restrictions on how they can deliver items; UPS, for example, can't deliver to post office boxes. But however you ship the item, always tell the buyer which carrier you're using so they'll know what to keep a lookout for. This is especially necessary when an item is sent insured or registered—the buyer will need to be available to sign for the package or be able to visit the carrier's depot to pick it up.

Now, also in the spirit of good communication, the seller asks for confirmation from the buyer when the package arrives. That shows not only that the seller is interested in seeing the transaction come to completion, but also that they're concerned with the buyer's satisfaction. That spells good customer service in my book and is often a successful invitation for future business.

# Ship Shape

Here, the ball is clearly in the seller's court. The seller has received the buyer's payment and the buyer is excitedly awaiting that coveted prize. It would be a shame if what arrived was some bashed-up, broken-up wad of cardboard and duct tape that only indicated the item, somewhere inside the mess, was a goner.

It doesn't have to be this way, though. Shipping items is easy these days. Even the novice seller can ship items safely and securely, looking like a pro in the process. There are plenty of helpful supplies out there to make shipping auction items as simple as sealing an envelope (no licking required).

## Assessing the Item

Of course, you can't tell how to ship anything until you know what it is you're shipping. Size of an item, inherent value, and fragility all play a part in how an item should be packaged. Take a look at each of these characteristics and see how you might decide to prep an item for the journey to its new home.

- **Size of the Item.** Sometimes, size does matter. When shipping, size is what determines what sort of shipping materials you should use. Small to medium-sized items (like a book, a CD, or a video) are easy to ship safely. Smaller boxes are readily available that are quite sturdy and hold up well in transit. A little cushioning around the item (such as bubble pack or packing peanuts) usually guarantee safe passage. Larger items—framed art, sculpture, anything generally larger than a board game—require larger boxes and more interior cushioning or may even require the services of a professional packaging service. Remember that the larger the box gets, the weaker the cardboard is likely to be, plus there's more of it to be dropped, kicked, stacked, or otherwise mishandled. Don't be afraid to call in the pros if you fear you can't guarantee safe delivery by your own efforts.

**WARNING!** Let the buyer know if something's changed in the way you'll be shipping the item. If it's an unusual item, the buyer will probably already have inquired about your shipping arrangements. (You will, won't you, buyers?) If the original shipping method or costs change during the packing preparation, be sure to discuss it with the buyer to determine if there are any further circumstances that need to be understood, accounted for, or paid for. Keep talking, folks.

- **Value of the Item.** Treat it with loving kindness, especially if it commands a king's ransom. Naturally, you'll want to insure an item of high value (with the buyer's consent unless you, as seller, are footing the bill), but the best kind of insurance is the kind you'll never claim. Expensive items should be packaged appropriately, adding additional fortification or cushioning to protect the item from mishap. Be especially aware that insurance claims will only be honored *if* an item was properly packaged in the first place.

  But if it's a lower-value item, don't go bananas boxing it up to withstand mortar attack. True, you should pack it up for safe delivery, but overpacking an item could make it excessively heavy and result in postage charges (charged by weight) more costly than the item itself. That's hard for a buyer to swallow.

- **Fragility of the Item.** Though I don't always recommend stamping "fragile" on the outside of a package (it seems to provoke bored package handlers, in my opinion), I would bolster a package properly if what's inside is prone to breakage. The best method here, besides a sturdy outer box and extra interior cushioning, is to use the box-within-a-box method. A fragile item should be carefully wrapped in bubble pack and inserted into a sturdy box. That box should then be placed in a larger box with plenty of cushioning between the wall of the outer box and the inner box inside. Chances are, if packed in this manner, fragile items can survive their trek. Packaging in this way is also acceptable in insurance claims.

## Getting Supplies

Once you've determined how you're going to package an item, you'll need the right supplies. Surprisingly, packing supplies are easier to come by than most people realize. Consider these sources for all things shippable:

- **Direct from the Carrier.** Most major carriers will provide packaging for your general shipping needs, and often it's *free*. The USPS has a wide variety of free Priority Mail and Express Mail packaging (boxes, envelopes, and tubes) that will cover most any shipping need. Better yet, you can order these supplies in bulk online at **www.usps.gov**, and it will be delivered right to your doorstep. Other carriers also provide free packaging if you ask. Why is it free? The free packaging is emblazoned with that carrier's particular service, and using it constitutes a promise to pay the appropriate service fee depending upon the packaging you select. If you have further packaging needs, the major carriers will also sell additional supplies. So if you're looking for convenience and low cost, start with the carriers you use.

- **Other Businesses.** If you work in an office or frequent any stores in your area, you'll often be treated to a nice assortment of free packing supplies—the stuff en route to the dumpster. No, this isn't considered *dumpster diving*, provided you don't crawl into the dumpster itself to retrieve them. You can find a lot of ready-to-use boxes, often already filled with bubble pack or packing peanuts. Just be sure the box is still sturdy and clean. Oh, and be sure it's OK to take this stuff, or you could be accused of a corrugated crime.

- **Office Supply Stores.** And if your needs are even more specific and the freebies you find won't ensure a packed item will make the trip safely, visit places like OfficeMax, Office Depot, and other such office supply stores. I will warn you that you could be spending a few bucks for what you need, but that might be a small price to pay if it keeps that item safe and sound.

- **Your Own Doorstep.** If you're buying stuff yourself, it's hopefully arriving in some sturdy packaging. Just reuse that. Again, be sure anything you reuse is still sturdy and clean. If so, then once again, the packing supplies you need are being delivered right to your doorstep.

And what other supplies might you need, besides boxes and interior cushioning, to become a self-sufficient shipper? Here's the laundry list of supplies I keep on hand:

- Clear shipping tape (have lots of rolls of this stuff around; it's the *duct tape* of the shipping world). A self-cutting dispenser is a real bonus here.

- Various-sized pieces of corrugated cardboard to use for stiffening (especially necessary for oversized envelopes containing pictures or other flat items).

- A sharp (but safe) utility knife.

- A box of 9"x12" (or larger) manila envelopes.

- A box of standard legal-sized envelopes.

- Sharpie permanent marking pens or other good medium line markers for addressing packages.

- Blank white paper (like 8.5"x11" printer paper) for writing thank-you notes to buyers or even to use as box labels.

- Blank self-adhesive address labels (these are really icing; I use the blank white paper for this and just tape it down to the package).

## You-PS (Your Parcel Service)

If you have your shipping shop all stocked and ready to go, you should have the makings of a small distribution center. Keep it clean and organized, and be sure you have a large enough flat area (table, workbench, or other clean surface) to package your little bundles of joy. Try to keep from using a garage floor or anyplace that might be dirty or grimy—you don't want to unnecessarily soil a buyer's item.

Package the item up as carefully and solidly as possible. Slightly overstuff the interior cushioning but not to the point where the item inside could become crushed (don't forget the box-within-a-box trick). Close up the ends of the package, prior to securing them, and give the package a shake. Do you hear anything moving inside? If so, you might need to add a bit more cushioning. Of course, if you're certain the item can't possibly be damaged, then perhaps it will be OK.

**IN MY MIND** How 'bout a "thank you" to the buyer? I've always enclosed a handwritten note in my packages just to sort of bring the deal to a close. I usually write something like this:

```
Hi Mark,
Here is your 1972 Mickey Mouse Watch. I hope it will meet
or exceed your expectations.
Thanks for bidding.
Best,
Dennis
```

To me, the note is a nice long-distance handshake that lets the buyer know you're glad they chose your auction in which to bid. I've received packages from sellers with just the item and nothing else, and it feels kind of impersonal to me to not finish the deal with a smile and a thank-you of some sort.

When you're satisfied the item will be safe in transit, use a good postal-weight packing tape to secure the box flaps, along the middle and across the ends. If the package (box or envelope) has some self-adhesive on it, think about whether it will really be strong enough to endure travel. If you have any doubt, add an extra strip of tape just to be sure.

**GET A CLUE** Hey, Houdini—don't gum up that package *so* securely that the buyer will have to wrestle the item from its impenetrable tomb. Overpackaging can often result in an item being damaged during the unpacking process. Make it secure, but don't make it a challenge.

One final point about packing: don't overpack an item to the point that the packing material is going to raise the price of postage higher than it needs to be. It's great to protect an item for safe shipping, but don't end up costing the buyer more than they need to pay if a bit more conservative packing will still ensure the item makes the trip safely.

## Determining the Cost

After you've been shipping stuff for a while, you'll have a good feel for what postage will cost. You'll actually need to determine this up front so you can properly charge the buyer when you request payment. If you're new at this, you have a couple of options to be sure you're charging correctly for postage.

First, you can package up an item and take it to the carrier's office or outlet and have it properly weighed. They'll give you the cost of postage at that time, which you can relay to the buyer to include with their high bid. You can also purchase your own postage scale (mainly for USPS shipping) where you can weigh items in your own home. There are different sizes of scales to choose from, depending upon the size and weight of the packages you intend to ship. If you're really going into hard-core selling, you can purchase a nifty postal meter that weighs and prints postal tags. These hook up to a phone line, and you'll be billed for your metering on a monthly basis.

Many people "estimate" postage costs. That's fine if you're using a generally static-cost service (like USPS Priority Mail, which costs a $3.20 flat rate for envelopes and packages up to two pounds, $4.30 for parcels up to three pounds, $5.40 for parcels up to four pounds, and so on. When you visit **www.usps.gov**, you'll find several different cost charts and rate calculators (domestic and international) that will help you accurately assess postage costs. Actually, I find using the Priority Mail service is easiest because of the standard costs and the fast delivery, but you should choose whichever service you like best.

**IN MY MIND** What happens when you've received payment, packed up the item, and trudged off to the carrier's office only to find out it will cost more than you thought to ship the item? Do you ask the buyer for more money? No, no, no! In cases where the cost ends up being higher than estimated—in my opinion—the seller pays up. That's just the cost of doing business. If you were the buyer, how pleasantly would you respond to a request for a few more bucks before the package will be sent? That's what I thought. For the seller, it's a lesson to be more accurate when estimating postage costs or finding more cost-effective (though not less effective) methods of safe shipping.

On the other hand, what if you overcharge the buyer for postage? Well, in my experience, if the buyer was overcharged more than a couple of dollars (shame on me for making such a gross error, by the way), then I'll send the money back. Really. It's annoying to a buyer to receive a package that allegedly cost $5.40 in postage and the package's postal meter only reads $3.20. That teeters on the line of rip-off. Use good customer satisfaction methods, and remember how you'll want to be treated when you're the buyer.

## Do You Charge for Anything Else?

This can be a bone of contention among buyers and sellers at online auctions: should a seller charge a buyer for things like "handling," "supply costs," "packing and posting time"? Well, ask a buyer, and they'll probably say no. Ask me—as both a buyer and seller—and I'll say no, too. Though some may disagree, I contend there is a true *cost of doing business*. I think someone once said, *"You have to spend money to make money."* Chances are, a successful seller is making decent profit at the auctions. Why try to squeeze out a few more dollars from a buyer? An astute buyer will see they're being significantly overcharged and probably won't bid at your auctions again. One of your best sources of regular income as a seller is to attract repeat customers. Yes, the big mail order businesses charge shipping *and handling* all the time, but they're paying people to do the work and renting space for them to do it in. That's a whole different deal from spending part of an evening in your back room to make sure you keep your customers happy.

So when I'm charged $6 for "postage and handling" though I know full well what I'll receive will cost no more than $3.20 (and don't even try to pull the "third-class quickie" on me), then I'll realize the seller is getting greedy, and I'll bid elsewhere in the future.

**IN MY MIND**

Well, if I had a soapbox I'd mount it for this next point: I've heard from sellers who claim they bear a lot of expense in bringing items to the auctions. They have to spend time researching items, finding them, procuring them, making them presentable, storing them, listing them, and on and on and on. My response: I blow the raspberry on 'em. As a seller myself, I know the work that goes into listing items for auction and the eventual exchange: that's part of the business. I don't feel my buyers need to bear any unnecessary expense because of how I've chosen to make some income.

I don't mean to be insensitive to the beliefs and opinions of some sellers out there, but really, folks. Buyers will gravitate to the sellers who offer the best service, the best quality items, and at the best terms and prices. Squeeze for too much, and you'll only end up squeezing yourself right out of business.

**DID YOU KNOW?**

For your information, hidden costs at auctions are a borderline scam game. See Chapter 14 for the low-down on this and other dishonest deals.

## The Waiting Game

And then you wait. The buyer waits for the package and the seller waits to hear from the (hopefully) satisfied customer. It can be a tough wait, especially for an excited buyer, so once more, keep the dialog flowing. When the seller ships the package, it's good business to contact the buyer via e-mail to announce that the goods are on the way:

> Subject: Your item is on the way: 1972 Mickey Mouse Watch
>
> Hi Mark!
>
> I just wanted to let you know your item is on the way. It's traveling via USPS Priority Mail, and I'd expect you'd receive it within a few days.
>
> I hope you'll be satisfied with the watch. Please let me know when you receive it.
>
> Thanks again for bidding.
>
> Best,
>
> Dennis Prince
>
> dlprince@bigfoot.com

So now the buyer knows the item's on the way, and is probably feeling better that the deal is about to come full circle. If it was agreed the item would be sent via some traceable carrier method (such as USPS Express Mail or UPS), it's a nice touch to include the tracking number in the e-mail message. That way, the truly eager buyer can track the item's journey from door to door. (Most carriers' web sites provide package tracking online.)

When the item does arrive, the buyer should inspect it right away (yeah, I know, try stopping them, huh?), and if satisfied, get back to the seller via e-mail that the deal is done:

> Subject: Package received: 1972 Mickey Mouse Watch
>
> Hey Dennis!
>
> The watch arrived today—it's great! Better than I had originally expected.
>
> Thanks for auctioning such a terrific item. Now if only I could tell time on an analog watch. J
>
> Best,
>
> Mark
>
> makrmaldrill@buyer.net

But what if the item takes a while to arrive? Then what? First, get communicating . . . *again*. It's possible the seller couldn't get the item out the day promised. It's possible the carrier attempted to deliver the item but no one was home to sign for it (which they sometimes try even if no signature is required)—check to see if the carrier left a "delivery attempt" note. And sometimes a package might take a bit longer than normal, and it's really no one's fault. In fact, carriers won't even begin to trace an item until after three or more weeks have elapsed. In the meantime, don't start suspecting one another; just keep the communication flowing and work together to resolve the problem.

GET A CLUE    If you fear you're in the midst of being ripped off (as buyer or seller) keep your cool and be very methodical in your next steps. Of course, I'll ask you to wait until Chapter 14 where I'll go into this sort of situation in detail.

Though I may sound like a broken record (and there are a lot of those usually up for auction), I'll say it again: 99.9 percent of all auction deals are transacted smoothly and happily. Be of good faith.

# Reaching Out and Speaking Up

So far, you've read a lot about working with others, being trusting and trust-worthy, and communicating till you're blue in the face. It all sounds so nice but a bit too *Rebecca of Sunnybrook Farm*-ish, maybe? Call it corny, wistful, or even naive, but it's true that the folks at online auctions must exercise some old-fashioned values to get along effectively in cyberspace. So that raises the next question: "Fine, but how can I be sure I won't be a patsy just waiting to be steamrolled by aggressive online thugs?"

In this chapter I'll focus specifically on auction dealings with others in cyberspace and how you can help keep events relatively in line. You'll see that there are plenty of ways to engage in pleasant transactions while maintaining your stan-dards of good behavior, both yours and others'. The key, as you'll soon see, is knowing where you can air your feelings—good and not so good—about other folks at the online auctions. Yes, *feedback* is what I'll be talking about here. You've probably heard about it and might be wondering how it works and how effective it really is. It's quite effective, and you'll need to know the best ways to use it to keep your auction activity upbeat and on track.

## First Impressions and Last Rites

Just a quick reminder here about online communication. In cyberspace no one can see you smile and no one can hear your tone of voice. Always be careful to use a simple and professional style when communicating. If you're a bit of a joker, you might be misperceived as a bit of a jerk. A sense of humor is great thing to have online; in fact, it's almost required to keep everyone from taking little ups and downs too seriously. However, if you're engaging in first-time communication with someone, be polite and straightforward at first. Soon, if you're striking up a nice friendship, then you can loosen up and have a bit more fun. Since you can never be sure of the disposition of the person on the other end, I maintain it's safest to play it cool at first.

If you're too abrupt or brash in your communications, others could avoid you in the future—that is, this deal you work with the other person could be the first and last as far as they're concerned. Since the auction community is built on trust and mutual respect, you'll find more success and a have better time when you keep attitudes in check. Remember that e-mail is notorious for being misinterpreted—don't let an unfriendly, though maybe unintentional, e-attitude precede you.

## I'll Show You My Feedback If You'll Show Me Yours

*"All right, Mr. Manners. So I'm prompt and pleasant in my dealings. Why such a big deal about all this? Do I really stand to gain more for being so peppy and polite?"*

You're darned right you do. Why? People talk about you and me and everyone else they deal with at the auctions. What are they talking about? They're sharing their experiences with you so others can determine if you're a good apple or a bad egg. They're all congregating at the virtual auction kiosk known as the feedback forum.

The premiere person-to-person auction sites offer a *feedback forum* or similarly named area where auction users are encouraged to comment on one another. It's a sort of online referral system, and it can build you up or rat you out. Feedback forums are the heart of auction communities. Anyone and everyone who is about to deal with you can read the cyber-report card you're issued.

## Feedback in a Nutshell

Feedback forums are special places at auction sites where you can input a positive, negative, or neutral comment about other users you deal with. It's a points-based reward system where positive comments earn you one point, negative comments subtract a point, and neutral comments have no effect. All auction users are encouraged to participate in posting feedback, sharing with others the good news or bad news of their dealings.

Do these points matter? Sure, because the accumulation of points is what tallies up as your *feedback profile*. The higher your rating, the better perceived you will be. Most sites even offer visual rewards of stars for higher-performing users. Many users covet these stars of recognition and work very hard to earn your trust and positive feedback, hoping to further heighten their starry reputation.

When you find an item you want to bid on, you'll want to check the seller's feedback to see if other buyers have been satisfied with him or her. If you're selling, you might be interested to read the feedback of folks who bid on your item, determining if your high bidder is someone who regularly follows through or flakes out. In these feedback forums, people are talking and everyone's listening.

Of course, the key to feedback is participation. If the users don't post feedback, everyone's at a loss to learn who's who. There's considerable concern out there that crooks are lurking in the auction wings. Yes, it's true that some thugs are looking to crash the party. However, if they're going to try to pull a fast one at the auction, chances are the feedback spotlight will ferret them out. All auction users must register to bid or sell. This allows the rest of the community to speak up and speak out about what their fellow auction-goers are up to in the virtual parlor.

## How to Post Feedback

It's quite simple, actually. Suppose you just completed a transaction with a seller. You paid quickly and got a great item. You're both happy with the deal, and you used excellent communication to see the whole thing through. For obvious reasons, you should reward that other person with a positive feedback note. Visit the site's feedback forum and post the comment for your newfound friend. You can choose what flavor your comment will be—positive, negative, or neutral—and you have somewhere in the neighborhood of 100 characters to sing that person's praises. How 'bout something like this:

"Great buyer. Paid promptly. Terrific e-mail communication. Recommended to all."

"Excellent seller. Item just as described. Fast delivery. A+"

When you post a positive note, you'll see the recipient's profile rating increase. And your own rating will probably increase soon after: people *like* getting positive feedback, and that provides an added incentive to return the favor. (Don't go overboard, though; in general, positive feedback only boosts the rating once for each individual. You can't give—or get—25 juicy rating points for one good deed.)

Keep in mind that the comments you leave will be read by others. If you want to praise a user, be sure the comment you leave briefly but clearly explains their overall performance. The sample notes you've just read make it clear how the buyer and seller performed in the transaction. That's the kind of information other potential buyers or sellers will hope to find when they review a user's feedback comments.

Finally, some auction sites allow feedback in direct reference to an actual completed auction and also in a more general manner without reference to an auction. Why the difference? Clearly, the most valuable and most telling feedback is that where others can see a real transaction has taken place. General comments are fine, but they're more of a feel-good sort of thing and don't always convince others that good dealing is going on. Both types of feedback are welcome, but the transaction-specific feedback is the most revealing. Post that sort of feedback whenever possible.

**GET A CLUE**  Transaction-specific feedback is restricted to the seller and high bidder in an auction. Others not involved in the auction (even outbid bidders) are usually prevented from posting transaction-specific feedback. It makes sense since these folks presumably weren't involved in the final exchange.

## But What If It Was a Bad Deal?

Though I've assured you the vast majority of exchanges go well, sometimes a deal goes sour. Then what? Should you rifle off a round of bad feedback? Perhaps, but proceed cautiously.

Negative feedback carries a lot of weight at auction sites and can often overshadow a bevy of positive notes. The added impact is because people typically avoid saying anything bad about each other. Though there are some exceptions, many people avoid getting into confrontational situations, online or otherwise. A negative comment, then, means some aspect of a deal went so far wrong that someone felt overwhelmingly compelled to air their complaint to the entire community. Therefore, many sellers and buyers flat out refuse to deal with auction goers who have excessive negative comments or have earned an overall negative feedback rating. Those negative comments show that someone is to be avoided.

**WARNING!** Most auction sites will boot you out of their auction galaxy if your feedback rating goes too deep into the negative numbers. At eBay, for instance, any user who earns a feedback rating of -4 will usually be sent packing. This is serious stuff, and if you're serious about auctioning, treat this with care and consideration.

**IN MY MIND** Of course, you'll hear tales of lunatic auction goers who fire off negative feedback and harassing e-mails at the first sign of trouble or inconvenience. It's true, there are some trigger-happy people out there just waiting for an excuse to unload, but I still maintain those types are the exception. Of course, if you've been on the receiving end of some explosive character, I'll have a hard time convincing you it doesn't happen often and it's really nothing to be too concerned about. All I can say is to keep your communications clear and professional even if the other person is operating with a short fuse. Contact the auction site for assistance if you need to. Above all, endure: this, too, shall pass.

Now, with all I've said about the importance of two-way communication, I could hardly advise you to post a negative feedback comment at the first sign of trouble. In fact, negative feedback should be considered a last resort when all else fails. If a deal seems to be running astray, communicate! If you're a buyer and haven't received your item, contact the seller—there might be a reasonable explanation. If you're a seller and haven't received a payment, contact the buyer—again, perhaps there's a reasonable explanation. Above all, try to keep the lines of communication open. Most mishaps can be resolved through some dedicated partnering. But if you've tried all of that and still fear you're being shammed, follow these steps before heading off to post your frustration:

1. Collect all of your messages to the other person up to this point (it's always a good idea to copy yourself on your correspondence).

2. Review the auction site's instructions about resolving conflicts and disputes. You might find some intervention or gain information about helpful organizations such as the Postmaster General, Better Business Bureau, or others (don't laugh—this could be mail fraud).

3. Contact the other person one more time to explain your dissatisfaction and the potential action that you're considering taking (contacting help organizations, reporting the incident, posting a negative comment).

4. If you're still left in the cold, proceed as you indicated and also post the negative comment.

 **DID YOU KNOW?** Some sellers clearly state in their listings that they'll quickly post negative comments about buyers who don't honor the deal. Ask any seller who's been burned more than once and they'll tell you that doing so is issuance of "fair warning." Usually, it's no bluff and a line you'd best not cross.

The key to leaving a negative comment (the community often refers to them as *negs*) is to focus on the problem, not the person. Something like this:

"Buyer never paid. Never responded to payment-due e-mail requests. Caution."

"Item not as promised. Seller refused refund. Ignored my attempt to renegotiate."

Never, ever, post personal attacks on another user. No matter how angry you might be, you could land yourself in the murky depths of libel. Remember that the community is looking for clear information about your dealings with others. Describe exactly what happened, keeping incensed comments about the no-goodnik's physical attributes, breath, or mother out of the exchange.

And what can you expect if you post a neg? You could receive one in return—it's called *retaliatory feedback* and is usually volatile and unkind. To the community's eyes, it signals a breakdown in communications and commitment from either or both parties involved in the dispute. It's sad when this happens. Some sites allow responses and follow-ups to negs, and a wise auction goer witnessing the event will read both sides of the story, usually finding the truth somewhere in the middle.

**GET A CLUE** All major person-to-person sites restrict negative feedback to completed transactions and can only be posted by the seller and high bidder involved. They also prevent anyone from posting multiple negs about the same user, eliminating *food back bombing*.

But there's still a ray of hope. Some negs are posted out of immediate frustration and misunderstanding. Often, two auction goers can find resolution after the flames of fury have died down. In such cases, each user can post responses and follow-ups explaining the misunderstanding. Those should be followed with a positive note that will work to offset the previous neg.

**IN MY MIND** Y'know, you don't necessarily *have to* leave a neg. I've been in situations where buyers have stiffed me. Sure, it's frustrating, but luckily it's never been for high dollar amounts, nor has it been too much hassle for me to relist my item. If that's your situation, you might be better off letting it slide and chalking it up to the other person's irresponsibility. Watch for them in your next auction (remember Yahoo! Auctions has the bidder blacklist) and stop them at the front gate.

If you feel you must leave a comment though you're not really hopping mad, consider the neutral comment. People *do* read them, and they do have an impact, though much less than a neg, of course. Again, stick to the facts, and use it as a firm prod to let that other person know that they're in the dog pound as far as you're concerned.

## Should I Read Between the Lines?

Oh yes. When you're out there bidding and selling and encounter others with nice feedback ratings, take the time to pop in and read the actual comments. Many sites offer quick statistics on the number of comments received by a user, including how many are good and how many aren't. You might feel good about a user with a rating of 75—that is, until you visit their comments and find the number is really the result of 100 positives and 25 offsetting negs. I'm not encouraging distrust—far from it—but I am encouraging you be fully informed.

## Can Feedback Be Faked?

Well doggone it if someone hasn't figured out a way to skirt the system. Yes, feedback has been faked before. There was a time when negative feedback bombing was a frequent occurrence, two users getting into an all-out feud and often saying some very colorful things. Most sites have put controls in place to prevent that, and most will suspend users who post even one vulgar or otherwise offensive negative comment.

But when feedback is faked, it's usually on the other end of the spectrum. Some users have devised methods to artificially boost their positive ratings. Fearing the path to negative noncommission or overly eager to build a stellar rating, sneaky users can sometimes collude with one another to post general positive notes in hopes of boosting their perceived online reputation. Two forms of such *feedback abuse* (which it is) exist: feedback shilling and feedback padding.

- **Feedback shilling** involves dishonest users who work with others to post bogus positive feedback. Some users have even secured additional user IDs and posted false feedback for themselves. This is typically the method used by crummy users struggling to avoid being booted out for too many negs. Whether an act of collusion or self-perpetuated, when revealed, feedback shilling is usually a ticket to site suspension.

- **Feedback padding,** on the other hand, is just an attempt to quickly beef up a feedback rating. The user, again in collusion with others or through use of ill-gotten additional user IDs, might not necessarily be trying to rip others off. They might just be impatient about the time and effort needed to respectably gain a fair rating. Regardless, it's wrong and could result in site suspension.

## So Does It Really Work?

Though some may disagree, most ardent auction users believe in the feedback system. Hey, everyone would like to read nice comments about themselves. More important, good feedback spells better business and greater trust for those who work hard to achieve it. Yes, some dishonest ones will try to circumvent the process, and others will say a feedback comment can't force anyone to behave a certain way. That's true, but the real power behind a feedback system is that it works something like a Neighborhood Watch program. The serious auction users want to keep their online streets clean and are incredibly vocal when some undesirable tries to set up an unsavory shop. Remember, though, the key to success is through your active participation.

## Building a Better World Online

If you think all this talk of good manners, stellar behavior, and feedback Brownie points is a bit sappy, I'd beg you to think again. Remember that more than half of U.S. citizens have yet to venture onto the Internet. Many of them wish to join in the online fun, but simple fear and uncertainty keeps them away. Online retailers, auction sites, and consumer advocate agencies are eager to develop methods and programs that will provide greater security and confidence in those millions of would-be surfers, bidders, and sellers. Good online behavior can only help in that effort.

It seems to me that everyone who's already online has a responsibility not only to keep their virtual havens clean and safe but also to make them attractive to potential new visitors. That guy who's been afraid to log on might have a bundle of great stuff he'd like to sell or a wad of cash he won't mind spending. If you set the example and stay involved and informed about what's going on where you play, you have a greater chance to make the virtual world a better place. The undesirable element is out there, but I've always believed there are far more good people than bad.

# Auction Scams, Shams, and Other Flim-Flams

Every paradise has a dark cloud that passes overhead from time to time. Online auctions are not immune to the effects of evil doers and crooked creeps. Though I've shown you a lot of the good online auctions have to offer, I feel compelled to inform you equally of the things that go *bump* online.

As the auction sites continue to grow, advance, and improve with each passing month, so do the online scoundrels' ways of fooling the unaware. The key to combating the auction outlaws is to stay informed. Auction scam artists can be pretty clever, but here you can learn just what those creeps are up to and how you can spot a cheat from a mile away.

If the negative press you've heard about online auctions is what's been keeping you on the sidelines, take some time now to learn what's really behind the hype. You might be surprised to find out a little investigative work of your own is all that's needed to reveal a rip-off.

**DID YOU KNOW?** I'm sorry to tell you that online auctions have been identified by the National Consumer's League (**www.natlconsumersleague.org**) as the number-one forum for online fraud. Rounding out the top five scams were general online retailing, computer equipment and software, Internet services, and work-at-home schemes. But none of those areas *have* to be fraudulent, and more and more online businesses are teaming up with consumer groups to put more safety in cyberspace.

# What Makes Them Think They Can Get Away With It?

If they can catch you napping, they'll steal your shoes. Presumably all crooks are drawn to people who are unaware, unprepared, or inattentive. Crooks look for the easy target and typically shy away from anyone who shows signs of being alert and on the lookout. If a crook can pull the wool over your eyes without much resistance or fear of being found out, you're a prime target. Therefore, get informed, look alive, and let these cyber-prowlers know you're onto them.

## Who's At Risk?

Many people new to online auctions believe the buyers, those who must faithfully send out their money, are the ones who'll be scammed. True, most auction victims are buyers, but sellers are also exposed to deception. As you read the rest of this chapter, you'll see that buyers and sellers alike need to become informed and take steps to protect themselves from online auction ne'er-do-wells.

## The Seven Deadly Scams

How can you be armed and ready? Read along, and I'll explain the most frequent con games played in the online back alleys. If you know how the rules are being bent, you can call the foul the moment you see it—and probably send the Shady Grady packing.

## Shill Be Comin' Round the Auction

The most common auction fraud is known as *shill bidding*. It's one of the easiest to commit and works like this: a seller has an item up for auction, but there is less bidding activity than their greedy little mind had imagined. If you're the current high bidder, you might see yourself getting a good deal on a passed-over prize. Just as the auction's about to end, there's a flurry of bidding, and your maximum bid is nearly eclipsed . . . but not quite. Suddenly, the great deal turned into your maximum bid or very near. What happened?

It's possible that a seller had a *shill* drop by the auction to bid it up before the auction ended. A shill could be a seller's cohort in crime or could even be the same seller under the guise of an illegal alternate user ID. In some cases, the shill might outbid the current high bidder, but clever shills will bid in smaller increments to push you to your maximum without putting themselves over the top. Remember, when two bidders bid the same amount, the first bidder to have offered that amount will win. That could work against you if a shill pushes you to the brink then quickly retreats when they find your maximum outbid their identical bid.

If a shill accidentally outbids a bona fide bidder, the seller can simply relist the item later. Beware, though, if the seller contacts you anyway and says "that no good deadbeat" wouldn't pay, and would you like the item at your high bid instead?

To spot a shill, you'll need to be able to recognize these warning signs:

- Last-minute bids just barely fail to eclipse your reigning status. (They could be legitimate, of course, but if there are a lot of them in very small increments from the same bidder, there's a fair chance of fraud involved.)

- After you're outbid, the seller informs you that the item's available if you want it. (Especially when the seller says, "Oh, I have two.")

- There are feedback comments in the seller's profile where others allege that shilling is taking place.

If you think you've been shilled, do some investigative work:

- Was the last-minute bidding cast by several bidders, or maybe just a single bidder taking multiple pokes at you?

- Check the seller's other completed auctions: do you see the same bidder or bidders placing last-minute bids but rarely winning? Do these bidders seem to bid in many of the seller's auctions and few (or no) others?

If you can provide reasonable proof that you've been shilled, contact the auction site immediately. This is illegal stuff, and if the auction site concludes a shill was at work, the user will get the boot but quick. But don't just work in an after-the-fact fashion; knowing how shilling is done, your best preemptive strike is to always review a seller's feedback and possibly search on some of their completed auctions for any signs of shilling. If you think you've been shilled in a seller's previous auction, never visit that crook's listings again. They might or might not actually be dealt with by the auction site (many users complain auction sites aren't tough enough on the baddies), but at least you'll know who to avoid in the future.

## A Protective (and Perplexing) Shield

Next in line is *bid shielding*, and this is one that snowballs the seller. It's a method by which auction bidders work together to snag an item at a low price while shielding it from other potential bidders. Two or more bidders will target an item to be shielded. One bidder places a bid backed up by a high maximum. A second bidder comes along and places a ridiculously higher bid that drives the price of the item up beyond a reasonable market value. Any other honest bidders will see the item is overvalued and will pass on it. Just before the auction ends, the second bidder suddenly pulls out of the auction, which drops the item's high bid value down to that of the opening bid—the one made by the "shielded" bidder. The auction ends, and the seller is cheated out of the chance to have made a better profit while the shielded bidder picks the item up dirt cheap.

You can often identify bid shielding in the same manner as bid shilling: bidders work together on a frequent basis (or a dishonest buyer repeatedly uses multiple user IDs). Sellers can reveal a shield scam when, after being a victim of a shield, they do some quick looking to see if these bad bidders have been playing the same trick at other auctions. If the shield can be proven, the seller should report the shielders immediately to the auction site. As a protective step, again, check the feedback that could indicate previous shield shenanigans. If the shield scam has already been committed, a seller should either blacklist (at Yahoo! Auctions) or otherwise take note of the collusive bidders and block them from any future auctions. If the creeps come around, their bids should immediately be canceled by the seller (a seller's prerogative at person-to-person auctions).

## Fabulous Fakes . . . Aren't

If you know what you're buying is a reproduction, that's one thing. However, if you're misled that the mineral water you're drinking came from high atop a snowy peak when it actually came from a garden hose, then you're being ripped off. The same thing happens occasionally at the auctions: a shifty seller tries to pass off bogus knockoffs as the real thing.

There's nothing wrong with selling reproductions (*re-pops*, as they're sometimes called)—it's a reasonable way for collectors to acquire items they admire at a fraction of the price of an original. However, trouble brews when the reproduction is passed off as an original at original prices. Not even the scam is original—it's one of the oldest deceptions in the book.

Whether it's artwork, printed matter, autographs, or even bogus Beanies, cheap imitations aren't so cheap anymore. In fact, with the advent of technology in manufacturing and imaging, re-pops are getting harder and harder to detect. Your best bet for protection here is to truly know your item and ask plenty of questions of the seller *before* you bid. If a seller ever replies ambiguously or claims they're "pretty sure it's original," you can be pretty sure it's not. You might have difficulty returning an item to a seller and getting your money back by claiming it to be a fake. The seller can assert that "all sales are final" or accuse you of doing a "switch and return" (another type of auction rip-off). For these reasons, this sort of situation can result in a battle royal. Be sure up front, and avoid sellers who seem to offer near-perfect items that should be nearly extinct.

## This Ain't No Swap Shop

Here's another scheme that sometimes afflicts sellers. Consider a seller who auctions an item, the buyer pays, the seller ships it, then the buyer reports it's damaged or isn't what the seller described. The seller, wanting to please every customer, may agree to a return and refund, but what comes back from the buyer is *not* what the seller originally sent—it's the same *kind* of item, but not the same one the seller shipped. It's the old switcheroo from a buyer who's looking for a free upgrade. Bad news.

The switch is usually easy to detect; good sellers are almost intimate with each nuance of the items they sell. A seller who strives to photograph and faithfully describe each item they offer will detect when something returned is not what originally left the seller's ownership. To head off this tactic, sellers who accept returns usually stipulate "items returned in same condition will be cheerfully refunded." If the seller has good photographs of the item (you should always have such photographs and keep them until after the sale is truly a done deal), he or she can use them to confirm a switch-off by a bamboozling buyer. If there is a dispute, the seller can offer to reroute the switched item back to the buyer or have both parties take it up a notch to actually prove their case. If a seller is adamant about the condition of the original item sent and has pictorial proof, chances are the bad buyer will know it's a futile case, retreating to the shadows while muttering, "Curses, foiled again!"

## Every Picture Tells a Story, Don't It?

Pictures are almost a standard requirement at auction sites to show potential bidders exactly on what they will (or won't) be bidding. Photos provide a healthy dose of realism—except when a seller posts a bogus photo or one so retouched that it's a far cry from what's truly being offered. What's a bidder to do?

If you bid on an item, win it, and receive something that only vaguely resembles what you expected, get in touch with that seller right away. But first, return to the auction listing and snag a copy of the auction ad and the accompanying photo (if still available); you might need this information to plead your case. Hopefully the seller will realize the potential of being ratted out or earning a neg, and will return your money quickly.

How do you detect a doctored photo? First, review the photo for authenticity. If the item is so well presented that it looks like it came from an advertisement, it just might have. Beware. If the picture doesn't jibe with the way the item's been described, ask questions of the seller. And if the photo looks overly bright, sharp, blocky, or anything else that suggests a jimmied jpeg or garnished gif, you might want to shop elsewhere.

Sellers are free to clean up their item images and should do so to give the best representation of their item, but should stop short of overdoing it. In fact, sometimes a digital image of an item can end up looking better than the original without any editing applied. In those instances, sellers should tone down the image to avoid false representation.

## Making (Up) the Grade

Though beauty is in the eye of the beholder, grading the condition and quality of an item calls for some objectivity. Many times, ambitious sellers describe the items they sell as "near perfect," "mint in box," or "excellent condition." However, this terminology shouldn't be tossed around lightly; hard-core collectors are paying through the nose for gem-quality items and are plenty perturbed when one seller's trash turns out to still be trash when it arrives at their abode. Though sometimes this is nothing more than an amateurish mistake on a new seller's part, some sly dogs out there are quite adept at gilding the lily—hoping a less-savvy buyer will let it slide.

The most difficult aspect of grading items, and one that has plagued collectors for a long time, is agreeing on a universal grading system. It's yet to be done, and the grading terminology differs from commodity to commodity. If what you bid on is advertised as "mint in box" but what arrives is "mess in box," contact the seller and see if you can agree to an exchange. An abrupt "No!" from the seller indicates they were deliberately attempting to pull a slick willy. But if it was an honest mistake, most sellers will work with you.

As a buyer, your responsibility is to fully study any images or descriptions of items before you bid. If you have doubt, ask plenty of questions: *"Is the packaging damaged?" "Is that a water stain I see in the image?" "Does this item show signs of fading?"* Ask all the questions you can (within reason) to determine if it's of the quality you're after.

**IN MY MIND**   On a couple of occasions I bought items a certain seller described as "mint in box" and "near-mint in box." Unfortunately, neither item turned out to be of the quality that I'd describe in that manner. The seller cheerfully agreed to the first return, apologizing for my dissatisfaction. The second time, though, the seller asked if I could provide my interpretation of "mint." He agreed to the return, but was a bit perplexed that I wasn't satisfied. After all, from his point of view, he'd answered my pre-bid questions with the truth as he saw it.

I suppose I am a bit of a stickler for quality in some items, but the moral here is both the seller and I learned that our interpretations of grading terminology differed significantly. You might run into the same situation yourself someday.

## When the Mail Doesn't Go Through

And here's the one auction newcomers tend to fear the most: when they send money and never receive the item they've paid for. It's a tempting scam for new crooks, though it's one of the most heavily penalized offenses. If someone takes your money then fails to deliver the goods, they've committed mail fraud and that's a federal offense. That Postmaster General door you see at your local post office isn't just a trim-and-paint facade. The person on the other side of that door is out to bust mail mischief. Take a look at the Wanted sheets the next time you're at your local P.O.—you'll see plenty of people wanted for mail fraud.

If the item you paid for doesn't arrive, keep your cool. Gather up all correspondence with the seller thus far. Contact the seller again and explain you have yet to receive your item. If the seller claims the item's been lost in transit, you'll need to work with him or her to have the claim filed for the return of your money. If the seller never actually sent the item, filing a claim on your behalf amounts to an attempt to defraud the carrier. Again, go directly to jail. But if the seller ignores you, contact the auction site, contact the Postmaster General, and possibly the Attorney General. In some cases, a collection agency can be called in to rough up the offender (well, get to the bottom of the situation, anyway).

The best protection is to know who you're buying from. If it's a new seller and the price warrants, you might consider using an escrow service. If it's an established seller, check to see if others have complained about this sort of thing before. It's uncommon for a good seller to have a single lapse of judgment, then quickly return to the straight and narrow path. But if it *is* an honest-to-goodness mix-up, keep the dialog flowing and work with the seller to clear up the mess.

## Is There Anything Else I Should Know?

Yes, there is. First, I'll repeat myself yet again by saying that such scams are the exception, not the norm. Don't overwhelm yourself with the fear that you're going to be the next sucker. With millions of buyers and sellers out there, odds are you'll be just fine.

Next, be informed. Though I already mentioned this, your understanding of the auction place and its user protections, and your knowledge of who you're dealing with, is tantamount to insurance for your safety and success. Understand how the rip-offs are run, and you'll sniff them out nearly every time.

If you do wind up on the bad end of a bad deal, keep calm. Assess the situation, do your investigative work, and make every attempt to work with the other person to solve the problem. Above all else, *never* issue any threats or even any statements that can be construed as threatening. In those cases, the finger of blame will most likely single you out, not the real crook.

Don't be afraid to ask for help if you need it. The major auction sites are working hard to beef up their security and help for their users. Many offer insurance programs for buyers who don't receive merchandise or get stuff that bears little resemblance what they thought they were buying. If your site offers such a program, use it!

If you're being scammed or fear you're about to be, contact the site and ask for assistance. Trust me, they don't want bad publicity any more than you want to be victimized. Be aware that site investigations will most likely move slower than you'd like—it's the nature of the beast. However, if you allow an incident to go unreported, you let a crook run free to scam another day. Don't let that happen.

Now, take a deep breath, then breathe out. I've painted some ugly pictures for you here, but only to inform, not to alarm. What I've outlined is from my experience, research, and belief. Always do what you feel is best, and always seek out the best help you can find if you think an auction has gone awry. But keep smiling.

# Part IV

## Tips, Tricks, and Traps

CHAPTER 15

# Pastime or Full-Time Job?

By the time you read this chapter you've no doubt been surfing the sites and looking at what these terrific auctions have to offer. Perhaps you've been actively bidding on items—that's good. Maybe you've been carefully surveying the sites to see how many other people are bidding—very astute. Maybe you've seen stuff up for auction that's just like what you have in your garage, basement, or attic, and some pretty hefty prices are being paid for it—that's *very* encouraging. Maybe you're thinking you can make a profit by buying and selling yourself—that's almost a certainty. So why not go for it, and make auctioning a full-time pursuit?

Whoa, there. Slow down a moment.

Before you strike off to make your auction fortune, it's a good idea to reflect on what you've seen. People seem to be making money hand over fist out there, and it looks so easy. In addition, they're making these riches in a fun environment, selling fun stuff. It looks like a definite calling for anyone looking to cash in, right? If there's a life of leisure and riches out there, why shouldn't you stake your own claim in the gold rush? But keep in mind the costs involved in what the auction pros are doing. They're working hard and expending time, money, and effort. If you want to tap the auction flow, that's great, but wait until you've had a chance to chew on the food for thought I'm serving up in this chapter.

Before indelible dollar signs form in your eyes or you decide that you're going to scoop up every choice goodie that crosses the virtual podium, plant your feet firmly and decide *why* you've come to the auctions. Are you here for fun or fortune?

**IN MY MIND**   This chapter is mainly directed at auction newcomers. If you're an established dealer and have successfully developed a livelihood in retail sales, perhaps even face-to-face auctions, then you've already learned the reality of this sort of business. Moving online is apt to add a lot more profit than work to your life. If, however, you're considering going into the auctions as a full-time endeavor based on all the hype you might have heard, this chapter will help you see some of the hidden aspects of living that "simple life."

## Preserving the Magic

Many people dream of the perfect job, one at which you can make lots of money doing what you love most. It's doubtful that very many kids grow up with aspirations of filing forms, going to staff meetings, or refilling napkin holders. Whether screening and reviewing movies, trekking around the world to buy and sell rare artifacts and ancient treasures, or writing and selling books about favorite hobbies, that "perfect job" is what many are reaching for. (For the record, writing books is no breeze, OK?)

To a lot of people, online auctions present the potential to make a great living while performing such enjoyable activities as learning new software, surfing the Internet, and buying and selling the kind of stuff they enjoy. But is this "path to riches" going to be as romantic when you must trudge it day after day, night after night, knowing the bill collectors have very little interest in how much fun you're having? Before you realize it, that passion just turned into work and, and a grind being a grind, can quickly sour you on that which you once savored.

This is the reason that many collectors and hobbyists keep their pastimes as just that: pastimes. They know the minute they put time limits and dollar values on what they love, they run the risk of killing the fantasy. Consumed by the need to make a living, some folks soon look past the inherent beauty or nostalgic tug of an item, more concerned with how fast they can sell it and for how much. Soon, the once-enjoyable treasure hunt becomes nothing more than a never-ending quest for *inventory*. To me, that's not as enjoyable as savoring one's newest addition to a collection (unless, of course, you collect *money*).

Perhaps you won't have this problem. Perhaps you can turn a hobby into a business without turning the dream into a nightmare. Some can, but most can't. And if you do succeed at profiting from your passion, it might surprise you to find other "passionists" who are trying to keep their hobby a hobby and not a business venture. What does that mean? Well, it means you could find little support from collectors who want to find great stuff and would like to do it at a reasonable cost. Mentioning your "cost of sales" to hobbyists might make them feel exploited. Mentioning that all prices are firm or all auctions have reserve prices is likely to send your would-be buyers elsewhere to do business with someone who's less pressured and less pressuring. It's not to say that anyone is wrong for trying to make a living in collectibles or antiques or any other resale business, but buyers who love the hobby are not interested in being gouged to help you pay your rent.

**IN MY MIND**  *Hey! Is this author down on dealers or something?* Not at all. Actually, dealers are doing a fine job delivering some great items to the auctions and elsewhere. But I will say that some dealers do a better job than others in keeping the magic alive. Find a dealer who truly enjoys what they're selling, and you'll find them to be a joy to work with. Perhaps auctioning is just a sideline sales venue for them (a *very* good one, by the way), and they have enough experience in reselling to know that high prices often translate into low sales. If pressured to make ends meet with each sale, the dealer will probably find less satisfaction with what they do and might find fewer satisfied customers in the process. That would be a shame.

Dealers and resellers are terrific for the different hobbies and interests, but the truly good ones know they won't always be able to pay the rent on a single huge transaction, nor will they try to make a killing on every sale. The really good sellers will work to keep customers happy and satisfied, knowing that those who feel they were treated well will probably come back again for another purchase. *That's* how steady income can be gained.

So don't misunderstand me—if you want to start up a virtual business at the online auctions, that's great. But if you quit your day job to strike it rich online, understand the pressure of making a steady income week after week.

It might be the unseen twist that turns your passion into pain, making it just another job, and an uncertain one at that.

## If You Love It, Can You Bear to Part with It?

Here's something else to consider: if you're a long-time collector or hobbyist and decide that buying and selling fun stuff will be your road to income, be sure what you buy is something you can sell. I'm not talking about demand for an item, but rather what happens when you find many terrific things in your inventory and realize you can't bear to part with any of them. This is a quandary for hobbyists: they fall in love with their inventory, and their business tends to get heavy on buying and light on selling. This is especially true when a seller finds initial success and then has the capital to invest in items previously out of reach. With the funds to shop, the seller could slip into purchasing higher-cost items with a subconscious desire to own them rather than sell them. That won't contribute to the profit statement at the end of the month.

So should sellers only deal with junk they don't care about? Emphatically, *no!* A seller who is less than thrilled about what they sell is usually less than motivated when selling it. Though the rule is not universally applied, sellers really should deal with the items in which they are most interested and knowledgeable and in which a market of buyers will also be interested. I'll typically shy away from the seller who, when asked about an item, might reply "*I don't know what it is, but it's ten bucks if you wanna buy it*" (an actual quote I heard at a show several years ago). Conversely, I love to talk with the seller who has a wealth of knowledge about what they're selling, an obvious enthusiasm for it, and a genuine interest in helping a fellow collector make a purchase that serves the passion.

## How's Your Inventory Look?

Here's something to consider: if you begin to make reasonable profits at online auctions, how will you ensure a steady inventory to keep it up? If you clear a profit and intend to sell professionally, you'll need to decide how to reinvest your profits wisely to help your business grow. When you hear other entre-

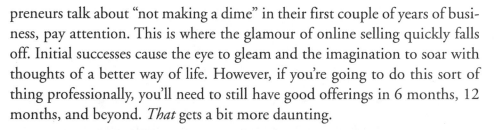

preneurs talk about "not making a dime" in their first couple of years of business, pay attention. This is where the glamour of online selling quickly falls off. Initial successes cause the eye to gleam and the imagination to soar with thoughts of a better way of life. However, if you're going to do this sort of thing professionally, you'll need to still have good offerings in 6 months, 12 months, and beyond. *That* gets a bit more daunting.

I've heard stories and talked to other online enthusiasts about making a run for an online income. They're encouraged by early successes but soon find their endurance waning, not to mention their inventory. According to these folks (and my own experiences bear them out), online auctioning is very time-consuming when you're working to maintain a steady supply of things to sell. Though you may feel you have an attic full of treasures, it's the true treasures you'll usually sell first for good money. After that, you might be trying to sell less desirable items, and your auction income may quickly fall off. This is especially true in the collectibles arena. Many collectibles command such a high price because they're no longer being produced. That's great when you have the item, but it poses a real problem when you go looking for more. Take into account that the condition of collectible items will vary, and you'll see how that causes your final income to swing dramatically in the auction marketplace.

If you have items that you produce yourself (artwork, castings, photographs), you stand a better chance of keeping an inventory that isn't subject to the scarcity and condition issues of collectibles. If you have access to manufactured products (as a reseller), then you'll probably be fine because your items are often newly manufactured—provided you can keep a pipeline of supply open month after month. Whatever you decide to sell full time, make sure you'll have a reliable full-time inventory to keep your business afloat.

## If You've Got the Time, We've Got the Place

If you make a go of the auction business, be sure you understand how you'll be spending your time day in and day out. By no means is it a job where you can kick back and just watch your auctions accumulate gobs of cash while you giggle with glee. You don't have time for that—there's a lot of other work to do.

First, expect that you'll spend somewhere in the neighborhood of 8-12 hours daily on your business if you truly want to succeed. Online auctioning success is directly influenced by the amount of time and effort you put into it. Here's what you'll need to do constantly to keep your boat afloat:

- List plenty of new items regularly (at least three times per week).

- Obtain and maintain new inventory regularly.

- Keep records of your business outlay versus your auction income (how else will you know if you're making money?).

- Continually research commodity trends and shifts in demand.

- Attend to bidders' questions.

- Maintain auction listings if changes are required.

- Keep up on auctions that have ended and send payment due notices.

- Prepare and package sold items for shipment (this could be a daily routine depending on when payments are received).

- Travel to the carrier's office to ship your items.

- Follow up on late payments.

I'm not making this stuff up; supporting an auction business is hard work! If you spend more than a couple of hours on a given night *just browsing* the auctions, consider how much more time and effort is required when you decide to sell full time. Again, I don't wish to discourage you, just enlighten you. This isn't always a walk in the park.

## Who's Driving This Ship?

Now here's something I have to make clear: at the auction sites, sellers really don't control the environment. Think about when a site's server crashes for 22 hours—no sales. Imagine a site temporarily closing for upgrades or design modifications—no sales. Consider a site that's difficult for bidders to navigate or has site policies that aren't very inviting—you get the idea. At online auction sites, unless you're an employee and have an impact on the direction of the site, you're relegated to working with whatever the site offers—or doesn't offer. As a seller, you're setting up your shop where the virtual landlord can do as it pleases regardless of your needs as a salesperson.

To help ensure that your sales goals won't be undermined (intentionally or otherwise) by the hosting site, you really need to choose your sales venue (or venues) wisely. Look for the sites that seem to have the best performance and reliability (though anything could happen when computers are involved). Look for the sites that have a strong user base—that usually indicates a site with good policies and features. Look for a site that polls its users (bidders and sellers) about what they'd like to see added, improved, or removed from the site format. But remember that the site owners are always in the driver's seat and can make decisions on what *they* believe is best, not on what *you* believe is best. For a business owner, that's a lot of power to let the virtual landlord hold.

## Economy

Obviously, I am a hobbyist. I seriously investigated becoming a full-time seller and quickly changed my mind. I realized the steady income I could pull in from a regular employer was far more reliable than the ebbs and flows of auction income. The world economy can be up or down, and that will take your auction earnings potential for a ride. While a regular employer might be able to buffer you from temporary swings in the economy, the auction market is more susceptible to bad economic times. If money's getting tight out there, people will respond by trimming out the unnecessaries in their budget, which can spell trouble for auction sellers.

If you're going to make a go of the auction business, be sure you have a backup plan to keep you going when times get tight (and expect they will on occasion). Be sure your inventory stays replenished and that you can comfortably sell items at lower prices while still bringing in a profit. Also keep a safety net of cash or other liquid assets you can fall back on when profits shrink.

## Who Invited Murphy?

This little discussion will perfectly footnote that last lecture to the expectant e-businessperson. For some reason, it's almost impossible to figure why some auctions work well and some fall flat—not just the different auction sites, where there are way-ahead leaders and struggling followers, but even within the offerings of single sites. Just when you think you know why that last auction of yours did so well and how you'll firmly position yourself for many more, your theory gets blown to pieces.

Consider this: you see an auction for an item—maybe something rare or something trendy—and it pulls in a hefty final bid. You've got some of those items, and you're expecting to make a similar profit when *you* auction them. However, when your listings go live, bidding is often only three-quarters, one-half, or less than what the other person's auction drew. What happened? Clearly, there were two or more people interested in that item when it showed up on the auction block. A battle ensued, and the seller raked in a tidy profit. However, by the time you came around to make your score, the battle was over and everyone left. Maybe it was an impassioned bidding war, maybe it was a perceived shortage, it was a here-today-gone-tomorrow fad that ended as quickly as it came. Whatever it was, if you pinned your hopes on bringing in the same profits with a whole boxload of that item, you might be stuck with just the boxload instead of a box of money. Incidentally, look around and see how many other opportunists saw the same high-priced auction, and how many of them jumped at the chance to list their newly-recognized treasures, too. Suddenly, you're trying to make a fortune in the midst of a market glut. Bummer.

IN MY MIND Call me superstitious, but I've always found that I do extremely well when I least expect to make a profit on an item. And when I'm full of excitement and anticipation, I'll get a lousy response. When that happens, I often wonder how I'd be feeling if I had the added pressure of *having* to make a certain profit just to keep bread on my table. Maybe you've figured out the secret to consistently high sales, but I haven't.

## Enjoy the Ride and the Thrill of the Chase

For me, the enjoyment of the auction comes from my ability to take it or leave it. If I choose to buy something for the sheer fun of it, I have a great time. If I sell an item to bring in a few bucks to offset my auction buys, I'm doing well. And if I decide to simply surf about the sites to see what's out there, I can do so leisurely without any other pressures. Most important, if I decide to turn off the PC and take the family to the park for the day, I can do so without the nagging feeling that I should be "working the auctions." What I really value is the freedom to make the auctions whatever I want them to be and whenever I feel like it. I love a treasure hunt, and however long it takes me to find what I'm looking for, I enjoy the things I see and the people I meet during the journey. If you're new to auctions, I'd suggest you coast along for a while and just enjoy the scenery, stopping off from time to time to buy or sell. Later, if you see a true opportunity and are determined to make your fortune, then you can take the plunge into full-time auction life.

C H A P T E R 16

# Put Your Money Where Your Mouse Is

Well, you've seen a lot out there to bid on. If you don't want the auctions to take over your life and drain your wallet, you'll need to keep an eye on your bidding to determine if you're still on the right track. The auctions are great fun, but it's easy to become distracted from your original aspirations, getting caught up in the flurry of bidding that goes on.

GET A CLUE  If you're a seller, this chapter will offer some salient points you'll probably want to take note of. Don't skip past this one too quickly.

## What Were You Really Looking For?

How many times have you wandered into Home Depot, Wal-Mart, or Price Club to purchase a specific item? You venture in with a $5 bill—more than enough to cover your planned purchase—but are immediately distracted by great stuff, incredible bargains, and just about anything imaginable shrink-wrapped into a two-pack. Before you know it, you're guiding a shopping cart to all corners of the store. Soon, you roll up to the checkout stand with hundreds of dollars of stuff, and in a flash of plastic you hear, *"Do you need help loading all this into your car?"* By the way, did you get that little item you were originally there to buy? I thought not.

It's the same story at online auctions, though sometimes even worse. No, the auction's not bad, per se, but it's easy to get distracted as you browse the virtual aisles and begin wanting that, and that, and those, and some of these. But online, it's even easier because all your shopping and bidding is done with the click-click-click of your PC's mouse. Bid on this, bid on that, bid, bid, bid. Just don't forget, you'll have to pay, pay, pay soon. My goodness—how much stuff did you bid on, anyway? Gulp.

## Work Within Your Means

When you're out there bidding, you'll do well if you can set some limits. Limit the amount of time you'll be surfing the auctions or limit the number of items you'll bid on in the span of a week or a month. Most important, limit the amount of money you'll plop down in the virtual auction parlors. Remember, this includes the maximum bid you've committed, not just the current high bid value. If you've put a high maximum bid out there, chances are it will be met before the auction ends. Be sure you can cover that amount comfortably and *never* think *"nobody's going to bid this much."* Remember Murphy's Law? Murphy seems to be an avid bidder, too.

## Know When to Quit

Then there's the time when you should just hang it up and walk away. If you're winning an auction and have some maximum bid amount still protecting your claim, that's great. However, if bidding heats up on the item you're after, it could get costly. When you're outbid in an auction, you then have to decide if your current maximum bid really is the highest amount you can afford to pay. If it is, let the auction go—there's always a chance a similar item will show up later or at a different site. This is easier said than done—I know from firsthand experience.

If you're outbid, you can become so enthusiastic about *winning* that you can forget how much money you're committing to the item. You could end up paying way too much for an item—more than the market value or more than you could ever recoup if you choose to resell it later. You could also end up bidding above your means, winding up in the very sticky situation of having to tell a seller you can't pay. *That's* definite trouble because you'll be deemed a novice and an irresponsible bidder. You might even get some negative feedback for it.

Understand that it's common for newcomers to want to bid on everything they see. Resist the temptation. A large percentage of the items you'll see really will come around again. Though it's hard to believe, especially when something you covet shows up on the auction block, many items make the rounds again and again. Take heart when you have to step away from an overpriced auction—many other sellers will see the price paid for the item, and the site may soon be flooded with more of the same. And at the next round of auctions, it's not often that the item will achieve the same price level—the first one to show up usually brings out the highest bidders. But after the big spender pays through the nose, the rest of the folks can get one too and usually at a much lower price. Be patient and be true to your limits. Trust me—it will pay off in the long run.

## Keep Realistic Expectations

Don't get disgruntled when you can't seem to get that "killer deal." There are a lot of bargains to be had, but getting the satellite dish for $9 or the ultra-rare Beanie Baby for a single dollar just doesn't happen much. With all the bidders flocking to the auction sites, it's a wonder that anyone still maintains you can get steals every day.

Your best bet is to decide what it is you're looking for, then research the item's availability, variations, and current market value. Then, with that knowledge, strike off to the auctions and work within those parameters. If you save a few bucks, excellent! If you pay market price, that's still not a bad thing provided you got what you wanted. But if you're on the verge of paying too much in the heat of bidding, ask yourself if you're willing to pay high this go around. If you really want the item now and are willing to pay more, then decide to do just that. If you'd prefer to pay a fair-market price, wait for the next one to come through. It might be weeks or months until you see another, but chances are one will show up.

GET A CLUE    This is a great way to fend off hype. If you're desperate for an item and the price is soaring, try to hold back. In a month or so, it could be that the fad has worn off, the item is in plentiful supply, and you can get yours for a much better price. Of course, you'll also find out if the fad has faded in your own mind as well, and it was the hype or rumors of potential profit that got you all riled up in the first place. Given more time to consider the item, you might learn *you* no longer want it, either. Furbies come to mind when I think about fads that are here one day and gone the next.

## Don't Give the Proxy All the Power

This follows the earlier discussion about setting spending limits. Remember that your bid is your commitment to purchase an item. Your maximum bid is your commitment to pay up to that price. The proxy system used at an auction site will only do what you tell it to and will only bid as much money as you give it. Proxy systems don't keep tabs on your daily affairs and don't realize when you've had a change of heart about an item. It may sound sarcastic, but I only mean to be kind—the proxy system can spend your money very quickly. It's a real blemish on your record when you withdraw a bid (and some sites don't even allow bid retractions), so you want to be sure you've set a reasonable limit and are prepared to let the proxy spend every dime you give it.

## Short- and Long-Term Gains

Be sure to consider the reason for your purchase before you bid. If you're buying for personal ownership—maybe for a collection or as a special gift for somebody—you might be inclined to pay more for an item. If ownership justifies paying more (maybe more than current market value), then that might be a good buy as far as you're concerned. However, if you're buying for resale, you'll need to be strict in how much you spend for an item. Remember, true resale is only successful if you can achieve some sort of profit in the process. If you pay market value or higher for an item, you'll have a difficult time getting any profit from hiking the price up when you want to sell it. (And you might even have trouble getting back what you spent if you've paid at or over market value.) Resellers have to be particularly conscious of their spending limits if they're going to be successful in bringing in a regular profit.

# When Bids Go Bad

Sometimes, life happens while you're making other plans. You could be happily bidding away when something around you changes and you're suddenly unable to honor your bids. Yikes! What should you do? What *can* you do? Well, before you panic, here are a few tips on what to do if your bids ever need to be reeled back in.

I caution you, though, that this is not advice presented to give you an easy way out of your auction commitments—far from it. However, since "stuff" happens, it's wise to know how to proceed, avoiding as much thrashing about as possible for both yourself and the seller.

**WARNING!** If you're at a merchant site, you might not get the chance to pull your bid, no matter how much you need to do so. Remember, the merchant sites often have your credit card on file and will charge to it if you win. In that case, you either carry the balance on your card until you're in better financial health or you attempt to return the item for a refund after it's arrived. And some merchant sites carry a policy of "all sales final" on closeout or refurbished merchandise. Bid carefully.

# Something Suddenly Came Up

What happens if an unexpected financial crisis befalls you? Whether you like it or not, you're in the prickly situation of not being able to honor your bid. Now what can you do? Is there any hope?

Well, if yours will be a sad song, don't wait to sing it to the seller. That is, when you find yourself in the position where you can no longer honor your bid, contact the seller immediately. If there's time left in the auction, the seller still has a chance to get other bids even after you've retracted yours (again, provided the site you're bidding at supports bid retractions). Be honest with the seller regarding why you can't pay, and the seller may let you off the hook. Many sellers are regular people and can be very understanding when things don't go as you planned. Just communicate quickly, honestly, and apologetically—you may be surprised at the empathetic response you'll get.

If the site doesn't allow bid retractions (or bid cancellations by the seller), still communicate the situation to the seller—there might be an opportunity to cancel the auction and relist the item, though this could definitely cut into the seller's potential profit and time.

GET A CLUE    Sellers, remember to see if the site you're selling at offers listing fee refunds for times when auctions go bad. Buyers, if you're bumming out of a bid and the seller doesn't know about listing refunds, be sure to let them know. That could help you get off easier.

But if the auction's already ended and you find yourself fundless, communicate to the seller as fast as you can. Again, be honest and apologetic. If yours is a good reason, the seller might still be understanding and could work with the next highest bidder in an effort to salvage the auction. The site might offer a listing fee refund or a free relisting to the seller. If yours is a short-term situation, you and the seller might be able to reach an agreement to delay the purchase until you're back on your financial feet. This is definitely an act of true generosity by the seller, so don't default a second time. And, *don't* get caught bidding on other auctions while the seller's waiting for you to pay up.

## What If I've Changed My Mind?

A financial setback is one thing, but changing your mind after you've bid is just irresponsible. I don't assume you'll ever do this, but you should be aware that some bidders actually do. Some bidders see the auctions as a game and will occasionally bid for the fun of it. Those bidders don't retain registered status for long. But, at times, bidders will change their minds about what they've bid on. Though I could never guarantee the seller's response, if you feel you must back out for this reason, then start communicating. Remember, if there's still time in the auction, let the seller know you're pulling out as quickly as possible. If the auction's over, you're going to be in a more sticky predicament. The seller's expecting that high bid and isn't going to be very happy about your being careless with your bidding. The seller might let you off the hook, but might also drop a neg in your feedback profile. Don't get upset—you had it coming if you backed out just because you didn't want the item any more.

## Are There Valid Reasons for Pulling Out of an Auction?

Actually, there are. Auction sites and auction communities generally hold that you can rightfully retract a bid if you made a mistake in your maximum bid value (you bid $1,000 when you meant to bid $100) or if the seller modified the description of the item after you bid and now the item seems to be something other than what you originally envisioned. Those are understandable circumstances, and if the site allows retractions, you should feel comfortable in retracting your bid.

 GET A CLUE A note to sellers: Take care when you modify or add to the description of your item after bids have been received. Whether the changes are truly significant or not, a bidder can contend that your actions were justification to pull a bid. There aren't many bidders out there hoping for this loophole, but take care in what you change and when you change it.

## Your Solid Gold Guarantee

So what's the best thing you can bring to an auction? Your good word. Though it may sound corny, your guarantee is the best thing to present to others at the auction sites when you decide to bid and sell. With all the concern these days over the safety and reliability of dealing with strangers, your ability to ease the concerns of those you'll come in contact with speak volumes and probably garner you a greater share of the online community's trust and respect.

CHAPTER 17

# Bidding and Selling Strategies

If you want to achieve auction greatness, you'll need to fill up your tool belt with bidding and selling strategies. Following are some of the key things you'll want to consider as you embark on your auction adventure. Comb through the tips that follow and consider how each might fit in with your intentions, your personality, and the way you plan to approach the auctions. Though not all of these strategies are foolproof (what strategies are?), these tried-and-true techniques will help you hit the ground running and get more out of your auction investment.

## Bidding Tips and Tactics

If you're at the auctions to make a buy, consider these bits of advice to guide you in your endeavors.

### Spread the Wealth

If you bid exclusively at a single site, you could be passing up great deals or unique items available elsewhere. At some of the less-traveled sites, eager sellers may be willing to let an item go for far less than what that same or similar item is commanding in a bidding war at another site. Plus, at the less-traveled sites there is less competition, too. Often, sellers institute reserve prices to make sure the potentially light site traffic doesn't cause them to take a loss on an item. However, many sellers at smaller sites are interested in making a sale and that might be your opportunity to find better deals.

## Use Selective Searches

Time is money at the auctions as much as anywhere else, so you'll want to be sure you spend yours as wisely as possible. When you're buying at online auctions, whether for resale or for your personal collection, a smarter search can save you time as opposed to laboriously browsing through category after category, detail page after detail page. If there's something you're looking for, search for that specific item. Use the site search tools and scan item titles for specific key words: dvd player, 8-track, wedgewood, *Mad* magazine, or whatever. You'll quickly find out whether what you want is there or not.

Then, to save even more time, put the site's search-bot to work scanning the listings for you while you're away doing something else. If the site has a "personal shopper" or "auction watcher" or whatever it might be called, set it up with your search criteria and let it notify you when it finds a match.

GET A CLUE  These search-bots are especially useful when you're looking for so many items that you often forget to search for some of them. To avoid missing an auction that you forgot to search for, let the search-bot "remember" for you.

A final note about searches: use spelling variations in your keyword searches. Not all sellers are the best spellers, and you could miss a great item (and a great bargain) when a misspelling prevents it from showing up on your search results. Move the vowels around and use common misspellings for the key words you're entering. More often than not, you'll find hidden treasures that others might not see. That spells "bargain" for you.

## Going, Going, Grab It!

Wanna get some good deals? Search the listings for auctions that are due to end within the hour. A lot of items are offered at the auctions, and a lot of them get passed over entirely. Many auctions close without receiving a single bid. Barring

the ones where the seller has a ridiculously high reserve on the item, these might be the auctions where you can score big by being the only bidder. Check the sites' sections of auctions that are about to close—look for *Going, going, gone* or *Auctions ending soon* links (or however your favorite site labels them).

**WARNING!** If you're going to grab something this way from a site that uses automatic auction extensions, be sure you place your bid before the final five- or ten-minute window arrives. If you bid in those last few minutes, you'll needlessly extend the end of the auction and add more time for someone else to come along and battle you for the item. By then, the bargain hunt's usually over.

## When to Bid First

Bidding first is a good strategy if you want to stake your claim and let other bidders know that you're minding an item. Sometimes, a first bid can claim an item, especially when it has a generally accepted value. If an item typically sells for, say, $20 and rarely any more, be the first to lay down that 20-spot (maybe a dollar or two more), and you'll signal to other bidders that "this item is taken." If it's an item that's relatively available at the auctions, most bidders will move on to the next one rather than pay too much trying to outbid you. Oh, and don't forget the 10-percent first-bidder discount offered at Amazon auctions.

## Outbid the Outbidder

If you're determined to win a particular auction, one way to fend off others is to immediately outbid them if they outbid you. When you immediately outbid another bidder, it might be intimidating enough to shoo them away. This is no bullying tactic, it's just a way to communicate that you're watching the auction closely. Some bidders might decide to stick around and battle you for it. Some might come back near the end of the auction for the final stand. Some, though, might see you want the item and will switch to another item instead. This is especially effective when you can pony up a sizable maximum bid that others will chip at but few will top. After a few auto-outbid messages from the auction site, the other bidders will see your determination, by proxy.

## Win It with a Penny

When you bid, always use odd values: $10.37, $45.96, and so on. Sometimes, a bid of $10.01 can be all it takes to beat another bidder who put a maximum of $10. Remember the auction sites usually impose preset bid increments, though many will allow you to bid with an extra bit of loose change. If your bid is enough to top a current bidder's maximum, the bid increment policy typically won't come into play. This is a great strategy to beat out the "round dollar bidders" while also shaving a few bucks or more from the final value by beating out the site's bid increment function, too.

## Bid Big

Though it might not sound like a true strategy, sometimes winning comes down to spending. Whether you plan to bid early or bid late, you might win only if you bid *big*. In physical auction houses, big bidders use what's called a *jump bid:* it's a big bid that far surpasses the current minimum bid increment the auctioneer's asking for. A well-timed jump bid can typically knock off any other bidders who are trying to nickel and dime the auction to death. A jump bid can, in a single move, outbid the maximum bids of those small fish. At the same time, a jump bid can make it apparent that there's a bidder in the parlor who isn't afraid to drop some serious bucks, and one jump bid can be followed by another from that bidder if someone else attempts to hang on. So, the equivalent to the jump bid in virtual parlors is a healthy maximum bid. If you've got the funds, a big bid could be enough to assure you of the win.

## Explore the Joys of Sniping

This is the bid many online auction goers have heard about, though many still aren't sure how it works. Think back to the discussion of eBay in Chapter 7, where I explained that sniping is achieved by using two browser windows: one holds the bid that's ready to be cast while the other monitors the auction clock. When the final moments of the auction approach, the bidder can cast that final bid in hopes of beating out the current high bid with no time left for the outbid bidder to react.

Sniping is as much a sport as it is a tactic. To some snipers, it has evolved as an art form. Placing well-executed snipes is something to marvel at, and whether you're sniping or getting sniped, a snipe well done is something to admire. The goal is to leave as few seconds as possible in the auction after your bid has been registered (and, of course, to become the new high bidder in the process). The key to sniping, though, doesn't revolve around luck, and it doesn't require a stopwatch to time it. The key to sniping lies within the site's response time (often affected by your Internet connection and even your PC's processing power) and a keen sense of intuition. You have to be aware of how fast the auction site is responding to your mouse and keyboard commands. Sometimes the site will respond quickly to your actions; other times it can be sluggish. The key to delivering a late snipe without having the auction actually end mid-bid is to acquire a feeling for how much time you'll need for your snipe to be delivered, recognized, and registered by the auction site. But if you're truly skilled and can deduce how much time it takes for your bid to register, you can deliver some amazing snipes with only scant seconds left before the end of the auction. Personally, I've delivered what I consider to be pretty impressive snipes—those with "zero" seconds left in the auction (a perfect snipe) and others with only split-seconds left (a "screaming" snipe). But, don't forget that a snipe can be beat out if there's still time for others to squeak in after the site registers your bid (and others could be sniping right alongside you) or if your maximum bid still fails to top the current high bidder's. Don't be surprised to see a popular item double or triple in price within the last 30 seconds of the auction. However, if you've done your homework, know how much it might cost to become high bidder, and deliver a last-second snipe, you can walk away a winner while others are wondering what just whizzed past them.

**IN MY MIND**   Sniping carries a certain load of controversy with it. Some auction goers believe sniping should be disallowed (and many auction sites don't even let it happen, having *all* auctions equipped with automatic auction extensions). Anti-snipists contend sniping robs a seller of additional profit, whereby an outbid bidder might bid again if there's still time to do so. However, the pro-snipists explain that sniping adds excitement and drama to the auction, and it's often sniping itself that draws many bidders to certain sites. And a truly determined sniper will usually deliver a double-barreled snipe backed by a high maximum bid. Get two or more snipers in the action, all toting high maximum bids, and the seller stands to make out quite well.

## Mix It Up

Don't forget variety. Use several bidding techniques as you work the auctions. A bidder who *always* bids early stands a greater chance to lose auctions. Likewise, a bidder who *always* snipes becomes known among other bidders, prompting them to bid higher or begin sniping as well (remember, most sites allow users to review bidding activity of other bidders, which makes it easy to identify the bidding practices of others). And if you always bid an extra penny, some will square off with you by throwing a dime onto their bid. So try to use a variety of bidding techniques based on the understood value of an item, its scarcity, and how popular it might be. If you come at auctions from different bidding angles, you stand a better chance of keeping others guessing at how, when, and where you might strike next.

**DID YOU KNOW?**   Some auction-goers make it a practice to follow other bidders around to see what they're bidding on. These "bid stalkers" let others find and bid on items of mutual interest. The stalker will review what the "stalkee" is bidding on and might sneak in and snipe at the last minute. This isn't any sort of illegal activity (and the term *stalker* sounds more sinister than it truly is), but many bidders complain about doing all the research only to be bid against at the end of the auction by someone who was just riding their coattails. If you think someone's stalking you for particular items, those might be the kinds of items to snipe.

## Pay Quickly

Not really a strategy, but if you pay for your items quickly, you'll be well perceived, and your feedback rating will grow accordingly. In addition, a seller who is pleased with your performance might be inclined to inform you of future auctions for the items you're looking for. Sometimes a seller will even offer an item to you directly, avoiding the whole auction process. Depending on the price of the item, this could translate into better buys for you.

On the other hand, if you don't pay quickly, not only does the seller become annoyed (maybe even inspired to leave accurate and negative feedback), they might also offer the item to someone else. Snub a seller, and you could even wind up blacklisted. Bad news.

## Post Feedback

Again, not truly a buying strategy, unless you consider how valuable a good reputation can be, a seller's and your own. At the auction sites that offer a feedback forum, be sure to post positive feedback for a good seller in a timely manner. The seller will reciprocate if you've done a good job holding up your end of the deal. In the long run, good buying feedback will show you to be trustworthy and committed. If and when you decide to sell at the auction sites, that will all add up to a stellar feedback rating that will draw more bidders to *your* auctions.

## Selling Strategies

If selling is what you're into, then consider these words of wisdom to help you save time, effort, and headaches—leaving you more time to count your profits.

## Know Your Stuff

Before you list your items, be sure you *know* what they are. Though this may sound obvious, you'd be surprised at how many sellers list items without actually knowing what it is they have. Not knowing your stuff will have a double-edged result: if you don't know you've got a real treasure, you could sell it for far too low a price; if you *think* you know what you have but you're wrong, you'll wind up looking either like a raw novice or a rat. Either way, bidders don't like bidding with sellers who are uninformed: it gives them little confidence that they'll truly receive what they're paying for. However, if you are an expert or manage to become one quickly, bidders will trust your expertise and might return to your auctions again and again because they know you deliver the real deal.

 **GET A CLUE** If you make a mistake in an auction and a bidder points it out to you (usually via e-mail), consider modifying the listing to include the new information. Other bidders will be pleased to see that you're honest and are trying to provide the best information for the auction's duration. Oh, yeah—don't forget to thank the person who provided the clarification.

## Do Your Market Research

If you want to get the best profits from your merchandise, you'll need to offer the best merchandise. Shop the different auction sites to see which one caters best to the kinds of items you'll sell. Don't just look at which sites have the most antiques, artwork, or toys, but check to see where most of the bidding is taking place. Check for completed auctions in the category where you might list your item. Look for how many of the auctions actually got bids. When you find where the bidders are, see how much they're actually bidding. An auction is a great place to determine current market value for whatever it is you want to sell. If you can't find an item just like yours, look for something close to it (same time period, subject matter, or whatever). A close cousin to your item might be enough to consider when trying to determine what you have might be worth.

## Craft Tempting Titles

The fish won't bite if you don't bait the hook properly. The same goes for auction listings and the titles you give them. Remember that usually the only bait you can offer the bidders is a promising item title. Unless your auction is featured in some special photo area of an auction site (which usually costs more in listing fees), it will be up to your well-crafted title to halt bidders in their tracks and beckon them in to learn more about your special item.

When you develop an item title, try to put as much descriptive information into it as space allows. You're usually limited on how many characters you can use, and it's rare to get more than 100 characters to make your best pitch. Therefore, make sure your title has the information that helps a bidder decide whether or not to drop by your auction. Here are examples of a good title and a not-so-good title:

**Good:**   1973 Thermos-brand Mint PARTRIDGE FAMILY lunchbox w/ Near-Mint thermos

**Not Good:**   Lunchbox and thermos from Partridge Family—GROOVY!

The first title gives a potential bidder information about the item, its year of origin, and its condition. The second description doesn't tell as much about

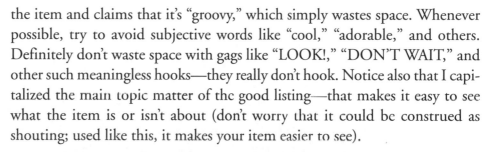
the item and claims that it's "groovy," which simply wastes space. Whenever possible, try to avoid subjective words like "cool," "adorable," and others. Definitely don't waste space with gags like "LOOK!," "DON'T WAIT," and other such meaningless hooks—they really don't hook. Notice also that I capitalized the main topic matter of the good listing—that makes it easy to see what the item is or isn't about (don't worry that it could be construed as shouting; used like this, it makes your item easier to see).

Most important, include key words that might be used in a bidder's search. Actually, both titles above have decent "hit words" such as "Partridge," "Partridge Family," "lunchbox," and "thermos." The good title also has "1973" (lots of '70s collectors out there, by the way). The good title works better, though, because it immediately lets the bidder know this isn't some busted, rusted, bashed-up box. Spend enough time looking at crummy items, and you'll appreciate the condition in an item's title—your bidders will, too.

## Give Detailed Descriptions

Once you've gotten the bidders in to look over the details of your item, offer the most useful information you can muster. You're acting as a salesperson now, and here's where you can make your perfect pitch. Be sure to restate what the item is, and go into appropriate detail about the item's completeness. Condition is a big deal to bidders, so don't skimp on describing the beauty of the item while also pointing out every flaw and defect. It's at this point bidders decide whether to bid or not, and if you don't provide an accurate and comprehensive description, they might pass over your otherwise great item or—equally bad—might bid with higher expectations than you'll truly deliver. For the Partridge Family lunchbox, a good description might read like this:

```
From the 1973 television series that starred Shirley Jones and
David Cassidy, here's the original Thermos-brand metal lunchbox
from The Partridge Family. This box features colorful illustrations
of Shirley Partridge and her musical mop-tops, including a stage
shot on one face and the famous multicolored family bus on the
other face. There are more illustrations of each of the kids along
the sides. This box shows extremely little wear and is virtually
rust-free. There are a couple of minor scratches near the handle,
```

and the box hinges are just a bit sprung. The box still closes
fully and without strain. Good gloss all the way around with a bit
of luster loss near the latch.

The thermos is the first-issue metal thermos with the wrap-around
photo of the family on stage. The glass inside is unbroken, and
there is only a minor scratch below the "T" in Partridge. The
original gloss is 90 percent present with some loss near the top of
the thermos. The stopper is present, and the cup-cap has just a bit
of wear on the top.

Sure, that's quite a bit of explanation, but you don't want to leave too much to
interpretation. If you err in your description, you want to be overly harsh
when grading and otherwise describing your item—that reduces the chance
of disappointment when the package arrives.

**GET A CLUE**    As a rule, I determine a grade for what I sell, then bring it down half a grade just
to be safe. For example, if I think my item deserves a grade of 8 out of 10, I'll
describe it as 7.5. By this method, I'll be more certain that the buyer will find the
item exceeds expectations rather than the other way around. Of course, don't be too
harsh when you grade your item or bidders will pass on it thinking it's in poorer condition
than they were looking for.

**WARNING!**    Spelling counts! Be sure you use good spelling and good grammar in your
item descriptions. Nothing hollers "incompetent" louder than gross errors
in the text of an item description. There aren't a bunch of snobby bidders out there, but if
your description sports misspellings in every other word, bidders might wonder about
the accuracy of the item you're attempting to describe. Take your time, and reread your
descriptions for correctness.

## Post Pictures

Definitely include pictures in your auctions to get the best possible results.
Pictures have pretty much become required fare when auctioning at the person-to-person sites. All you need is a digital camera (you can get them as low
as $200) or a scanner (you can get those as cheap as $60) to capture auction-

ready images of your items. Get an image host such as AuctionWatch, Yahoo!Geocities, or your own Internet service provider and upload your pictures to the Web. (Remember that some sites offer free image storage on their own servers, too.) Review the auction sites' listing forms to learn how you can reference your item's image.

If you don't think you want to mess with pictures, keep in mind that many bidders these days won't even bid on an item unless there's an accompanying image. With so many auctions going on, this is an area where bidders can be choosers. Just be sure any image you present is clear, large enough to view, and doesn't distort the actual condition of your item. Remember, the image is there to illuminate the truth, not bend it.

## Price For Persuasion

Pricing is difficult—bidders want a bargain, and sellers need a reasonable profit. As a seller, your goal is to attract bidders with an enticing price while keeping in mind the amount you've invested in the item versus what you believe bidders will potentially pay.

Low opening bids always entice bidders, especially the bargain hunters. Though you might start an item at a low price, that doesn't necessarily mean your final take will be low, too. Actually, some of a seller's best bidding comes from those who jump on an auction with a low starting price and then get "hooked." In most auctions, a bidder who has chosen to participate quickly develops some sort of emotional tie or desire for the item. When others come by to battle for the item, most bidders will accept (even enjoy) the competition and fight for the item. If yours is a popular or otherwise desirable item, expect that it will probably reach its market value before the auction is over.

 WARNING! Remember, the market is a volatile place. Things that were hot one day can get iced over the next. If you have trendy items to sell, sell 'em while the trend is hot.

If you're anxious to make a big sale and start your auction at a high opening bid (regardless of whether the item supports such a value), don't be surprised to see bidders pass you by in droves. Most bidders don't mind paying market value for an item, but few will engage in the bidding if you don't offer a bit of room for them to potentially get a better-than-average deal.

Many bidders avoid reserve price auctions like the plague. In those cases, some bidders contend they may as well just pay the seller's asking price rather than waste their time trying to figure how much the seller really wants. Don't shy away from using reserve prices, but save them for truly valuable items or those in which you fear you might not recover your original investment. *Don't* use reserve prices all the time just to ensure you make outstanding profits; bidders will quickly recognize your strategy and avoid your auctions.

## Answer All Questions

If a bidder (or potential bidder) asks a question, answer it quickly and completely. These are potential customers, and you need to give them exemplary service. Sometimes, bidders ask questions just to see how responsive you are in an effort to determine how you might behave when the auction's over and they're waiting on delivery of the item.

When a bidder asks a question give some extra information if you think the bidder is unclear about more than just what they're querying. Add just a bit of sales pitch, too. Without trying to manipulate the bidder or misrepresent the item, your enthusiasm could be just what the bidder needs to help them decide that yours is the best auction in which to bid.

## Announce Your Guarantee Policy

Here's one that perplexes sellers: should you offer a money-back guarantee? Most long-time sellers offer such a policy but stipulate that the item *must* be returned in the same condition as shipped. For sellers who sell a lot, guarantees don't pose much threat to their overall auction income (though the rework can be a bit bothersome). However, the sellers who do offer such guarantees can oftentimes attract *more* bidders since the guarantee shows they have nothing to hide and nothing to fear regarding the quality of their merchandise.

If you don't want to get into the returns business, clearly state that "all sales are final" in your item descriptions. This may or may not be a turnoff to bidders (depending on how faithfully you describe the item), but at least the bidders will be clear about your policy before they bid.

## Post Feedback

Just as when you're the buyer, post feedback quickly after the auction has closed (after the exchange of goods). Buyers who felt they were treated well and got positive feedback from the seller will probably come back for repeat business. To a seller, repeat business often spells repeat success.

# Do You Think I Have a Problem?

Now you have a feeling for online auction places, you know how to find the things you're looking for, and you have a nice array of tips and strategies to boost your success. But will you have control as you venture into online auctions? Will you bid wisely or wildly? Will this new hobby pass the time or fill it? Will you know when you've had too much? It's true that online auctions are exciting, but what happens when people get *too* excited about them?

Believe it or not, one of the newest and perhaps most threatening trouble spots in online auctions can come from you. Have you ever heard of Internet addiction, and have you heard of what it can do to individuals and families when it takes over? In this chapter I'll explain what Internet addiction is, how it can affect you, and how you can determine if you've been spending a bit too much time online. More to the point, I'll show you how online auctions are actually having negative effects on some people, threatening to turn their otherwise-normal lives upside down.

This discussion is going to be a bit more somber than what you've read thus far, but this is an important topic and one of which every auction goer should become familiar. I promise not to take the wind out of your sails, but I want you to understand the growing seriousness of online auction addiction.

# What Is Internet Addiction?

It's no wonder so many people want to get online and stay there: everywhere you turn, someone is heralding the arrival of *the new site to visit*. So much to buy, so many games to play, and so many new people to meet—you can't experience it all in just an hour or two, and that's when troubles arise.

Addictions are usually defined as any behavior that becomes more important than family, friends, or work. Often beginning as hobbies or even experiments of curiosity, some behaviors can become so compelling and compulsive that they throw normal life out of balance. Through addiction, a person's hobby or curiosity can sometimes develop into what's termed an "abnormal preoccupation." Granted, this is a simple definition for a complex problem, and a growing number of psychologists have turned their attention to behavior disorders attributed to Internet usage.

For a time, some argued it was merely the newness of the Internet that had many users surfing for hours on end, predicting that when the newness wore off, hours of usage would decline. Unfortunately, that argument has fallen flat. Psychologists have seen and treated clients who confess they have become addicted to the Internet, spending far too much time surfing while hurting themselves and others around them.

It started in chat rooms, where users were able to find new friends and even lovers online. "Cyber relationships" became a way to share interests and observations with others, rather than with people in the real world. Then came networked gaming, where players could log on and play Doom and Quake 24 hours a day, pitting their skills against other players. Eventually, addictions to online sexual materials raised its ugly head, and even online shopping has become a problem for "shopaholics."

Dr. Maressa Hecht Orzack is a clinical psychologist and founder of Computer Addiction Services (**www.computeraddiction.com**). Having studied and treated addictive behaviors for over 15 years, Orzack suggests that "our society is becoming more and more computer dependent not only for information, but for fun and entertainment." And while many innocently wonder what they would do without their computer (speaking from the perspective of general productivity), others have become downright addicted to computer and Internet use to the extent that they suffer symptoms of withdrawal when they're away from their PCs for any extended period of time (sometimes for as little as a few hours).

New terminology like *internet addiction*, *net compulsion*, and *cyberaddiction* has been coined to identify addictive online behavior, and it can affect people of all ages. Compulsive online behavior is no gag, and according to a growing number of psychologists, it's become more prevalent than you might realize. In a 1999 Q&A session, Dr. David Greenfield, an addiction expert at Psychological Health Associates in Connecticut, recognized how the Internet is fast replacing opportunities for physical interaction between people—interaction that Greenfield sees as crucial for good psychological health. Human contact on the Internet, as Greenfield observes, is not a suitable replacement for the real thing.

DID YOU KNOW? In 1997, a national story broke about a woman whose compulsive use of the Internet caused her divorce and led authorities to take away her children. Her estranged husband complained that she spent as much as 12 hours a day online. The police took custody of the woman's children—aged 2, 3, and 5—and the woman was charged with three counts of child endangerment.

## What Makes the Internet So Addictive?

In a word—freedom. The Internet has been built upon a foundation of free thought, free expression, and the freedom to pursue whatever it is that interests you. To a great extent, online freedom is not inherently evil, and there have been many legislative battles to keep the Internet a non-regulated forum for the exchange of information, ideas, and just about anything else. However, the dark side of online freedom is that it presents an unreal world where users are free to do whatever they choose, as often as they choose, and with whomever they choose without any repercussions or responsibility (after all, it's just a computer screen, right?)

Psychologists are finding that many Internet users become addicted due to the fact they can assume any identity or achieve (supposedly) complete anonymity in their online exploits. Internet users can assume whatever name, age, background, or appearance they choose when they interact with others. Usually, this isn't too problematic, but for some people, living in the faceless online world can produce serious personal troubles.

Dr. Kimberly S. Young, founder of the Center for On-Line Addiction (**www.netaddiction.com**)has observed, "Internet users, especially those who are lonely and insecure in real-life situations, take [online] freedom and quickly pour out their strongest feelings, darkest secrets, and deepest desires. This leads to the illusion of intimacy, but when reality underscores the severe limitations of relying on a faceless community for the love and caring that can only come from actual people, Internet addicts experience very real disappointment and pain."

Freedom is what has forged the Internet into the thriving new tool of our current culture. And, in my opinion, the freedom to interact with others without prejudgment or prejudice has advanced the sharing of information and the development of online friendships. Unfortunately, this freedom can be misused and abused, either through seemingly-innocuous online relationships, explicit sexual discussion and dependency, and even cyber affairs.

## Can Online Auctions Be Hazardous to Your Health?

It's true that online relationships can damage real-world relationships, but how does all this relate to online auctions? Actually, online auctions are classified as having the same addictive potential as gambling: there is the stimulation of the surroundings (casinos compared to flashy auction sites), the thrill of the game, and the euphoria of winning.

To many seasoned auction goers, auctions have already become an addiction. Many people treated for internet addiction have conceded that online auctions give them an actual high. It's widely documented that shopaholics actually experience escape from real-world pressures and temporarily mask deeper depression when they go shopping. However, as Greenfield notes in his book, *Virtual Addiction*, "Most of us have experienced the pleasant sensation we get after buying something. Unfortunately, that feeling is short-lived and may be followed by a sense of guilt or remorse, perhaps leading us to return the item. . . . Yet we often repeat this pattern of buying and feeling remorseful, in spite of the negative feelings it may bring." Compare Greenfield's observation with the bidder who bids but never pays or who asks to back out of a bid obligation. Though this isn't always a sign of someone who's addicted to online bidding, there could be a deeper problem at hand.

**IN MY MIND** By no means does this last point suggest you should begin practicing amateur psychology when one of your deals falls through. In fact, it would be highly unwise to ever accuse another person you might deal with of having addictive behavior. This information and opinion are merely being offered for your consideration.

There was a time when shopaholics would need to get dressed and travel to the store or shopping mall to feed their need to buy. Now, online retailing is not only incredibly convenient, but it can also be tremendous trouble for others. No longer is there the usual travel time to head off an impulse buy. Online the buy is immediate (most often through the use of a credit card), but the financial impact isn't felt until some time later. Greenfield recalls a client who fell under the spell of online shopping and, when she received her credit card statement, was shocked to learn she had spent $15,000 over the course of a month.

It's easy to understand the lure of online shopping: you can shop at any hour and have your purchases conveniently show up on your doorstep within a few days (in fact, for some shoppers the absence of a package on the doorstep can compel a shopaholic to get online and buy something else). But at online auctions, there's the added draw of shopping for the best deals or delivering the most strategic bids. Some psychologists have explained that their clients who profess to be "addicted" to online auctions often bid for the sake of the win as opposed to the actual item being offered. "They're buying to try to make themselves feel good, but it can never really make them feel good enough," states Dr. L. J. Rambeck in an article published by CasinoWire.com. Many auction goers are addicted to the process—the game—and sometimes lose sight of the fact that they will need to pay for the item in the event they emerge victorious.

DID YOU KNOW? Did you know that feelings of excitement and victory actually trigger the release of a neurochemical in our brains known as *dopamine*? The exhilaration people feel when they score a win (at auctions or casinos or wherever) is a short-lived feeling brought on by dopamine. Unfortunately, this intense, temporary satisfaction can also become addictive.

But even if you're clear that it's the stuff you're after at online auctions and not just the win, there is still a danger of finding far more stuff than you imagined and being tempted to own it all. Consider the auction sites you've seen in this book with their thousands and even millions of items up for bid every day. Unless you're focused on exactly what you want to find, you could easily begin "window shopping" for just about anything. On a mild level, browsing can cost you more time and money than you originally intended, but for some it can spark an obsession to find and own just about everything. That's the double-edged sword of online auctions: you're relatively assured to find what you're looking for, but you can also expect to find far more than you should ever attempt to own. The thrill of finding something at an online auction you never thought you could own and immediately placing a bid to bring it home (often on an impulse) can spell trouble.

## What Are the Warning Signs?

Subjectivity gets in the way when trying to determine if there's an addiction afoot. Often the most difficult question is, When have you crossed the line from "normal" to "addicted"? Reassuringly, there are signs to look for to determine a potential addiction to the Internet and online auctions. Dr. Orzack encourages patients concerned with Internet or computer addiction to determine whether they have experienced or exhibited one or more of the behaviors in Table 18-1.

---

## Table 18-1

**Psychological Symptoms**

- A sense of well-being or euphoria while at the computer

- An inability to stop the activity

- Craving more and more time at the computer

- Neglecting family and friends

- Feeling empty, depressed, or irritable when not at the computer

- Lying to employers and family about activities

- Problems with school or job

**Physical Symptoms**

- Carpal tunnel syndrome

- Dry eyes

- Migraine headaches

- Back aches

- Eating irregularities (such as skipping meals)

- Failure to attend to personal hygiene

- Changes in sleep patterns

---

*Source*: Computer Addiction Services (**www.computeraddiction.com**)

Dr. Young takes the assessment of addictive behavior to a level that focuses directly on online auctions, providing the list of potential trouble signs noted in Table 18-2.

## Table 18-2

- Do you need to bid with increasing amounts of money in order to achieve the desired excitement?

- Are you preoccupied with auction houses (thinking about being online when offline, anticipating your next online session)?

- Have you lied to friends and family members to conceal the extent of your online bidding?

- Do you feel restless or irritable when attempting to cut down or stop online bidding?

- Have you made repeated unsuccessful efforts to control, cut back, or stop online bidding?

- Do you use auction houses as a way of escaping from problems or relieve feelings of helplessness, guilt, anxiety, or depression?

- Have you jeopardized or lost a significant relationship, job, or educational or career opportunity because of online bidding?

- Have you committed illegal acts such as forgery, fraud, theft, or embezzlement to finance online activities?

*Source*: Center for On-Line Addiction (**www.netaddiction.com**)

It's okay to spend time at online auctions (or just online in general), and you can expect to log many hours as you learn about and perfect your auction activity. Expect that your early experiences at auctions will take longer, mostly due to your need to register and become familiar with the site. It's not necessary to immediately fear or suspect addictive behavior as you learn the ropes or begin to more fully enjoy the Internet.

GET
A
CLUE
Greenfield makes note of the "novelty factor." He claims it's not unusual for new surfers to log as many as 10 hours a day online when they begin their first ventures into cyberspace. For most individuals, the newness of the experience soon wears off, and time online typically decreases as well.

If you're of the mind to make online auctions a full-time venture, then you'll definitely be spending much more time online than most other folks. After all, you'll be busy learning site features and rules, investigating hot-ticket items, and building your inventory.

However, if you begin to exhibit some of the warning signs previously listed and become increasingly concerned about your time online (especially when friends, family, or employers begin to take note of it), you might need to reassess your activity. If you think auction (or Internet) addiction can't happen to you, I beg you to think again. Online auctions are great fun—I don't deny that. But online auctions can easily become that drug you need when nothing new or exciting has happened within the last week, the last day, or even the last hour.

GET
A
CLUE
I'd love to tell you that sellers are immune to overzealous online auctioning, but they're not. For sellers, it's equally thrilling to see folks bid on their items. It suggests their items have value, often being translated into the seller's feelings of personal value and worth. Sellers also have to be careful to avoid the pitfalls of auction addiction such as selling everything in sight, speculating excessively on goods that might or might not sell, becoming depressed or irate when bids received don't match up to (unrealistic?) expectations.

IN
MY
MIND
Hey! Has this been some sort of cruel joke? With all this potential for addiction to auctions and the Internet, have you been led down a merry path only to have the rug pulled out from under you? Simply, no. This book wasn't designed to lull you into online auctions only to threaten you with auction addiction at the end. Remember, I love online auctions, millions of others love online auctions, and there are great times to be had at online auctions. But, like anything else in life, it all has to be done while exercising *moderation*. It all comes down to *balance*. As with any endeavor, you'll do best if you balance your activities so that no one effort overpowers or squeezes out other important activities from your life or the lives of those around you.

## Is There Hope?

Remember, if you enjoy online auctions and begin to spend a significant amount of time at them, that's not necessarily a reason to panic, worried that you might be on the verge of addiction. However, if you're concerned that your auction and Internet activity might be getting the better of you, here are a few suggestions from Greenfield:

- Turn off the computer after each use. Having to restart every time may be enough of a delay to prevent you from logging on, surfing, and spending on a whim.

- Before you log on, decide exactly what you're looking for and go in with the focused determination to get that specific item.

- Try to avoid open-ended browsing—the temptation to buy on impulse could be too great.

- Develop a budget for your online shopping and stick to it. You might even consider an "online-only" credit card that has a low spending limit.

- Don't keep your online activities a secret. Let others know what you're doing. If need be, find and join a support group or seek counseling so you can further discuss your online activity (see the last section of this chapter for resources).

If you truly fear becoming trapped in the Web, shouldn't you just pull the plug completely and go cold turkey? Some have done that, but Orzack has noted that as a bit extreme and may only shift an addiction to some other behavior or substance. Instead, she suggests engaging in cognitive behavior therapy in cases where Net addiction has become particularly problematic. "[This approach] teaches the patient to identify the problem, to solve the problem, and to learn coping skills to prevent relapse." If at times Internet use becomes excessive, abusive, or addictive, correction might come in the way of breaking the compulsive pattern as opposed to cutting the cord entirely. Greenfield notes in *Virtual Addiction* that "it depends upon the degree and pattern of Internet abuse, along with one's personal circumstances in determining whether controlled use is possible." Therefore, to help yourself break potentially compulsive Internet use, Greenfield suggests these alternatives:

- **Take a break from technology**. Turn off the PC for a day or two or more. If you must log on, identify why, conduct your business, and then log off.

- **Develop other interests**. Just as your PC or the Internet became a new hobby, try a new activity with which to share your online time to possibly break the compulsive pattern.

- **Exercise**. Greenfield states he can think of no better recommendation that would have more positive effects than a healthy and regular exercise routine.

- **Shorten your Internet sessions**. Don't go cold turkey, but do impose time limits on yourself and stick to them. You might find you have more time each day catch up on what you've been neglecting, and you might learn how much leisure time you've truly been missing.

These are just a few of Greenfield's suggestions. If your problem is having serious and negative effects on your life and those around you, seek professional assistance as quickly as possible.

## Learning More about Online Addictions

Of course, I'm no credentialed psychologist, nor am I formally schooled in matters of obsessive, compulsive, and addictive behaviors. I have read and researched much of what has been published in the area of online addictions. If you want to learn more from the experts I've quoted in this chapter, I encourage you to look into the following resources.

## Web Sites

- Dr. Kimberly S. Young at the Center for On-Line Addiction (**www.netaddiction.com**)

- Dr. Maressa Hecht Orzack at Computer Addiction Services (**www.computeraddiction.com**)

- Dr. David N. Greenfield at Virtual Addiction: The Center for Internet Studies (**www.virtual-addiction.com**)

## Books and Articles

CasinoWire.com, "Net Auctions: Bidder Watch Out!" 12 March 1999 (www.casinowire.com/archive/99/mar/1317.shtml).

Greenfield, David N., *Virtual Addiction: Help for Netheads, Cyberfreaks, and Those Who Love Them* (Oakland, CA: New Harbinger Publications) 1999.

Young, Kimberly S., *Caught in the Net* (New York: John Wiley) 1999.

C H A P T E R 19

# Honorable Mentions:
# More Online Auction Sites

I promised I'd give you more, so here it is. In my years of auction going—and especially while preparing this book—I've sifted through just about all of the auction sites of merit out there. Though I gave you some detailed reviews of what I consider to be the best, here are the top runners-up that are also worth checking out.

**IN MY MIND** Before I go into some of these other sites, it's important to remember that diversity is key for hard-core auction buyers and sellers. Sure, most people think about eBay or Onsale when they think of online auctions. Unfortunately, when those big sites experience big problems or small inventories, auction goers realize they've put most of their eggs in very few baskets. While some of the sites in this chapter aren't the biggest or best, they offer alternatives to auction communities. Don't believe that eBay is the end-all auction site—its managers don't even believe that. Diversify, and you'll stand a better chance for success in the long run.

## More Merchant Auctions

- *CNET Auctions* (**http://auctions.cnet.com**). Online biggie CNET is best known as a source of computer commentary, online reports, and technical reviews. In May 1999, CNET threw its chips into the online auction realm. It boasts a "no Furby zone," commenting on the abundance of collectible sites. Here you'll find a good assortment of computer and electronic goodies to pore over. A nice bonus of this site: each auction item listing also has links to actual in-depth reviews of the item (features, durability, reliability). It's a nice touch and a worthwhile site to visit. Why didn't it make my top list? The site is still too new and doesn't have enough traffic and time under its belt. Still, it's one to watch.

- *DealDeal Auctions* (**www.dealdeal.com**). A fun name and a good site with a good selection of items, from home PCs to home audio to home and leisure items. The site has a nice design and a decent inventory. A neat little perk here is "Deal Bucks," with which you can earn virtual credits whenever you bid, recommend a friend to the site, or join DealDeal's affiliate network. Nice, but the site runs a bit slowly, and customer service seems to be on an extended coffee break. Worth a look, but it didn't completely clear the "top list" bar.

- *Haggle Online* (**www.haggle.com**). Sorry, but every time I hear the word "haggle" I inevitably think of Eric Idle and Graham Chapman bartering over a gourd in Monty Python's *Life of Brian*. Anyway, this engaging site is nicely designed and features a good selection. It's heavy on PC goods but balanced with home electronics, jewelry, and sporting goods. Strangely, after the large array of computer goods, the next highest-volume offering is in the "Adults Only" category. Customer service was a bit bleak, and the site seems schizophrenic about whether it wants to be a merchant site or a person-to-person site. Good items, though.

- *Egghead.com Surplus Auction* (**www.surplusauction.com**). With all the hardware auctions I've shown you, it makes sense to throw a bit of software into the mix. Interestingly enough, Egghead auctions offer both, providing a well-rounded auction-going experience. Egghead was a brick-and-mortar software shack until 1998 when it closed all of its physical stores to pursue a virtual presence instead. The site offers some great deals on software applications and other computer-related items. It's an eye-catching site but it's slow, and devoid of the usual online auction features (especially a proxy bidding system and outbid notification). Egghead announced a merger with Onsale in July 1999—that could be what it needs to beef up its site and jump into my top list.

## Person-to-Person Auctions

- *Auctions.com* (**www.auctions.com**). Formerly known as Auction Universe, Auctions.com is definitely a contender in the person-to-person realm, providing good site features and a respectable inventory (roughly 30,000 to 40,000 auctions at any given time). The site is straightforward in design and one of the easier sites to navigate. I have one gripe, though: I'd like to see the site lighten up on the animated banner ads—they're distracting, and they make me anxious to scroll down until they're out of sight. If you're selling, you'll be pleased to know that basic listings are free. If you want to add special features such as bold titles, showcase listings, or other upgrades, fees will be added for whichever of those perks you choose. Final value fees are only 2.5 percent of the high bid. Other features include the *Robo-bid* proxy system and an on-site escrow and insurance system, *Bid$afe*. Though bidding activity is rather light, Auctions.com is a key contender and is striving to give the other big dogs something to growl about.

- *Excite Auctions* (**http://auctions.excite.com**). Much like Yahoo!, Excite is another key Internet portal sites that decided auctions are good business. Excite Auctions is actually an outgrowth of the successful Excite Classifieds2000, an online classified ad service (hence, the site URL you see here). Excite Auctions offers a decent inventory of roughly 72,000 items at any given time, good features, a recently revamped (and much improved) site design, and 24-7 e-mail customer support, making it one of the well-traveled person-to-person sites.

- *CityAuction* (**www.cityauction.com**). Here's a site with a unique approach: it's designed to link up buyers and sellers in the same geographic region. Though it's not the grandest site in terms of design, inventory, or bidders, the concept behind it makes a lot of sense. So much sense that Ticketmaster recently purchased CityAuction, obviously in a move to team up ticket holders with ticket buyers for regional events. At CityAuction, you can choose from a list of links that will take you to auctions from sellers across the United States as well as across the world (there's a cool home page feature where visitors can enter their local zip code to find the auctions nearest their home town). The site is easy to use and navigate, unhampered by extensive design. (Is that a pro or a con?) You can typically find around

5,000 auctions or so on any given visit, which is on the low side, but the site does have some useful features like automatic e-mail notifications in the vein of *Personal Shopper* at eBay. Yes, it's still a fledgling effort, but I think the regional appeal of CityAuction will help it become a significant contender in the very near future.

■ *BoxLot Auctions* (**www.boxlot.com**). This is a new site that vies for the attention of general item auction goers. BoxLot has a simple design, though navigation gets a bit tricky (links don't always help you go back where you'd like to). However, the site does offer a decent inventory much like that of Auctions.com and approaching the levels at Amazon.com Auctions. Though the virtual shelves are stocked with plenty of categories, you'll do best if you're searching for collectibles (figurines, printed matter, and so on). All the same, BoxLot doesn't currently charge listing fees, and final value fees are quite reasonable. Bidding is rather sparse, but that can just be a matter of time, as auction-goers diversify their bidding and selling base. Give this site a look, though. I see potential here.

■ *Auction Addict* (**www.auctionaddict.com**). The name itself is enough to draw auction goers' attention. This is a nice little site with a happy feel. You'll find an easy-to-navigate design and little cartoon characters that remind me of a cross between the Monopoly millionaire and the Pep Boys. The inventory is a bit limited (only around 9,000 items when I last visited). There are quite a number of categories and subcategories; unfortunately, many subcategories had nothing in them. Seller-friendly Auction Addict doesn't charge listing fees, and low final value fees are only levied if the item sells at the auction.

■ *Gold's Auction* (**www.goldsauction.com**). Never heard of Gold's Auction? You're not alone, mainly since the site has only been officially "live" since October 1999. However, Gold's has been on the lips of the auction-going community the whole summer of 1999. Why? It's positioning itself as the eBay alternative. When the auction king suffered the annoying bout of site outages throughout the spring and summer of 1999, the folks developing the Gold's site saw the opportunity to provide an alternate venue to frustrated eBayers. Gold's began to conduct its online "beta test" in June 1999, encouraging new users to list items without any listing fees; the site was attempting to reach 50,000 items listed before it officially launched (it reached the 100,000 item milestone in early September). The site is similar in design to eBay (some say too similar), though it has incurred some launch delays due to some site instability and poor server response time. While some have bemoaned Gold's technical difficulties and delayed launch (it was supposed to have gone live in August '99), others see it as a sign that the site wanted to be sure its house was fully in order to avoid making promises it couldn't keep. eBay is keeping a close eye on this upstart site. You should, too.

## More Art and Antique Auctions

- *Sloan's Auctions* (**www.sloansauction.com**). Established in 1853 at 11th Street and Pennsylvania Avenue in historic Washington, D.C., it was originally known as Latimer and Cleary. In 1891, C.G. Sloan purchased the business and renamed it Sloan's. This is another of the fine upscale auction houses where you can learn about upcoming auctions and bid on publicized lots on the Sloan's Web site or in the regularly printed auction catalogs. Auctions are conducted in Washington, D.C., as well as at the newer location in Miami, Florida (opened in 1997). No, you can't bid online, but you can learn a great deal about this historic auction house and the fine items that it auctions. Absentee bids are welcome, and the site lists phone numbers you can call to learn more about Sloan's auctions and other high-end collector services. Nice site with a posh feel to it. I love these sites!

- *Artnet Auctions* (**www.artnet.com**). Impressive networked approach to the sale of fine art, furniture, and antiques. Artnet was originally devised in 1967 (according to the company-provided history) when company CEO Hans Neuendorf conceived a method to advertise available artwork beyond just single galleries. In 1996, Artnet.com came online to further that original vision, providing access to fine art and other significant pieces from hundreds of galleries and artists. Artnet.com is a consignment site and welcomes the participation of reputable dealers and art professionals to advertise, auction, and sell their items to the Artnet community. It's an easy-to-navigate site, rich in illustrations and photographs, that charges no seller's commission and only a 5 percent buyer's premium. You'll find modern, Impressionist, and early American artwork along with photography, 20th-century decorative art, and more.

## More Specialty Auctions and Other Venues

By this time, you can probably imagine how many more specialty sites are out on the Web. With over 400 sites today and more showing up every week, it's just a matter of searching for whatever interests you to see if an auction site exists that caters to your desires. Most often, you'll find a new site that fits the bill and, knowing what you now know about auctions, you can quickly assess the site to see if it's where you'll want to buy and sell stuff.

Yes, the auctions have much to offer mainly because there are so doggone many of them. But are auctions the only places online to find what you want? Absolutely not. There are many stones to turn over to find that special something that eludes you.

First, don't forget Usenet (remember, that's how I found online auctions many years ago). With so many specialized newsgroups out there, it's a venue you shouldn't overlook. Don't be surprised if you visit a group and most of the "For Sale" listings are actually auction ads that point you back to one or another of the person-to-person sites. However, you can still find many folks just looking to sell their stuff at fixed prices. It's first-come, first-served, so don't dawdle.

And don't be shy about stopping off at the major Internet portal sites (Yahoo!, Excite, Alta Vista, and others) and enter a search for whatever it is you're looking for. Enter "Beatles" and you'll find a wealth of sites where the Fab Four are celebrated and sold off. Search for "pottery" and you'll find a stunning number of sites devoted to classic claywork and more. Search for just about anything—if you like it, chances are many other people out there do too and have probably started up Web sites, chat groups, and enthusiast forums. The Internet is your oyster, and the beauty is that it practically drops the pearl at your feet. All you have to do is look, ask, and explore a little. And don't forget to have fun!

# Additional Sources of Information

Oh, I can hear the cries now:

*"But you didn't tell us everything about online auctions."*

*"I want to know more about selling."*

*"I want to know more about buying."*

*"I want to know more, more, MORE!"*

Excellent. I was hoping you would. Clearly, I can't provide every detail for you within the confines of this book. If I've done my job well, you have a good road map for striking off into the online auction terrain. But if the information I've provided has spawned even more questions than you had before, this appendix of references to more information may quench your thirst for knowledge.

**GET A CLUE** Well, pardon the shameless plug, but if you want to know the nuts and bolts of eBay, I invite you to grab a copy of my other book from Prima, *Online Auctions at eBay: Bid with Confidence, Sell with Success.* It's 500 pages worth of tips, tactics, and details of the largest person-to-person auction site on the WWW. Commercial over.

# Auctions in General

You'll find a lot of information about auctions and styles of bidding and selling at auction houses; some of it's on paper, some on the Web itself.

## Books

*Auctions: The Social Construction of Value* by Charles W. Smith; Berkeley: University of California Press, 1989.

This is a detailed, yet easy-to-read analysis of the business of auctioning. The author provides excellent narrative and examples of auctioning at work in global economies. If you're looking for more insight on how auctions play out and how they shape and direct market values, this would be the book for you.

*Auctions and Auctioneering* by Ralph Cassady; Berkeley: University of California Press, 1967.

This was my primer to auctions. Though I hadn't read this book until after I became well established in the online auction realm, the information that it provides filled in many of the gaps. Even though this book was published 32 years ago, the vast majority of information is still timely. Unfortunately, this book has been out of print for quite a while. That, of course, is a call to you treasure hunters and book finders to start the search for a copy. Don't forget to check your local public library, which was the first place I was able to find it.

*The Complete Guide to Buying and Selling at Auction* by C. Hugh Hildesley; New York: Norton, 1997.

This is a neat little book packed with firsthand insight that takes you inside the auction experience at high-end auction parlors. Author Hildesley has been a lifetime employee at Sotheby's and now holds an executive position at the firm. His book guides you through the do's and don'ts of auction-going, and then takes you behind the scenes to witness how auction items are obtained, how they're valued, and much more. This is a fun book that reads like a diary of one of the auction mainstays.

## Web Sites

If you're looking for auction information that's only a mouse click away from where you're currently bidding, try these sites.

- *AuctionWatch* (**www.auctionwatch.com**). A terrific site that's been around for some time, though it has recently undergone significant redesign. AuctionWatch offers auction goers help with their online auction problems. You'll find free image hosting, auction counters, and an auction search engine, plus plenty of help putting them to use. You'll also find a virtual library full of in-depth auction articles, features, tips, and commentaries. The site content is updated several times a week, and there's always some timely information to be gleaned. Finally, you'll find a public forum where you can share thoughts and reactions with others who've been bitten by the auction bug. AuctionWatch.com is highly recognized for the services it provides to online auction communities and has earned the endorsement of several online auction sites, including eBay and Amazon.com Auctions.

- *Gomez.com* (**www.gomez.com**). This site bills itself as "The eCommerce Authority." It fills those shoes pretty well, too. You'll find plenty of information about many e-commerce industries, including a special section dedicated to reviewing and rating auctions. You'll also find feature stories of interest to auction enthusiasts.

## Online Auction Search Sites

As I hinted earlier in the book, there are custom Web sites on the Internet that serve as your search portals to a number of online auction sites. Using these *meta-search* sites, you can send a search-bot off to find particular items across many different auction sites all at once. The meta-search result will tell you which items matched your search query and where those items are currently listed. Most meta-searches allow you to enter search key words that can be checked day after day. This is especially useful when you're looking for so many items that you might even forget to search for some of them when in the midst of an auction site. Slick, huh?

■ *AuctionWatch.com Universal Search* (**www.auctionwatch.com**). This is the newest search engine on the block, and it has a user-friendly feel. Simply enter your search criterion in the search window and click "go." The Universal Search will comb through the listings of over 300 auction sites and provide a listing for you with links to jump immediately to any item that you select. If you want even more control, use the Power Search to select a specific site to search, and how you'd like the results to be reported.

■ *Auction Sam* (**www.auctionsam.com**). This is another easy-to-use search agent. Upon your request, "Sam" runs off and searches multiple auction sites (you can select which ones) and looks for items with key words you specify. When it finds matches, it sends you an e-mail with the details.

■ *iTrack* (**www.itrack.com**). iTrack allows users to enter up to five search strings that can be checked several times a day for free. For a small annual fee, you can increase the number of search patterns the iTrack bot searches for. The best feature about iTrack is that it provides several types of intelligent searches: iTrack has been developed to work within the particular search algorithms used at a specified auction site (each site has a different way in which it reports search results). iTrack won't search multiple sites on a single request—its managers contend the differing site algorithms will result in poor matches.

■ *Bidfind* (**www.bidfind.com**). Here's another auction crawler with an agent (bot) that regularly visits over 300 online auction sites to continually update its auction item index. The result is a listing of more than 200,000 auction items. When you post your search at Bidfind, chances are you'll *find* what you want to *bid* on. Catchy name, too.

## Learn More about PCs, Web Browsers, and the Internet

I know I didn't go into the hardware and software aspects of surfing the wide open cyberspace. Here are some useful resources that will help you power up and dive into the online waves.

# Books

Here are a few books that I read and reviewed when I needed answers to pesky PC, software, and online questions.

*Upgrade Your PC In a Weekend, Revised Edition* by Faithe Wempen; Rocklin, CA: Prima, 1998.

A great guide for weekend warriors who want to rev up their PCs in a hurry. Written in a way that follows the flow of an actual weekend, Wempen's book guides readers through various hardware and software upgrading techniques that help squeeze more oompf out of any PC.

*Young at Heart: Computing for Seniors* by Mary Furlong; New York: McGraw-Hill, 1996.

I like to include this book in my list of recommended references just because it has appeal. Even if you're not a senior, you'll find some useful bits of information about computing. But for my senior auction-going friends (and I know there are a lot of you), get this book and get cozy with your PC—it's the best start for getting the most of those auction sites.

*Learn the Internet In a Weekend* by William R. Stanek; Rocklin, CA: Prima, 1998.

Here's a straightforward explanation of the Internet that everyone can understand. Even if you're a savvy Net ranger, author William Stanek delivers nuggets of wisdom that you might not have considered before. It's an easy and entertaining read.

*Supercharged Web Browsers* by Cheryl Kirk; Rockland, MA: Charles River Media, 1998.

This book is cool in that it takes on the battle over browser accessories and plug-ins and makes sense of the whole matter. From Microsoft ActiveX to Netscape plug-ins, this book helps a reader understand what the fuss is all about and which are the best tools to use for whatever the need may be.

## Web Sites

- *Using Netscape Browsers* **(http://www10.netscape.com/browsers/using/ index.html/)** Why look much further than the official Netscape web site? The URL above will take you to Netscape's online center, built with new users in mind. A bunch of great information, tutorials, and more are presented in a straightforward style. Check out this site if you want to be surfing like a pro in a fraction of the time it would take to plod along on your own.

- *Help Me: The Netscape Help Site!* **(www.geocities.com/Athens/Forum/ 5122/).** This is a great site that provides lots of help to Netscape Navigator users. It stays pretty current and even features an "update me" utility that sends you an e-mail message when the page changes.

- *The Web Developer's Virtual Library* **(www.stars.com/Software/Browsers/).** Stars.com is a virtual treasure trove of all things cyber. On this particular Web page, you'll find a great rundown on *all* of the different Web browser applications. The contributing authors at Stars.com really know their stuff; you should go there . . . *now!*

# Internet Safety and Good Practices

As promised in Chapter 3, here are some resources if you're a bit Net-anxious or otherwise wish to fully know what you're about to jump into (or are already waist-deep in) on the Internet.

## Books

*I Love the Internet But I Want My Privacy, Too!* by Chris Peterson; Rocklin, CA: Prima, 1998.

Author Chris Peterson takes you on an eye-opening journey through cyberspace and beyond, helping you understand how much of your personal information is already out there and what you can do to restrict it. I highly recommend this one.

*Protect Your Privacy on the Internet* by Brian Pfaffenberger; New York: Wiley, 1997.

Another fine book about online privacy and how to protect your sensitive information. The author doesn't inspire you to panic, and you'll learn some good lessons about how to guard yourself in the online wilderness.

## Web Sites

There are a lot of home grown and professional sites about matters surrounding Internet safety on the Web. New sites are always springing up, but here are a couple that I find to be consistently useful and fun to visit.

- *CyberAngels.Org* (**www.cyberangels.org**). You can quickly tell by the name that this is the online home of the Guardian Angels. Regardless of how you feel about them as an organization, this Web site has a lot of good tips and commonsense advice to protect yourself and your family online.

- *Federal Trade Commission: E-Commerce & the Internet* (**www.ftc.gov/ bcp/menu-internet.htm**). Well, you know the FTC means business and is interested in keeping your online business safe. This URL links to a specific section with the FTC's Consumer Education area. There are a bunch of great articles and analyses that you'll find enlightening in regard to online trading. If you're so inclined, visit **www.ftc.gov/ftc/consumer.htm** as well— it's not all Net related, but it's good consumer information all the same.

## Price Guides and Useful Publications

There is a magazine out there for virtually every interest or hobby. Just visit the magazine rack at your local bookseller or do a search on the Internet. You'll find specialty magazines and publications that cover everything from antiques to toys, action figures to Lomo cameras, music to movie memorabilia, and just about anything else you could possibly want to buy or collect. I can't even attempt to list them all here, but there's a gang of 'em. The nice thing about these publications is that they're all embracing the online auction world, and quite often will speak directly to online auction enthusiasts.

# Seldom Asked Questions

With *frequently asked questions* being asked so . . . frequently, it's likely that those questions are getting answered. I hope you've found the answers to most of your questions within this book already, or if not, that you've located the official FAQ pages of the auction sites covered herein.

But what about the questions you don't yet know to ask? What about those issues you haven't yet thought of but may soon be facing? What about the questions that the auction sites tend to overlook? Well, for you, I offer this list of *Seldom Asked Questions*. These are questions (and their answers) about those aspects of online auctioning that I've learned to anticipate through experience but you might have yet to run across. So, without further ado, let's jump into the *SAQ* (sorry, couldn't resist that one).

**Q:** *What if I unknowingly bid on and win stolen goods? Am I culpable in any way?*

**A:** No. Ill-gotten goods are out there, and they're being peddled all the time. When a case of software "falls off a truck" and someone starts selling it at auction, they're the ones who risk prosecution, not you. You're at risk only in that what you're buying will probably not be warranted or supported in any way. If you find an auction where expensive bulk items are being moved dirt cheap, then you might suspect sticky fingers.

**Q:** *Should I reveal the reserve price I've set on one of my auctions if someone asks?*

**A:** This one's really up to you. If your auction's stalling (not getting any bids) and someone inquires about your reserve, it might help generate interest if you pass along the information. If your auction's seeing a lot of action but the reserve hasn't been met, just say to anyone who asks, "It's nearly been met" or "I expect it will be met with the next bid." Reserve prices don't have to be treated like deep dark secrets, but it's not required that you reveal them if you don't want to.

**Q:** *If the buyer doesn't request that an item be insured during transit, who's responsible if it gets damaged?*

**A:** That's a toughie. If neither the buyer nor the seller discuss insurance, then you have both agreed (though unspoken) that you'll both be responsible for the item's safe travel and arrival. If damage occurs during shipping, it would be unfair and unethical for the seller to expect the buyer to "suck it up," nor would it be appropriate for the buyer to expect a full and expedient refund for the damaged item. If neither party discussed insurance explicitly, then the best thing to do would be to share the cost of damage: either the buyer sends back the item and the seller reimburses 50 percent of the final price, or the seller instructs the buyer to keep the item and they both agree on a reasonable refund to offset the damage. The real lesson here is that sellers should always state that insurance will cost extra upon the buyer's request. That way, if the buyer waives insurance, then that buyer will be 100 percent responsible for any damage to the item in transit.

**Q:** *Will insurance cover damage to any item, regardless of how it was packaged for shipment?*

**A:** No. The major carriers, upon receiving an insurance claim from a customer, will request to see the damaged item and the package it was shipped in. Clearly, if a glass snow globe was sent in a brown paper sack secured with duct tape, then it's unlikely that the carrier will consider that insurable. The responsibility here rests with the seller to properly package an item so it has a reasonable chance of arriving in one piece.

**Q:** *What if an unexpected situation arises and I can't honor my high bid in an auction? Can I cancel my bid without being thrown in auction jail?*

**A:** This really depends on which auction site you're dealing with and what circumstances have caused you to default on your bid. Remember, when you're dealing with the retail, wholesale, and surplus auction sites, they will have your credit card on file. You'll be billed regardless. However, if you need to cancel a bid or made an error when you bid, you can usually contact someone at the auction site's customer service branch to see if you can cancel your bid provided the auction hasn't yet ended.

For person-to-person auctions, you can cancel your bid, but you'd better have a really good reason for doing it. Sellers at these auction venues are generally compassionate, and they realize that stuff happens. They might cut you some slack. But if you abuse their good nature or have a history of backing out of bids, you'll probably feel their wrath and, if word gets back to the auction site in the form of multiple complaints, you'll probably be barred from using the site.

**Q:** *At the end of a reserve price auction where the reserve price isn't met and I'm the high bidder, do I have to pay the seller's reserve price anyway, whatever it is? Does he have to sell to me? Can both of us work out a mutually-agreeable price?*

**A:** If a reserve price isn't met during the regular course of an auction, then neither the high bidder nor the seller are required to make the exchange. The high bidder can contact the seller to ask about the reserve price to see if it's within reach, although the seller still doesn't have to sell even if the buyer offers the reserve price. The seller can contact the high bidder to either sell at the high bid price or see if the high bidder would like to raise the bid to meet the original reserve price. Both parties can go offline to see if a mutually-agreeable price can be met, which is frequently what happens in this sort of situation.

**Q:** *If I wait until the last minute to bid, don't I run the risk of not getting a bid in at all, especially if there are any technical difficulties or if the seller decides to close the auction early?*

**A:**  Correct. Waiting until the last minute to deliver a snipe bid is exciting and does have its strategic rewards, but you do risk missing out on the auction entirely. Problems with your PC, problems with your Internet connection, or problems with the auction site servers could all rear their ugly heads and cause you to miss out completely. This is why you shouldn't develop the habit of exclusively bidding by way of the snipe strategy.

**Q:**  *At the retailer and wholesaler auctions, why are some items listed with an "all sales are final" policy? Isn't that a lousy customer service policy if I'm dissatisfied with what I've won and purchased?*

**A:**  That's a good question, but there's a good reason for the policy. Many auctioned items are overruns, refurbished equipment, or surplus. The seller or consignor needs to get rid of this stuff and, unless it's a D.O.A. (dead on arrival) situation (item is not operational in part or whole) or damaged in transit, you'll be hard-pressed to get return privileges simply because you changed your mind. Be sure that the item you bid on will be the item you truly intend to buy and keep.

**Q:**  *If sniping seems to evoke love-hate responses from auction communities, why do some sites allow it to happen?*

**A:**  From my perspective, the snipe adds thrill and excitement to the auction experience. There's something about the flow of adrenaline and the thumping of your heart as you prepare to deliver a well-executed snipe. Sites that allow sniping know this, and they recognize it as an attraction to many of their regular users. To eradicate sniping would probably mean disenchanting many users. There are many auction sites that don't give users the ability to snipe, and those are the sites you should use if you prefer not to dance the last-minute mambo.

**Q:**  *I haven't bid at an auction site for several months now and probably won't any time soon. Is it safe to leave my account open with my credit card information in it?*

**A:**  Even though the site you've bid at is secure, as a rule you should never leave a stale account sitting around where your credit card information can be found. Remember the eBayla bug, and how some shady users were

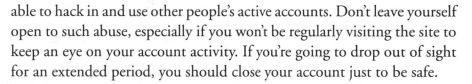

able to hack in and use other people's active accounts. Don't leave yourself open to such abuse, especially if you won't be regularly visiting the site to keep an eye on your account activity. If you're going to drop out of sight for an extended period, you should close your account just to be safe.

**Q:** *Do I have any return privileges at the auction sites?*

**A:** Different sites will have different policies about returns, and you should review each site's policies before you ever place a bid. Most sites will honor returns for damaged or lost goods, but that's usually it. At person-to-person sites, it all depends on the policy stated by the individual who's selling the item you're interested in. If the return policy isn't stated in the item description, send an inquiring e-mail message to see what the policy might be. If you're bidding on items listed "as is" or "all sales final" . . . well, there's your answer.

**Q:** *That's it! I'm getting nowhere trying to resolve my dispute with an auction seller. If I go direct to the Federal Trade Commission (FTC), they'll help me, right?*

**A:** Well, that's what the FTC and the Better Business Bureau are there for, and it sounds pretty impressive when you let it be known that you're going "right to the top" to resolve your matter. However, the reality is that these organizations will take in your claims, but they typically don't have the bandwidth to take care of each and every one of us on an individual level (unless the situation is particularly flagrant). These agencies will move into action when they see a recurrence of bad activity and the site operator doesn't appear to be making an effort to improve the reliability of the site or its users. Work with the auction site first, and do your very best to resolve the situation directly with the other person using calm and factual communications.

**Q:** *The seller says I need to pay sales tax for the item I won. He must be a business owner, right?*

**A:** Usually, but be careful. Some less-than-honest sellers could be trying to squeeze a couple more bucks out of you without planning to pay the tax themselves. If you're in doubt whether you should be paying a sales tax (especially if the item isn't being shipped within the seller's home state), then ask for the seller's business license number. That number can be easily verified by contacting the licensing department of the county or city that issued the license (this is all public information). If the license number you've been given isn't on file, then you should refuse to pay the additional amount requested, and you could even pursue reporting the seller for mail fraud.

**Q:** *I just won an auction for a very small item, but the seller is requiring an additional $6 for postage. What's with that?*

**A:** Yeah, that gets me steamed, too. Some sellers state that they want to be covered for shipping *and handling*. I disagree with that, especially when dealing on a person-to-person basis. There's a cost of doing business that must be absorbed to a certain extent. There's also a loss of return customers when sellers try to weasel an extra buck or two. If you think you're being overcharged for postage (especially if specific postage costs weren't noted as part of the auction's description), then ask how the seller determined the cost and see if there is an alternative method to get your item delivered to you at a lower cost. That's a fair inquiry to make, and both buyer and seller should be comfortable discussing it.

**Q:** *If I want to make a decent profit as an online auctioneer, does that mean I need to carry all the hot items that everyone's clamoring for?*

**A:** Not necessarily. Sure, if you have rare, hard-to-find items that everyone's clawing after, you'll probably turn a tidy profit. However, if you're only making a few dollars' profit on your auctions but you're hosting hundreds or more each month, then you can do the math yourself. A lot of bidders are looking for inexpensive items to bid on and win. Don't feel it's a waste of time to sell items that sell for less than $5 or $10. If you're making a profit and have a large inventory, then you can do just as well as the big-ticket-item sellers. It'll just take you a little longer to see the same gains.

**Q:** *Is there anything I can do to guarantee that my auctions are successful?*

**A:** Well, there's nothing I can offer to absolutely guarantee that your auctions will be successful, but there are many ways to improve your success rate. Be sure to use good item descriptions with searchable words included.

Be sure you provide detailed descriptions of your items, and be sure the spelling and grammar are up to par. *Include pictures!!* This is one of the key features that makes some auctions more successful than others. Most of all, watch other auctions and try to determine what has made them successful and why you might have been attracted to them yourself.

**Q:** *Which is the better strategy, using only one auction site to buy or sell from or using multiple sites?*

**A:** There are two schools of thought here. If you use a single auction site, then you develop expertise using it, and you develop a relationship with that site's auction community. You can easily keep abreast of site improvements, problems, or policy changes, and you can adjust your activities (buying or selling) quickly. You'll learn who many of the other bidders and sellers are, and you'll be better able to monitor the auction activity as well as the hot-ticket items that flow through the site.

However, you can increase your customer base (if selling) or increase your odds of getting better deals (if bidding) by shopping the other sites. Some of the less-traveled sites might have better deals due to the smaller user base. When selling, less-traveled sites might also mean less competition for the item you're selling, and you could spur a bidding frenzy on your "exclusive" item.

**Q:** *I keep hearing it's best to use a credit card to pay for my auction winnings. How come?*

**A:** Clearly, credit cards offer you the most protection since you can dispute the charges if troubles with a seller arise. Also, many credit card issuers offer increased buyer protection by way of automatically increasing manufacturer warranty periods or providing reimbursement for damaged or dysfunctional items. Check with your credit card issuer to get the full details of whether your purchases will qualify for these added benefits.

**Q:** *What if a seller asks for cash payment? Is that a cause for suspicion?*

**A:** If anyone requests payment by cash *exclusively*, then beware. Cash cannot be traced or recovered if the recipient suddenly drops off the face of the earth. It is OK to send cash if *you* suggest it, and most sellers worth their salt will first discourage it but will also treat that particular transaction with special attention due to the sensitivity to accusations of fraud.

**Q:** *If I can get the items I want to bid on for the same or better prices at retail outlets, why bother with the auction?*

**A:** Well, only you can answer that question. This is the kind of question that forces you to take a reality check. Are you really bidding wisely out there, or are you just caught up in the game? Do some comparison shopping before you bid and even after you've bid. Find out what a particular item costs on the retail circuit, then set your bidding activity not to exceed the cost of buying the item from a direct-sales site or local business.

# Index

## Numbers

**30-Minute Flash auctions,
    FirstAuction.com,** 106
**48-Hour Featured auctions,
    FirstAuction.com,** 106
**501(c)(3)(Recognition for Tax
    Exemption) form, charity
    auctions,** 179
**9-to-5er, described,** 61

## A

**absentee bidding, Christie's,** 167
**absolute price auction, described,** 63
**accounts, closing to prevent
    unauthorized use,** 81
**acronyms, described,** 40
**ActionWatch image host,** 291
**address labels, shipping uses,** 235
**advertisements, Amazon.com
    auctions,** 150
**age-controlled community,
    described,** 120
**Amazon.com auctions,** 50
    advertisements, 150
    auction insurance, 150
    AuctionGuy rating, 151
    bidding process, 147
    Bulk Loader, 150
    clientele statistics, 144–145
    cookies, 145
    customer support, 151
    development history, 142
    Dutch auctions, 146
    feedback forum, 150
    First Bidder Discount auctions, 146, 283
    HTML support, 149
    inventory types, 144
    LiveBid auctions, 146–147
    My Auctions feature, 151
    navigation techniques, 147–148
    notification process, 149
    offering items for sale, 149–150
    outbid notification, 147
    registration process, 144–145
    Reserve Price Auctions, 146
    screen elements, 142–144, 148
    search techniques, 147
    seller fees, 149
    small business-to-person concept, 142
    Sotheby's partnership, 157
    Straight auctions, 146
    Your Auctions tracking tool, 206
    zShops, 150
**animated auctioneer, bid.com,** 99–100
**announcements, eBay.com feature,** 130
**annual fees, online auction assessment
    factor,** 58
**anonymity, Internet addiction
    development reason,** 297–298
**appraisals**
    Butterfield & Butterfield, 171
    Christie's, 167
    International Society of Appraisers, 157
    Sotheby's, 163
**ARPANET (Advanced Research Project
    Agency Network), Internet roots,** 6
**Artnet auctions, described,** 311–312
**ascending price auction, described,** 63
**atrium auctionarium, described,** 4
**attachments, security concerns,** 38
**Auction Addict, described,** 310
**Auction Alerts, Yahoo! Auctions,** 140
**auction certificates, student good
    citizenship awards,** 20
**auction commissions, online auction
    assessment factor,** 58
**auction culture**
    Golden Rule, 66
    netiquette, 66–67
    professionalism, 66
**auction insurance, Amazon.com
    Auctions,** 150
**auction lots**
    Biddington's, 173
    Butterfield & Butterfield, 170
    Christie's, 165–166
    Sotheby's, 161–162
**auction tracking**
    buyers, 206–208
    closed auction data availability, 208
    sellers, 208–210
    spreadsheet uses, 207–210
**Auction Watch, Biddington's tracking
    service,** 175
**Auction Web** *see* **eBay.com**
**AuctionGuy ratings**
    Amazon.com Auctions, 151
    bid.com, 102–103
    Biddington's, 175–176
**Butterfield & Butterfield,** 172
    charity auctions, 185–186
    Christie's, 168
    eBay.com, 130–132
    FirstAuction.com, 109
    Onsale.com, 88
    Sotheby's, 163–164
    uBid.com, 95–96
    Yahoo! Auctions, 141
**auctions**
    *See also* online auctions
    combining with the Internet, 10–13
    described, 20
    development history, 3–6
    duties, 20–21
    effects on the economy, 17–18
    participants, 18–19
    U.S. Treasury, 18
**Auctions.com, described,** 309
**authentication, specialty auction
    advantages,** 189
**authorized, described,** 31
**Auto-Bid, Biddington's proxy
    system,** 175
**automatic auction extension**
    Onsale.com, 86
    uBid.com, 93
    Yahoo! Auctions, 138
    disadvantages, 283
**auto-outbid messages, bidding
    tactics,** 283

## B

**Babylon, auction development
    history,** 4
**Baker, Samuel, Sotheby's development
    history,** 159
**bargain hunter, described,** 60–61
**barter, advantage over fixed-price,**
    20–21
**Beanie Nation, specialty auction,**
    192–193
**Berners-Lee, Tim, WWW (World Wide
    Web) developer,** 8–9
**Bid Buddy, bid.com,** 100–102
**Bid Butler, uBid.com,** 94
**Bid Maker, Onsale.com proxy bidding
    system,** 87
**bid shielding, described,** 254

bid summary, FirstAuction.com, 108
Bid Watch, Onsale.com feature, 87
bid.com
    animated auctioneer, 99–100
    auction automatic extension non-
      support, 101
    auction formats, 98–99
    AuctionGuy rating, 102–103
    Bid Buddy, 100–102
    bid Comments, 100
    bidding process, 100–101
    category links, 97
    credit card number issues, 98
    Deals of the Day link, 99
    Dutch auctions, 98–99, 101
    inventory types, 98
    item descriptions, 99–100
    live Dutch auctions, 99
    navigation techniques, 99
    Netcast auctions, 99
    non-cancelable bid policy, 101
    notification process, 102
    preset bid increments, 100
    publicly offered stock, 96
    registration process, 98
    screen elements, 96–97, 100
    search techniques, 99
    Top Bid auctions, 98, 101
    vendor relationships, 96
bidder blacklist, Yahoo! Auctions, 140
bidder ratings, Yahoo! Auctions,
    135–136
bidders
    *See also* shoppers
    deadbeat, 215
    finding for items, 288
    online auction advantages, 21–23
    types, 60–62
bidding
    *See also* bids and shopping
    proxy system issues, 276
    realistic expectations, 275–276
    shill bidding scams, 252–254
    short/long-term gains, 276–277
    when to quit, 274–275
bidding strategies
    automatic auction extensions, 283
    bid within the last hour, 282
    bidstalkers, 286
    first bidder, 283
    leave feedback, 287
    outbid competition, 283

pay quickly, 286
selective searches, 282
sniping, 284–285
use odd values, 284
use several sites, 281–282
use variety of methods, 286
when to go big, 824
win with a penny, 284
Biddington's
    auction lots, 173
    Auction Watch tracking, 175
    AuctionGuy rating, 175–176
    Auto-Bid proxy system, 175
    bidding process, 173–175
    online escrow provider, 172
    registration process, 173–175
    screen elements, 173–174
bids
    *See also* bidding
    automatic auction extension, 86
    earlier bid prevails when two or more
      match, 86
    pulling, 277–279
    retracting, 86
Bids, Orders & Shipments,
    Onsale.com, 206
bidstalkers, described, 286
BoxLot auctions, described, 310
Broadband PCS services, auction
    participant, 19
Broadcaster.com, Hollywood Auction,
    183–184
Bulk Loader, Amazon.com auctions, 150
business reply mail, personal
    information gathering method, 32
Butterfield & Butterfield
    appraisal services, 171
    auction lots, 170
    AuctionGuy rating, 172
    bidding process, 171
    category types, 170
    cosigned items, 17!
    development history, 168–169
    eBay partnership, 157, 170
    HGTV affiliation, 170
    International Auctioneers affiliation, 170
    international offices, 169
    screen elements, 169–170
    site map link, 170
    Zing.com partnership, 170
Butterfield, William, Butterfield &
    Butterfield developer, 168

Buy Price auctions, Yahoo! Auctions, 136
buyer fees, untraditional sites, 158
buyer profiles, personal information
    issues, 31–32
buyer's protection policies, credit card
    issuers, 227
buyers
    *See also* bidders and shoppers
    auction tracking, 206–208
    checking seller's feedback rating, 224
    feedback forum profile, 243
    international transaction payment
      issues, 225
    mail fraud scam recourse, 258–259
    monetary transaction feedback profiles,
      222–223
    package received message format, 239
    pastime versus full-time job, 263–271
    payment considerations, 224–225
    payment method cost/convenience
      issues, 224
    payment protection issues, 224
    payment sent message format, 230
    proxy system issues, 276
    reproduction scam issues, 255
    scam risks, 252
    shill bidding scams, 252–254
    take-it-or-leave-it attitude benefits,
      270–271
    traceable payment method advantages,
      224–225
    unreceived item scam, 258–259
    winning bid notification process,
      212–213

**C**

cancellation request form, retracting a
    bid, 86
cardboard pieces, shipping uses, 234
careers, online auction as full-time job,
    263–271
carriers, packing supplies, 233–234
cash, payment method
    disadvantages, 225
cashier's checks, advantages/
    disadvantages, 226
casual drop-in, described, 61
catalogues
    Christie's, 167
    Sotheby's, 161–162

**categories**
  eBay.com, 122–124
  item types, 71–72
  merchant site types, 75–76
  subcategories, 71–72
**caveat emptor, person-to-person sites,** 115
**Center for On-Line Addiction,** 298
**charity auctions**
  501(c)(3)(Recognition for Tax Exemption) form, 179
  AuctionGuy ratings, 185–186
  Broadcaster.com Hollywood Auction, 183–184
  development history, 5
  eBay.com, 184–185
  Internet advantages, 178
  monthly contribution support, 180
  online donations, 180
  overhead cost issues, 177–178
  Universal Studios Charity Auctions, 182–183
  versus traditional fundraising methods, 177–178
  WebCharity.com, 180–182
  Yahoo!, 185
**chat rooms**
  eBay.com, 130
  Internet addiction development history, 296
  online auction success effects, 52
**children, auction participants,** 20
**Christie, James, Christie's founder,** 164
**Christie's**
  absentee bidding support, 167
  appraisals, 167
  auction development history, 5–6
  auction lots, 165–166
  AuctionGuy rating, 168
  bidding process, 166–167
  catalogues, 167
  category types, 166
  commissions, 167
  development history, 164
  Lotfinder, 166
  pre-auction exhibitions, 167
  screen elements, 165
  survey link, 167
**CityAuction**
  described, 309–310
  stock market effect, 51

**classified ads, versus Internet auctions,** 10–11
**clientele**
  online auction assessment factor, 57
  person-to-person sites, 114
  specialty auctions, 188–189
**CNET auctions, described,** 307–308
**COD (Cash On Delivery), advantages/ disadvantages,** 230
**Collecting Nation, specialty auction,** 191–192
**collectors, auction participant,** 19
**Collectors Universe, specialty auction,** 195–197
**comments, bid notes,** 100
**commissions**
  Christie's, 167
  escrow services, 228
  online auction assessment factor, 58
  person-to-person sites, 113
  untraditional sites, 158
**communications**
  end-of-auction message format, 214–215
  feedback forums, 242–249
  first impressions, 241–242
  package received message format, 239
  package sent message format, 239
  payment received message format, 231
  payment sent message format, 230
  seller thank you notes, 235–236
**communities of users, person-to-person site clientele,** 114
**community values, online auction assessment factor,** 58
**CompUSAAuctions.com, online auction site,** 50
**cookies**
  Amazon.com Auctions, 145
  described, 35–36
**cookies.txt file, described,** 36
**Creative Computers, Inc., ubid.com,** 88–96
**credit cards**
  advantages/disadvantages, 227
  bid.com registration issues, 98
  buyer's protection policies, 227
  merchant site payment method, 77
  SSL (Secure Sockets Layer), 58
  Yahoo! auction information requirements, 135–136

**customer service**
  online auction assessment factor, 58–59
  specialty auction advantages, 189–190
**cyberaddiction, described,** 297

**D**

**data encryption, online auction assessment factor,** 58
**databases, personal information storage method,** 32
**Davis, Cindy, auction certificate/good citizenship awards,** 20
**deadbeat bidders, described,** 215
**DealDeal auctions, described,** 308
**Deals of the Day link, bid.com,** 99
**descriptions**
  detailed, 289–290
  spelling importance, 290
**development history**
  Amazon.com Auctions, 142
  auctions, 3–6
  Butterfield & Butterfield, 168–169
  Christie's, 164
  eBay.com, 116–117
  Internet, 6–10
  Internet addiction, 296
  Onsale.com, 78
  Sotheby's, 159
  uBid.com, 88–89
  Yahoo! Auctions, 132
**documents, hypertext,** 8
**DOD (Department of Defense), ARPANET development,** 6
**dopamine, described,** 300
**dos and don'ts list, described,** 71
**dumpster diving, described,** 234
**Dutch auctions**
  Amazon.com, 146
  bid.com, 98–99, 101
  described, 64
  eBay.com, 121
  versus Yankee auctions, 64

**E**

**Easy Search, Onsale.com search advantages,** 87
**eBay elf, proxy bidding system,** 125
**eBay Foundation, described,** 185

**eBay.com**
active auction indicator, 124
age restrictions, 120
auction formats, 121–122
AuctionGuy rating, 130–132
bidding process, 125–126
Butterfield & Butterfield relationship, 157, 168–172
Categories banner, 122–123
category types, 122–124
charity auctions, 184–185
chat rooms, 130
core philosophy, 130–131
development history, 116–117
Dutch auctions, 121
eBay elf, 125
eBay Foundation, 185
Featured banner items, 124
Feedback Forum, 129
final value fee, 128
growing pains, 131
Help toolbar, 127–128
HTML support, 128
inventory types, 118
item descriptions, 124–125
My eBay personal pages, 129–130, 206
navigation techniques, 122–127
news/announcements, 130
notification process, 127
online auction development history, 49
outbid notices, 126
password selection, 120
proxy bidding system, 125
publicly offered stock, 117
registration process, 119–121
Reserve met note, 125
Reserve not yet met note, 125
reserve price auction fee issues, 65
Reserve Price auctions, 121–122
reviewing bids, 125
SafeHarbor, 129
screen elements, 117–118
search tools, 129
Sell your item link, 128
selling items, 128
site map uses, 127
sniping an auction, 126
Straight auctions, 121
subcategory types, 122–124
User Agreement, 120
user ID, 120
visitor statistics, 117

**e-gateway, described,** 45
**Egghead.com Surplus Auction, described,** 308
**electronic commerce**
reasons for success, 46–48
secure servers, 44
**electronic trails**
cookies, 35–36
IP address, 35
security issues, 34–37
**elliptical stream, described,** 22
**e-mail**
end-of-auction communication message format, 214–215
package received message format, 239
package sent message format, 239
payment received message format, 231
payment sent message format, 230
personal information gathering method, 32
spam issues, 37–38
successful bid notification, 86–87
winning bid notification process, 212–213
**emoticons, described,** 40
**emotions**
bidding yourself into bankruptcy, 77
controlling, 68–69
**end-of-auction**
communication message format, 214–215
notification process, 212–213
payment methods, 223–230
post-auction prep work, 215–216
rules & etiquette, 210–212
seller's shipping responsibilities, 232–238
waiting for merchandise, 238–240
which comes first, money or merchandise?, 221–223
**envelopes, shipping containers,** 234
**escrow services, advantages/ disadvantages,** 228–229
**e-shopper, described,** 48
**e-tailers**
described, 46
leveling of the playing field, 47
**etiquette, end-of-auction rules,** 210–212
**Excite auctions, described,** 309
**expectations, setting,** 67–68, 275–276
**expertise, specialty auction advantages,** 189

**Express auctions, Onsale.com format,** 82
**extended warranty, ubid.com policy,** 95
**eye candy, described,** 46

**F**

**FAQs**
online auction learning guides, 83
online auction success effects, 52
**farmer's auctions, development history,** 6
**FBI, Internet Fraud Complaint Center,** 42
**feature bloat, online auction assessment factor,** 59
**feedback**
abuse, described, 248
bombing, described, 247
described, 242–243
importance of leaving, 287
padding, described, 248–249
shilling, described, 248
**feedback forums**
Amazon.com Auctions, 150
described, 242–243
eBay.com, 129
faking, 248–249
online auction success effects, 52
person-to-person sites, 152–153
posting process, 243–247
profile ratings, 243
reading between the lines, 248
transaction-specific feedback, 244
**feedback post from seller,** 293
**feedback profile**
described, 243
monetary transaction history, 222–223
**fees** *See* **commissions**
**file attachments, security concerns,** 38
**file extensions, virus types,** 39
**files, cookies.txt,** 36
**final value fee, eBay.com,** 128
**first bidder, reasons to be,** 283
**First Bidder Discount Auctions, Amazon.com,** 146
**first impressions, importance of,** 241–242
**FirstAuction.com**
30-Minute Flash auctions, 106
48-Hour Featured auctions, 106

auction formats, 105–106
AuctionGuy rating, 109
bid comments, 106
Bid Summary, 108
bid-bot non-support, 107
bidding process, 106–107
development history, 103
earlier bid prevails, 107
Help desk link, 109
inventory types, 104–105
item descriptions, 106
keyword searches, 106
navigation techniques, 106
non-cancelable bid policy, 107
notification process, 108
Personal Pages, 108
preset bid increments, 106
re-bidding process, 107
registration process, 105
screen elements, 104
shipping list, 108
stock market effect, 51
toll-free help desk, 109
Yankee auction format, 105
**flaming, described,** 40
**flexibility, end-of-auction
etiquette,** 211
**fluff costs, online auction assessment
factor,** 58
**formats, online auction types,** 63–65
**fragility, item shipping
assessment,** 233
**fraud**
Internet Fraud Complaint Center, 42
National Consumer's League list, 41–42
security issues, 41–43

## G

**garage sales, versus Internet
auctions,** 11
**Gibson Global Auction, specialty
auction,** 201
**Golden Rule, described,** 66
**Gold's Auction, described,** 310–311
**graded items, scam issues,** 257–258
**Great Britain, auction development
history,** 5–6
**Greenfield, Dr. David , Internet
addiction studies,** 297, 305
**guarantee policy, announcing,** 292–293

## H

**Haggle Online, described,** 308
**handling charges, shipping issues,**
237–238
**HGTV, Butterfield & Butterfield
partnership,** 170
**high bids to win,** 284
**hobbyist, described,** 60
**home distribution center, packaging
uses,** 235–236
**HTML (HyperText Markup Language)**
Amazon.com Auction support, 149
eBay.com support, 128
**hyperlinks, described,** 8
**hypertext documents, described,** 8

## I

**image hosts,** 291
**insurance**
auction, 150
person to person sites, 115
**Internal Revenue Service, Recognition
for Tax Exemption form,** 179
**International Auctioneers, Butterfield
& Butterfield affiliation,** 170
**International Society of Appraisers,** 157
**Internet**
advantages, 14
ARPANET roots, 6
auction development history, 11–13
combining with auctions, 10–13
development history, 6–10
disadvantages, 13–15
distrust advantages, 34
future outlook, 9–10
growth rate, 9
IP (Internet Protocol), 8
knowledge source, 14
leveling the auction playing field,
25–27
NCP (Network Control Protocol)
development, 8
safety issues, 29–39
surfing time limit setting, 14
user types, 32–34
versus traditional methods of selling
cast-off goods, 11–13
Web browsers, 9
WWW (World Wide Web), 8

**Internet addiction**
alternative activities, 304–305
Center for On-Line Addiction, 398
described, 296–297
online auction potential, 298–300
physical symptoms, 301
psychological symptoms, 301
reasons for developing, 297–298
self-help treatments, 304–305
warning signs, 300–303
**Internet Explorer 4.0**
cookie preferences, 37
Web browser, 9
**Internet Fraud Complaint Center, FBI
agency,** 42
**Internet Shopping Network,
FirstAuction.com,** 103–109
**inventory**
letting-go issues for sellers, 266
online auction assessment factor, 57
reinvesting in, 266–267
**IP (Internet Protocol), Internet
development history,** 8
**IP address, electronic trails,** 35
**ISPs (Internet Service Providers),
spam avoidance messages,** 38
**item categories, described,** 71–72
**item size, shipping
assessment,** 232
**item titles**
bad ideas, 289
crafting, 288–289
**item value, shipping
assessment,** 233
**items**
descriptions, 289–290
grading, 290
posting pictures, 290–291
titles, 288–289
trendy, 291

## J

**Jump Start Tutorial,
uBid.com,** 91
**Just Glass, specialty auction,** 193

## K

**keywords, vary spellings,** 282

**L**

legal-sized envelopes, shipping
    containers, 234
links
    Christie's survey, 167
    Deals of the Day, 99
    end of auction, 283
    merchandise, 83
    site maps, 83
    topical, 83
listing fees, person-to-person sites, 113
LiveBid auctions, Amazon.com
    support, 146–147
Lotfinder, Christie's, 166
low bids to win, 284
low-opening bids, 291
lurking, described, 69

**M**

Magic Auction, specialty auction, 198–199
mail fraud, unreceived item scam, 258–259
manila envelopes, shipping
    containers, 234
manufacturers, auction participant, 19
marketing trends, personal information
    issues, 31–32
markets, checking for value, 288
marking pens, shipping uses, 235
McAfee's VirusScan program, virus
    scanning, 39
merchandise insurance
    Amazon.com Auctions, 150
    person-to-person sites, 115
merchandise links, Onsale.com
    navigation technique, 83
merchant sites
    benefits, 77
    bid.com, 96–103
    bid-pulling cautions, 277
    category types, 75–76
    CNET auctions, 307–308
    comparative pricing, 110
    DealDeal auctions, 308
    described, 75–78
    Egghead.com Surplus Auction, 308
    FirstAuction.com, 103–109
    Haggle Online, 308
    high confidence level, 76
    inventory gathering methods, 76

Onsale.com, 78–88
    payment methods, 77
    premier sites, 76–110
    uBid.com, 88–96
    versus in-store shopping, 78
    versus person-to-person sites, 113
    warranty issues, 77
meta data, described, 15
misspellings, search effects, 72
mistakes, acknowledge as seller, 287
Mohiuddin, Razi, Onsale.com
    developer, 49
money orders, advantages/
    disadvantages, 226
My Auctions
    Amazon.com Auction tracking, 151
    Yahoo! Auction tracking, 140, 206
My eBay, auction tracking tool,
    129–130, 206–209

**N**

National Consumer's League, fraud
    leaders list, 41–42, 251
NCP (Network Control Protocol),
    Internet development history, 8
negative feedback, feedback profile
    effects, 245–247
negs, described, 245–247
net compulsion, described, 297
Netcast auctions, described, 99
netiquette
    acronyms, 40
    auction culture, 65–67
    described, 39–41
    emoticons, 40
    flame avoidance, 40
Netscape Navigator 4.6
    cookie preferences, 37
    Web browser, 9
news, eBay.com feature, 130
newsgroups
    *See also* Usenet, 12–13
    auction item postings, 72
    described, 12
    postings versus Internet auctions,
        12–13
    specialty auction resource, 312
niche sites *See* specialty auctions
Norton's AntiVirus program, virus
    scanning, 39

notification process, end-of-auction,
    212–213

**O**

Office Depot, shipping container
    source, 234
office supply stores, shipping container
    source, 234
OfficeMax, shipping container source, 234
Omidyar, Pierre, Auction Web
    (eBay.com) founder, 49, 116–117
online auctions
    *See also* auctions
    Amazon.com, 50, 142–152
    Artnet auctions, 311–312
    assessment factors, 57–59
    Auction Addict, 310
    Auctions.com, 309
    Beanie Nation, 192–193
    benefits, 27
    bid.com, 96–103
    bidder communication benefits, 27
    bidder's advantages, 21–23
    Biddington's, 172–176
    BoxLot auctions, 310
    Broadcaster.com Hollywood Auction,
        183–184
    Butterfield & Butterfield, 168–172
    career endeavor issues, 263–271
    charity auctions, 177–186
    chat rooms, 52
    Christie's, 164–168
    CityAuction, 51, 309–310
    CNET auctions, 307–308
    Collecting Nation, 191–192
    Collectors Universe, 195–197
    community member alertness, 26–27
    competition between, 56
    CompUSAAuctions.com, 50
    DealDeal auctions, 308
    development history, 49–50
    dos and don'ts lists, 71
    eBay.com, 49, 116–132
    economic impact, 50–51
    Egghead.com Surplus Auction, 308
    elliptical stream, 22
    Excite auctions, 309
    FAQs, 52
    fast growing market, 55–56
    feedback forums, 52

FirstAuction.com, 51, 103–109
formats, 63–65
fraud self-policing policies, 42–43
Gibson Global Auction, 201
Gold's Auction, 310–311
Haggle Online, 308
impossible-to-find item availability, 27
international access, 27
International Society of Appraisers, 157
Internet addiction, 296–306
Just Glass, 193
leveling the playing field, 25–27
Magic Auction, 198–199
merchant sites, 75–110
National Consumer's League fraud
   rating, 251
Onsale.com, 49, 78–88
person-to-person sites, 111–153
Pottery Auction, 200
public bulletin boards, 52
reasons for success, 46–48
scam reporting, 259–260
screen elements, 159–161
seller's advantages, 23–24
Sloan's Auctions, 311
Sotheby's, 158–164
specialized search crawler issues, 73
specialty sites, 56, 187–202
StampAuctions, 197
stock market effects, 51
third-party authentication services, 157
Tickets.com, 197–198
uBid.com, 51, 88–96
Universal Studios Charity Auctions, 50,
   182–183
untraditional sites, 157–176
URLMerchant, 201–202
uses, 45
versus classified ads, 10–11
versus garage sales, 11
versus newsgroup postings, 12–13
WebCharity.com, 180–182
WineBid, 193–195
Yahoo!, 50, 132–141
**online commerce, retailer advantages,**
   **15–16**
**Onsale.com**
   at Cost items, 79–80
   auction development history, 78
   auction formats, 81–82
   AuctionGuy rating, 88
   automatic auction extension, 86

Bid Maker, 87
Bid Watch, 87
bidding process, 83–85
Bids, Orders & Shipments tracking
   tool, 206
earlier bid prevails, 86
Easy Search, 87
e-mail notification, 86–87
Express auctions, 82
Merchandise links navigation, 83
multiple quantity bid issues, 86
navigation techniques, 82–83
online auction development history,
   49–50
publicly offered stock, 79
Quick Buys, 82
registration process, 81
retracting a bid, 86
screen elements, 79–80
shipping method selection, 83–85
site inventory, 80–81
Site Map navigation, 83
telephone hours, 83
topical links, 83
tutorials, 83
vendor relations, 79
Yankee auctions, 82
**Orzack, Dr. Maressa Hecht, Internet**
   **addiction studies,** 296–297, 305
**outbidding competition,** 283

# P

**packets, described,** 8
**packing**
   home distribution center advantages,
   235–236
   office supply stores, 234
   overpackaging issues, 236
   supply sources, 233–235
   used containers, 234
**passwords, registration process,** 70
**payment methods**
   cash disadvantages, 225
   cashier's checks, 226
   COD (Cash On Delivery), 230
   credit cards, 227
   escrow services, 228–229
   merchant sites, 77
   money orders, 226
   personal checks, 226

seller's terms, 223
send quickly, 286
**penny, as bid amount,** 284
**permission statements, online**
   **purchasing issues,** 32
**personal checks, advantages/**
   **disadvantages,** 226
**personal information**
   business reply mail, 32
   closing accounts to prevent
   unauthorized use, 81
   electronic trails, 34–37
   e-mail response, 32
   online auction assessment factor, 58
   permission statements, 32
   product warranty cards, 32
   purchasing preferences, 31–32
   registration process, 69–71
   security issues, 31–32
   sensitive information request denial
   methods, 34
   shopping habits, 31–32
   telephone surveys, 32
**Personal Pages, FirstAuction.com,** 108
**personal shopping agents** *See* **search-bots**
**person-to-person sites**
   Amazon.com Auctions, 142–152
   Auction Addict, 310
   auction tracking search, 207
   Auctions.com, 309
   BoxLot auctions, 310
   category types, 111
   caveat emptor, 115
   CityAuction, 309–310
   clientele, 114
   communities of users, 114
   development history, 111
   eBay.com, 116–132
   Excite auctions, 309
   feedback forums, 152–153
   flea market comparisons, 112–113
   free merchandise insurance, 115
   Gold's Auction, 310–311
   listing fees, 113
   negative feedback restrictions, 247
   notification process, 212–213
   sales commissions, 113
   seller fees, 112–113
   undesirable element, 115–116
   user feedback, 115
   versus merchant sites, 113
   Yahoo! Auctions, 132–141

**physical symptoms, Internet addiction,** 301
**pictures**
  posting, 290–291
  scam issues, 256–257
**poker face, described,** 3
**politeness, end-of-auction etiquette,** 211
**positive feedback, feedback profile effects,** 243–245
**post offices, auction participant,** 19
**postings, feedback forums,** 243–247
**Postmaster General, mail fraud scam recourse,** 258–259
**Pottery Auction, specialty auction,** 200
**pre-auction exhibitions**
  Christie's, 167
  Sotheby's, 162
**premier sites, merchant sites,** 76–110
**pricing**
  low-opening bids, 291
  reserve prices, 292
  sellers issues, 291–292
**Priority Mail, shipping advantages,** 237
**privacy policy, online auction assessment factor,** 70
**private citizens, auction participant,** 19
**product warranty cards, personal information gathering method,** 32
**products, knowledge is important,** 287
**professionalism**
  auction culture element, 66
  end-of-auction etiquette, 211
**programs**
  McAfee's VirusScan, 39
  Norton's AntiVirus, 39
**proxy bidding, described,** 64, 125
**psychological symptoms, Internet addiction,** 301
**public bulletin boards, online auction success effects,** 52
**public resources, auction participant,** 19
**publications**
  Caught in the Net, 306
  Net Auctions: Bidder Watch Out!, 306
  *Online Auctions at eBay,* 126
  People Magazine, 185
  Surplus Record, The, 91
  Virtual Addiction, 298, 306
**punctuality, end-of-auction etiquette,** 211
**purchasing preferences, security issues,** 31–32

**Q**

**questions, answer quickly,** 292
**Quick Buys, Onsale.com,** 82

**R**

**Rambeck, Dr. L.J., Internet addiction article,** 299
**registration, information types,** 69–71
**re-pops, described,** 255
**reproductions, scam issues,** 255
**Reserve Price auctions**
  advantages/disadvantages, 292
  Amazon.com, 146
  described, 64
  eBay.com, 65, 121–122
  fee issues, 65
  Reserve met/Reserve not yet met notes, 125
  Yahoo!, 136
**response time, end-of-auction etiquette,** 211
**restoration services, Sotheby's,** 163
**retailers, auction participant,** 19
**retaliatory feedback, described,** 247
**retouched pictures, scam issues,** 256–257
**Rome, auction development history,** 4–5
**rules, end-of-auction,** 210–212

**S**

**S/R Auction, Inc., uBid.com partnership,** 91
**safe environment, Internet security initiatives,** 43–44
**SafeHarbor, eBay.com customer service/support,** 129
**scams**
  bid shielding, 254
  grade markup, 257–258
  National Consumer's League online auction fraud rating, 251
  online auction assistance, 259–260
  reproductions, 255
  retouched pictures, 256–257
  shill bidding, 252–254
  switch and return, 255–256
  unreceived items, 258–259
  who's at risk?, 252
**search-bots, described,** 72, 282
**search engines**
  online auction search results, 42
  specialty auction resource, 312
**searches**
  Amazon.com auctions, 147
  bid.com, 99
  charity auction returns, 178
  Christie's Lotfinder, 166
  eBay.com, 129
  FirstAuction.com, 106
  item category types, 71–72
  misspelling avoidance, 72
  Onsale.com Easy Search feature, 87
  person-to-person site auction tracking, 207
  search-bots, 72
  specialized Web sites, 72
  time saving feature, 62
  type used, 282
  vary spellings, 282
**secure servers, described,** 44
**security**
  buyer beware principle, 43
  closing accounts to prevent unauthorized use, 81
  cookies, 35–36
  credit card issues, 58
  electronic trails, 34–37
  file attachment concerns, 38
  fraud concerns, 41–43
  Internet Fraud Complaint Center, 42
  Internet user types, 32–34
  merchant site advantages, 77
  National Consumer's League fraud list, 41–42
  netiquette, 39–41
  personal information issues, 31–32
  privacy policy, 70
  registration information requirements, 69–71
  safe environment initiatives, 43–44
  safety in numbers, 30
  secure servers, 44
  sensitive information request denial methods, 34
  shopping habits, 31–32
  spam, 37–38
  SSL (Secure Sockets Layer), 58
  viruses, 38–39

**self-adhesive address labels, shipping uses,** 235
**seller fees**
  person-to-person sites, 112–113
  untraditional sites, 158
**seller's terms, reasonableness issues,** 223
**sellers**
  auction tracking, 208–210
  bid shielding scam, 254
  dealing with bid-pulling requests, 277–279
  eBay.com process, 128
  feedback forum profile, 243
  feedback rating, 224
  handling charge issues, 237–238
  home distribution center advantages, 235–236
  inventory considerations, 266–267
  letting go of your inventory, 266
  mail fraud scam cautions, 258–259
  market glut effect on profits, 269–270
  monetary transaction feedback profiles, 222–223
  online auction advantages, 23–24
  online auction employment benefits, 264–267
  package sent e-mail message format, 209
  pastime versus full-time job, 263–271
  payment received message format, 231
  reproduction scam issues, 255
  scam risks, 252
  server dependency issues, 268–269
  shipping responsibilities, 232–238
  site maintenance duties, 268
  switch and return scam, 255–256
  take-it-or-leave-it attitude benefits, 270–271
  thank you notes, 235–236
  underestimating/overcharging shipping costs, 237
  winning bid notification process, 212–213
  world economy issues, 269
**selling strategies**
  acknowledge mistakes in listings, 287
  announce guarantee policy, 292–293
  answer all questions, 292
  check all markets, 288
  check sites to see where bidders are, 288
  good descriptions, 289–290
  grading items, 290
  item titles, 288–289
  know your product, 287
  post feedback, 293
  post pictures, 290–291
  pricing issues, 291–292
  reserve price uses, 292
  spelling counts, 290
  trendy items, 291
**serious collector, described,** 60
**servers, seller's dependency issues,** 268–269
**services, online auction assessment factor,** 58–59
**Shaper Image, online auction component effect on business,** 51
**shill bidding, described,** 252–254
**shipping**
  cost determinations, 236–237
  handling charge issues, 237–238
  item assessment issues, 232–233
  item fragility issues, 233
  item value issues, 233
  packing supplies, 233–235
  Priority Mail service advantages, 237
  underestimating/overcharging, 237
**shipping list, FirstAuction.com,** 108
**shipping tape,** 234
**shoppers**
  *See also* bidders and buyers
  9-to-5er, 61
  auction culture, 66–67
  bargain hunter, 60–61
  bidder types, 60–62
  browsing time issues, 62–63
  casual drop-in, 61
  emotion controlling, 68–69
  expectation setting, 67–68
  hobbyist, 60
  loyalty issues, 47
  password, 70
  registration process, 69–71
  serious collector, 60
  user ID, 70
**shopping**
  distractions, 273–274
  merchant site versus in-store, 78
  WYSIWYG (what you see is what you get) activity, 48
**shopping habits, security issues,** 31–32
**site maps**
  Butterfield & Butterfield navigation, 170
  eBay.com navigation, 127
  Onsale.com navigation, 83
**site policies, online auction assessment factor,** 58
**sites, use several,** 281–282
**Sloan's auctions, described,** 311
**sniping**
  advantages/disadvantages, 285
  bidding method, 284–285
  described, 126
**snipists versus anti-snipists,** 285
**Sotheby, John, Sotheby's development history,** 159
**Sotheby's**
  Amazon.com partnership, 157
  appraisal services, 163
  auction development history, 5–6
  auction lots, 161–162
  AuctionGuy rating, 163–164
  bidding process, 162
  catalogues, 161–162
  development history, 159
  fully authenticated/graded inventory, 163
  online auction component effect on business, 51
  preview exhibitions, 162
  restoration services, 163
  world wide locations, 162
**spam**
  described, 37–38
  file attachment concerns, 38
  legal issues, 38
**specialty auctions**
  authentication advantages, 189
  Beanie Nation, 192–193
  clientele, 188–189
  Collecting Nation, 191
  Collectors Universe, 195–197
  customer service advantages, 189–190
  described, 56
  expertise advantages, 189
  Gibson Global Auction, 201
  Just Glass, 193
  Magic Auction, 198–199
  Pottery Auction, 200
  profit issues, 189–190
  smaller is better advantages, 188–190
  StampAuctions, 197
  Tickets.com, 197–198
  URLMerchant, 201–202
  Usenet as resource, 312
  WineBid, 193–195
**spelling, keywords,** 282

spreadsheets, auction tracking method, 207–210

SSL (Secure Sockets Layer), online auction assessment factor, 58

stability, online auction assessment factor, 57

StampAuctions, specialty auction, 197

state attorney general, fraud recourse, 42

Straight auctions
  Amazon.com, 146
  described, 63
  eBay.com, 121
  Yahoo! Auctions, 136

strolling, effects on spending, 63

subcategories
  eBay.com, 122–124
  item types, 71–72

survey link
  Christie's, 167
  personal information gathering method, 32

## T

telephone surveys, personal information gathering method, 32

Terms of Service, described, 70

Terms of Use statement, online auction assessment factor, 58

thank you notes, including with packages, 235–236

third-party authentication services, 157

thrill of the hunt, described, 72

Tickets.com, specialty auction, 197–198

time, item locating issues, 62–63

timing, bidding tips, 282–283

titles, developing for items, 288

Top Bid auctions, bid.com, 98, 101

topical links, information source, 83

traditional sites
  See also untraditional sites
  inventory types, 156
  movement to online opportunities, 156

transaction-specific feedback, described, 244

trendy items, sell when hot, 291

trust, monetary transaction between buyers and sellers, 221–222

tutorials, online auction learning guides, 83

## U

U.S. government, auction participant, 18

U.S. Postmaster General, mail fraud recourse, 42

U.S. Treasury, auction participant, 18

uBid.com
  auction formats, 92
  AuctionGuy rating, 95–96
  Auctions Closing This Hour link, 92
  automatic auction extension feature, 93
  Bid Butler, 94
  bidding process, 93–94
  category listings, 92
  development history, 88–89
  earlier bid prevails, 93
  extended warranty policy, 95
  item details, 93
  Jump Start Tutorial, 91
  multiple quantity bid issues, 93
  navigation techniques, 92–93
  non-cancelable bid policy, 93
  publicly offered stock, 89
  registration process, 91
  S/R Auction, Inc. partnership, 91
  screen elements, 89–90, 92–93
  site inventory, 89
  stock market effect, 51
  successful bid notification, 94
  Top 10 Specials link, 92
  vendor relationships, 88–89
  Yankee auction format, 92

Universal Studios, online auction site, 50

Universal Studios Charity Auctions, described, 182–183

untraditional sites
  See also traditional sites
  auction heritage education opportunity, 158
  Biddington's, 172–176
  Butterfield & Butterfield, 168–172
  buyer/seller commissions, 158
  Christie's, 164–168
  old-world auctioneering with Web designs, 157
  Sotheby's, 158–164

uptime, online auction assessment factor, 57

URLMerchant, specialty auction, 201–202

USA Networks Interactive, FirstAuction.com, 103–109

usage terms, online auction assessment factor, 58

Usenet
  See also newsgroups
  auction item postings, 72
  described, 12–13
  specialty auction resource, 312

User Agreement, eBay.com, 120

user ID, registration information, 70, 120

User Policy, described, 70

USPS, Priority Mail advantages, 237

utilities, auction participant, 19

utility knife, shipping tool, 234

## V

values, comparison checking, 288

venues, person-to-person sites, 112

viruses
  described, 38–39
  file extension types, 39
  security issues, 38–39

## W

warranty cards, personal information gathering method, 32

Watchlist, Yahoo! Auctions, 140

Web browsers
  enabling/disabling cookies, 36–37
  Internet development history, 9

Web retailers, online commerce advantages, 15–16

Web sites
  AuctionWatch, 72
  BidFind, 72
  Center for Internet Studies, 305
  Center for On-Line Addiction, 305
  Computer Addiction Services, 305
  discount retail, 110
  Infoseek White Pages, 31
  iTrack, 72
  McAfee's VirusScan, 39
  National Consumer's League, 251
  online auction reports/reviews, 59
  Real, 99
  S/R Auction, Inc.
  virus-hoax information, 38
  www.800.com, 110

webcams, described, 15
Webcharity.com, described, 180–182
White Pages, personal information, 31
white paper, shipping uses, 235
Whitman, Meg, CEO, eBay.com, 131
wholesalers, auction participant, 19
WineBid, specialty auction, 193–195
WWW (World Wide Web), Internet development history, 8
WYSIWYG (what you see is what you get), described, 48

**Y**

Yahoo! Auctions, 50
Auction Alerts, 140
AuctionGuy rating, 141
Auctions Help pages, 140
automatic auction extension support, 138
bidder blacklist, 140
bidding process, 137–138
Buy Price auctions, 136
category listings, 133–134
charity auctions, 185
credit card information requirements, 135–136
customizing winning e-mails, 140
development history, 132
free site, 132
inventory types, 134–135, 141
item descriptions, 137
Minimum Bidder Rating method, 136
My Auctions tracking tool, 140, 206
navigation techniques, 136–137
notification process, 138–139
offering items for sale, 139
publicly offered stock, 132
registration process, 135
Reserve Price auctions, 136
screen elements, 132–134
Sign Up Here link, 134–135
Straight auctions, 136
Watchlist, 140
Yahoo! Messenger service, 138
Yahoo! Messenger service, outbid notices, 138
Yahoo!Geocities image host, 291
Yankee auctions
described, 64
FirstAuction.com, 105
Onsale.com format, 82
uBid.com format, 92
Young, Dr. Kimberly S., Center for On-Line Addiction founder, 298, 305
Your Auctions, Amazon.com, 206

**Z**

Zing.com, Butterfield & Butterfield partnership, 170
zShops, Amazon.com fixed price selling, 150